Japan's Secret Service, fighting the world's most dangerous war—a silent war fought by invisible warriors...

Hideyoshi, the spy-master who unified a nation

Will Adams, Japan's first Englishman, the right arm of the Shogun

Admiral Yamamoto, mastermind of Pearl Harbor

The Mysterious Case of Charlie Chaplin's Spy Valet

Yoshiko Kawashima, whose exploits won her the nickname "Joan of Arc of Manchuria"

The Japanese Purple Machine, the cryptographic marvel that baffled the world

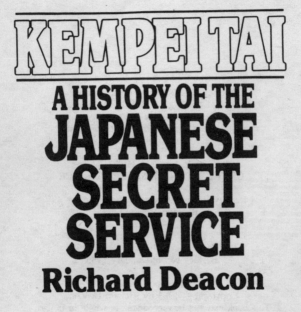

KEMPEI TAI

A HISTORY OF THE
JAPANESE
SECRET
SERVICE

Richard Deacon

BERKLEY BOOKS, NEW YORK

This Berkley book contains the complete
text of the original hardcover edition.
It has been completely reset in a typeface
designed for easy reading, and was printed
from new film.

KEMPEI TAI: A HISTORY
OF THE JAPANESE SECRET SERVICE

A Berkley Book/published by arrangement with
Beaufort Books, Inc.

PRINTING HISTORY
Beaufort Books edition published 1983
Berkley edition/January 1985

ISBN: 0-425-07458-7

A BERKLEY BOOK ® TM 757,375
Berkley Books are published by The Berkley Publishing Group,
200 Madison Avenue, New York, New York 10016.
The name "BERKLEY" and the stylized "B" with design
are trademarks belonging to Berkley Publishing Corporation.
PRINTED IN THE UNITED STATES OF AMERICA

Contents

1

Introduction

> "If you know yourself and know the enemy, you can win in battle...To defeat the enemy psychologically is the superior strategy. To defeat the enemy militarily is the inferior strategy"
>
> Sun Tzu

HAVING WRITTEN HISTORIES of the British, Russian, Chinese and Israeli Secret Services, and now the Japanese, it is interesting to make comparisons and to try to draw some constructive deductions.

One of the first points to make is that the histories of the two oriental secret services—China and Japan—involved far deeper and longer research than those of Britain, Russia and Israel. This is partly because oriental espionage dates back to a much earlier period than that of the Western World, but another important reason is that the agents of oriental powers are caught far less often than those of the West. Indeed, this latter fact is perhaps the cause of Western complacency about oriental espionage and explains why the Japanese Secret Service in all its ramifications was so consistently underrated for so many years.

The Intelligence Services of the rest of the world have been the subject of countless books, covering one aspect or another of their work. Those of the Japanese have, however, been very much neglected. To some extent this has been a result of their services having been underrated. But it also due to the fact that for the first half of this century a great deal of their espionage

was masterminded by secret societies outside the official security agencies.

Despite this apparent handicap to historians, there is considerable documentation on the activities of the secret societies
which have, of course, long since been disbanded. Unlike some
other nations, the Japanese regard spying as an honourable and
patriotic duty and, even in their reference books, do not seek
to hide the fact that some of their illustrious citizens have
indulged in espionage. In a Japanese edition of *Who Was Who*,
for example, there is this remarkable entry:

"ISHIKAWA, Goichi: Spy. Born 1866, died 1894. Sent to
China where he travelled to the Mongolian border. Active in
China in Sino-Japanese War, but captured by the Chinese and
executed in Tientsin. . . ."

I was fortunate in one respect in setting out on this quest.
Despite the fact that my country and Japan had been enemies
in a war in which I was personally engaged, I had no prejudice
against the Japanese people. Nor was this a case of hindsight,
or merely resulting from admiration for the splendid, disciplined manner in which the Japanese people had snatched an
economic victory out of a military defeat by hard work and
imaginative enterprise. As far back as 1934 in a book entitled
The Talkative Muse I wrote that "Japan is a nation to whom
every credit is due for so nobly introducing civilization to the
East. But, having introduced this civilization, is it likely that
Japan wishes to see the position she had fought for under-
mined?. . . It was deplorable, no doubt, that Japan could not
see her way to accept the Lytton Report [the League of Nations
report on the Manchurian Incident], but she not only has a
strong case in her favour, but is definitely to be sympathised
with. For, whether her methods of settling her problems are
right or wrong, there is little doubt that it would be in the
interests of the whole world to grant her certain powers in
Manchuria. Not merely would this mean a bulwark against
Sovietism for Japan, but China also."[1]

Objectivity is a desirable quality when writing any secret
service history, but very often it is not easily recognised in the
finished product. Until comparatively recent years it was considered unpatriotic to write critically of the history of British
Secret Service. Indeed, going back to 1932, the late Sir Comp-
ton Mackenzie was charged under the Official Secrets Act at
the Old Bailey in connection with his book, *Greek Memories*,
which was withdrawn from publication. It may seem unbe-

lievable that the prosecutor, Sir Thomas Inskip, accused Mackenzie of revealing "the mysterious consonant, 'C', by which the Chief of the Secret Service was known." A fine of £100 was imposed for that!

It is, fortunately, not quite so hazardous for secret service historians today. Generally speaking, it is recognised that some grave errors could have been avoided in the past thirty years if this subject had been less taboo several years ago.

The Japanese are not hypocritical like the British in this respect. They are much more forthcoming about the facts of life of their own secret service history. To present an objective picture of Japanese Intelligence one needs to bear in mind that what Japan was doing in the way of aggressive espionage in the 1930s can fairly be compared to what the British were doing under such celebrated spymasters as Walsingham in Elizabeth I's reign and Thurloe under Cromwell. In each case it was a period of intensive empire-building, first by Britain, then by Japan.

But, having made this point, to get a completely accurate picture of events, one has to realise that Japan in effect progressed from the seventeenth century to the twentieth in a mere 50–60 years. In the 1840s in Japan life was something like that of the 1640s in England. By 1910 she had become a highly civilised, modern world power. In the field of Intelligence the Japanese managed to achieve this shortcut in time by utilising a number of patriotic secret societies to supplement the routine work of their official security and intelligence agencies.

In comparing the world's secret services, no special common factor emerges. It is where they differ from one another that is instructive. Israel's Secret Service aims at the survival of Israel at all costs and perhaps the singlemindedness of this aim makes hers the most efficient of all modern Intelligence Services. Soviet Russia is as intent as ever on spreading disruption and anarchy throughout the rest of the world while pursuing a policy of communist imperialism. The American C.I.A., starting almost from scratch and lacking in previous experience except for what it borrowed from the wartime O.S.S., is still trying to find the right balance between a huge bureaucracy and an army of enterprising but not always wise agents in the field. British Secret Service has in the past fifty years, if not long before this, fallen victim to its own passion for secrecy. This has not succeeded in keeping the very secrets it most cherished, but on the other hand it has enabled it to be infiltrated much more easily by the Russians.

The Chinese Secret Service is in many respects the most enigmatic of all. Though belonging to a nominally communist government, it is totally unlike the K.G.B., or any other branch of Soviet Intelligence. In the past twenty years it has increasingly tended to avoid aggressive and illegal espionage, but to have sought intelligence mainly by legitimate means. For example, China acquired the knowledge to produce her own nuclear weapons entirely by keeping in close touch with all her physics students and scientists overseas and by diligently collecting all published material on the subject. This may have taken her far longer to obtain than it did Soviet Russia, but an interesting point is that there was not a single instance of China either bribing or in any way suborning scientists of other nations to betray secrets.

Japan is unique in that she has a far broader, more imaginative conception of Intelligence than any other power. Of all peoples of the world none more than the Japanese desire knowledge for its own sake. As in all other aspects of life, this has always been the basis of its Secret Service thinking. Japan has made herself one of the greatest of the world's powers today by applying intelligence-gathering to peaceful purposes, in other words using it to make the nation more prosperous. In the long run it could be greatly to the advantage of the Western World to heed this Japanese lesson and profit from it.

The original inspiration for Japanese intelligence-gathering dates back 2,450 years when Sun Tzu, the Chinese strategist, expounded his techniques of espionage. It was the quotation from his works made at the beginning of this chapter which became the prime axiom of Japanese Secret Service down the ages.

Many Japanese scholars have paid tribute to the intellectual debt which their nation owes to Sun Tzu, whose work, *Ping Fa*, or *The Strategy of War*, lays down so many principles of intelligence work which are still astonishingly applicable even in these sophisticated days. Not only have they studied *Ping Fa*, but down the years they have elaborated and adapted Sun Tzu's expositions in their own inimitable style and, let it be said, with far greater efficiency than the Chinese. One finds echoes of Sun Tzu in the speeches and writings of countless generals of Nippon. Even in medieval times his thesis that it was the better strategy to defeat the enemy psychologically rather than militarily came to be accepted by some of the warlords. Later under Toyotomi Hideyoshi, that brilliant unifier of the Japanese empire, it became the main theme of his policy.

Captain Malcolm Kennedy, who has written extensively on various aspects of the history of Japan and was a former British military attaché in Tokyo, attributed much of the success of Japanese intelligence during the Russo-Japanese War of 1904 to being "a result of generations of study of the axioms laid down by the two Chinese strategists, Wu and Sun."[2] Right up to the time of the attack on the U.S. Fleet at Pearl Harbor Japanese tactics for acquiring intelligence and putting it to practical use had been borrowed from *Ping Fa*.

Invariably when Japan borrows an idea from another nation she improves upon it. Thus sometimes the workings of her secret services have baffled her rivals. Occasionally Japanese Intelligence in action has been so blatantly daring and obvious that it has not been recognised for what it is. At other times it has kept so low a profile that the more complacent bureaucrats of other secret services have been foolish enough to propound the theory that Japan never had an effective Intelligence organisation.

To understand the motivation of Japanese Secret Service throughout history one needs to appreciate two distinct factors in the national character. The first was the strong spirit of independence and individualism which for centuries caused Japan to isolate herself from the outside world. This may have kept the nation backward for too long, but it also strengthened the national character, giving it a powerful impetus to survive and nurturing the patriotism of the people. The second and all-important factor was the intense desire for all kinds of knowledge, the inborn curiosity of the race. This amply compensated for the early isolationist tendencies and meant that, once Japan opened up contacts with the outside world, she was able to catch up with the achievements of other nations in an astonishingly short time.

In the twelfth century Japan was largely ruled by the Shogunate, a martial organisation which had its headquarters at Kamakura which was near the present capital, Tokyo. It was when the Shogunate authorities decided to isolate Japan from the rest of the world that the hostility of the rulers towards foreigners communicated itself to the people. Prior to this the Japanese had always shown great courtesy and hospitality to visitors from overseas. In the era of the Tokugwa Bakafu military government a huge team of official spies was recruited to keep constantly on the move up and down the country, watching and listening for any signs of revolt or criticism of the government. Any indiscreet comment or tactless action was liable to result in the arrest of an individual or even a whole family. Spying tended to become a national habit.

In those days there was an elite corps of Japanese spies, usually recruited from the *samurai*, or noble class, who practised *nijitsu*. In the Japanese-English dictionary a *ninja* is defined as "a *samurai* who mastered the art of making himself invisible through some artifice and is chiefly engaged in espionage." A *ninja* was also reputed to be able to walk on water and resembles a combination of James Bond and Batman.

Yet, quite apart from the espionage tactics of the Shogunate, the fact that the Japanese have a natural curiosity about all kinds of things has frequently led to their being suspected of spying, both by their own people and foreigners, when all they have been thirsting for is innocent knowledge. Spy scares have been frequent in the country largely because of this insatiable quest for even legitimate information.

The zeal for learning even extended to a passion for divination, or trying to ascertain what would happen in future. As the twentieth century draws to a close futurology is being regarded in some circles as a science and various institutes for predicting future trends by computer analysis are being set up in various parts of the world. If Japan is well ahead in such prediction techniques today, one need only look to the sixth century A.D. for a clue.

Fortune-telling has always been popular in Japan. Traditionally, the status of the fortune-teller has remained high even if today his or her counterpart may more often be a computer-operating futurologist using scientific techniques. The *onmyóshi*, as the ancient diviners were called, not only counted as a branch of the priesthood, but acquired the position of governmental advisers in the period when Nara was the capital. They were responsible to the Imperial Court in the early Nara period for making predictions for the future. It could be said that they were a vital link in a primitive intelligence system for not only were they required to forecast developments and events, but also to analyse information that was given them. Divination was regarded as being indispensable to secret service and a special section to conduct it was set up by the Imperial Court, the *Onyó Ryó*. It ranked as a department of the Ministry of Internal Affairs.

The *onmyóshi* were in effect a team of civil servants who were responsible to the *Dajokan* (Council of State) for presenting their forecasts and analyses. Governmental policy was thus formulated on their psychic talents which were chiefly dependent on the Japanese adaptation of Chinese astrological principles. The Japanese zodiac (*Junishi*) was divided into twelve signs exactly the same as the Chinese calendrical zodiac, but the methods of divination varied considerably. For the *onmyóshi* developed and laid down some twenty-six official methods of divination which were accepted by the Imperial Court.

When the Emperor Temmu was ruler for thirteen years until his death in 686 A.D., he not only introduced centralised government and curtailed the influence of the clans, but expanded the teaching of Buddhism and set up the *Jingikan* (literally, "Office of Deities") to signify the special relationship of Shinto worship, Buddhism and the ruling family. Temmu took a special interest in astronomy, a subject which in those early years was hardly distinguishable from astrology. He also began the compilation of the first histories of Japan, the *Kojiki* ("Record of Ancient Matters"). Some indication of the influence of the *onmyóshi* may be gathered from their carefully established links with the *Jingikan*. For the Office of Deities actually took precedence over the State Council and inside the *onmyóshi* was an hereditary office of divination, the *urabe*, who reported directly to the *Jingikan*. This relationship can perhaps best be explained by its British equivalent in which the head of the Secret Service has direct access to the Prime Minister of the day.

Among the twenty-six methods of divination were, apart from astrology and graphology, such well-established systems as palmistry, onomancy (a form of numerology) and rhadomancy (an unusual method of using a divining-rod). Some of the other systems related to meteorological and geological conditions. There was aeromancy (sometimes known as the mystery of *koku*) which made forecasts through a study of air, cloud and weather signs. Another of these twenty-six methods, still being studied and adapted in World War II, was austromancy, which in the Nara period was a primitive science of wind study.

Austromancy was given top priority in the *Onyó Ryó* and early on it was looked upon as a vital element in Japanese naval defence. The source of the wind, its force and effects were studied with great diligence with the intention of seeing how such knowledge could be used to the disadvantage of a potential enemy. *Kamikaze* (divine wind) was the name which the Japanese gave to the type of storm which helped them to check invasion attempts by Kublai Khan in the thirteenth century. On that occasion, in 1281, the weather aided the Japanese and a devastating typhoon played havoc with the Mongol fleets. Since then austromancy was developed into something much more scientific, though the magic of the phrase *Kamikaze* became a tradition of the Japanese Navy and austromancy is said to have played a useful role in strategy against the Russian Navy in the Russo-Japanese War at the beginning of the twentieth century. The word itself was often used in the press and on the radio in World War II when referring to the suicidal and daredevil attacks by Japanese pilots against Allied warships. *Kamikaze* Operations was the phrase used by Vice-Admiral Takijiro On-ishi, to describe many of these courageous, if foolhardy attacks. He made great play with the word *Kamikaze* in briefing his pilots, comparing their dive-bombing on to the decks of enemy ships with the havoc wrought by a typhoon, and conjuring up visions of the advantages which could be conferred on them by the God of the Winds, Fujin.

The same spirit of fanatical patriotism inspired the *ronins* (romantically-minded adventurers) who joined the various secret societies which sprang up in Japan in the latter part of the last century. It was their zeal for the national cause as well as their natural bravery which made them such first-class spies and collectors of intelligence. It is not easy to find a parallel in the Western World for a *ronin*. He was a soldier without a master, similar to a mercenary, but his motives were entirely patriotic and he would never sell himself to the highest bidder. There was something of the spirit of the Crusader about him and at the same time the fanaticism of a Jacobin. These societies eventually became the foundations of an all-embracing Japanese Secret Service. It was a service which by the 1930s had developed into a vast intelligence network spreading all over the world. It achieved something like total espionage more effectively than anything even Soviet Russia has organised. At one time, curiously enough at the very moment when Japan was moving further away from democratic government, it almost deserved the title of the People's Secret Service. For it was backed up by the people, often by those who were not even members of an Intelligence Service, by trade unionists and peasants as much as by *ronins* and professional Intelligence officers.

Secret service means different things to each nation. National conceptions of it vary enormously. Motivation changes over the years. While the requirements of national defence play a great part and sometimes a desire for aggression and empire-building can be an even more potent influence, quite often secret service in its modern sense—at least among genuinely democratic nations—can simply be a case of wishing to keep up with one's neighbours.

In short, secret service need not be sinister, though all too frequently it is. In this respect Japan, with its passionate emphasis on the acquisition of knowledge, may pave the way to a more peaceful and eminently sensible concept of secret service in the future. All the signs are there for those who wish to read them. Provided the world can avoid global war for another twenty years, it is possible that secret intelligence can become simply the acquisition of information which can help to produce more prosperity, which can show how to overcome food shortages in certain areas of the world, how to harness both science and the behaviour of human beings to improved living standards. Tokyo has already pointed the way to this future use of secret service in countless ways which do not seem to have been grasped by many other nations. An example has been set in that capital, the full implications of which have yet to dawn on much of the rest of the world—some Western Powers, the Soviet bloc and the Third World.

Cynics might say that this is an unjustifiably optimistic view in the light of Japan's actions in the 1930s and 1940s. Yet there have been very many Japanese statesmen who have always held views which encourage the pursuit of knowledge for peaceful purposes and cooperation with the rest of the world. In May, 1939, Prince Saionji, one of the most liberal of Japan's elder statesmen, told his secretary, Baron Kumao Harada: "Since the time of the Meiji Restoration it has been an accepted fact not to use such terms as 'Orient' and 'Occident' in opposition to each other. In spite of the dissolution of terms contrasting East and West by the honourable intentions of the Emperor Meiji, it is unpleasant to see the right-wing elements and militarists use them."[3]

2

The Spymaster Who Unified a Nation

> "The tale of Hideyoshi's life is one of the
> most wonderful records of the triumph of
> genius over highly formidable obstacles
> that Japanese history contains . . . Few more
> remarkable lives than that of Hideyoshi
> have been lived"
>
> Walter Dening

THE CHILD WHO was destined to become Japan's greatest general, if not her greatest statesman, was born on the first day of the first month of the fifth year of Tembun in the Japanese calendar (1 January, 1536). There was even a legend that a new star heralded his entrance into the world. His name was Toyotomi Hideyoshi.

At this period Japan was an isolated, neglected territory, totally uncoordinated, and reduced to misery and abject ruin after two centuries of internal strife. The various provinces which comprised the islands of Japan were ruled by some ten warlords or barons who spent their lives plotting against one another. Of these barons only three of them were near enough to Kyoto, then the capital, for them to establish any kind of relationship with the sovereign.

The Bakafu, a system of military rule which had been set up in the twelfth century, was still in existence when Hideyoshi was born. While it lasted, wrote Walter Dening, Hideyoshi's biographer, "the whole empire was one network of espionage . . . the fundamental principle of that system of government was suspicion."[1]

11

As a child Toyotomi Hideyoshi was fonder of sport than of books. He was intelligent, quick witted and had a surprising talent for reasoned argument for one so young, but as a pupil he was indolent. Quick to fly into a temper, he also rebelled against authority. Most contemporary accounts of him say that he resembled a monkey and was nicknamed as such. Yet portraits of him in middle age do not lend credence to this description: perhaps the paintings were intended to flatter him, even though legend proclaims that he was somewhat proud of being likened to a monkey. He was outstandingly successful in any sporting activity he took up, whether it was wrestling, jumping or climbing trees. Reprimanded at his temple school for his lack of concentration on religious instruction, he replied: "You priests are all a set of beggars. There is no reason why a brave child born in a world of strife should learn how to become a beggar." That comment reveals how at a very early age Hideyoshi felt instinctively that there was much to set right in his native country.

When he was twelve years old the priests expelled him from school for destroying a Buddhist idol. He is said to have carried out this action while addressing the idol in these words: "You are said to be a divinity that gives help to men. On this account you receive great honour from all who visit this temple. Food is supplied to you every day, but you seem to eat nothing. How can an idol that takes no food obtain strength sufficient to impart help to others? . . . you are no divinity, but you are a dumb idol and I will smash you to bits."[2]

After this episode Hideyoshi was dismissed from thirty-eight menial jobs in quick sucession. In his neighbourhood he was apparently regarded as unemployable, while his reply to this criticism was that he had a very low opinion of all his employers. Then he decided to try his luck on his own. Though he had condemned begging as a way of life, he set out on to the road while in his early teens, intending to survive by asking for alms, but anxious to find the kind of employment which offered a prospect of advancement. Within a very short time he had persuaded a gang of highwaymen to take him into their service. Koroku, the head of the gang, seemed impressed by the lad's quick wits and promised him food and shelter if Hideyoshi would seek out suitable houses to rob. So the youth went out scouting, studying the layout of various mansions, noting the weak points in their defences and, more important, the quickest means by which to escape from them.

Eventually one of the houses he had indicated was approved as a target for the gang. Hideyoshi not only showed his fellow conspirators how to scale the fence and open the gate, but led the way himself. When he got inside the house the inhabitants heard him and came rushing in his direction in the dark. Hiding behind a pillar, he had the presence of mind to throw a stone into an inside well, at the same time letting out a scream, making his pursuers think he had fallen in. While they ran to the well, Hideyoshi quietly escaped.

This display of initiative and self-confidence in one so young endeared him to Koroku, the highwaymen's chief, who eventually rewarded the boy by giving him a prized sword made by one of the best military craftsmen in the country. For a brief period he returned to his home, but Hideyoshi felt that if he was to fulfil his ambitions he must escape from this environment. His father was only a poor woodcutter and had no influence. He had long pondered on how he could get himself a post in the service of Oda Nobunaga, the most important of Japan's warlords. One way of achieving this was to find an excuse for calling on the homes of the illustrious. The chance to do this came when a priest asked him if he would join in a *fuda*—distributing mission. This was an annual event which consisted of selling cards on which prayers were written at the houses of the mighty.

While carrying out this task Hideyoshi was introduced to a wealthy retainer of one of the noble families of Imagawa. As a result he was offered a post as a servant to the family and, as an added inducement, lessons in fencing. Soon he became a highly skilled fencer. When he came of age his master suggested that he should settle down and marry. This he did, while still secretly planning to enter the service of Oda Nobunaga whenever the opportunity presented itself. He paid another visit to his parents and, so cheekily confident was he of his ultimate success, that he told them: "None of you need expect to hear from me. I will make arrangements that in case I die before my name is known all over the country, you shall be informed of my death. Otherwise you can take no news to be good news."

In 1558 he set out for a mountainous territory where he knew that Nobunaga had gone on a hunting expedition. With some difficulty, largely overcome by his bold and imperious manner, he succeeded in having an audience with the warlord. Nobunaga was duly impressed by the answers which young Hideyoshi gave to his searching questions and told him he could

join his retinue as a kind of odd-job man. Turning to his re-
tainers, Nobunaga jokingly commented: "We have had good
sport today. We have bagged a young monkey and can afford
to go home."

From them on Hideyoshi set out to do everything in his
power to impress on his master that he was equal to any task
he was given. Nobunaga soon noticed that Hideyoshi was always up and working long before anyone else, that he undertook
all jobs with great efficiency and, even more important, that
he was observant and able to give good advice. Soon Hideyoshi
was serving Nobunaga not only as an able officer, but as an
astute adviser who was often able to dissuade his master from
many impulsive proposals. The secret of Hideyoshi lay as much
in his originality of thought and his persuasive and forceful
tongue as in his military prowess. Wisely, he had taught himself
shogi, the Japanese game of strategy which is similar to chess.
It was a game highly regarded by all generals of the day, and
especially by Nobunaga, as an exercise in military strategy.
Hideyoshi proved to be singularly adept at this game.

The proof of Hideyoshi's wisdom and advice frequently
revealed itself in the military successes of his master. Nobunaga
gradually increased his authority over other territories and enlarged his dominions. Within a few years he became master
of a large portion of Japan, defeating his adversaries in a series
of battles in which Hideyoshi's talents showed to great advantage. Soon he was to become Nobunaga's leading general. A
natural leader of men, with the ability to win the confidence
of others, Hideyoshi established himself as much as a statesman
as an undoubtedly brave and resourceful soldier.

Nobunaga had not only established himself in Kyoto, but
built a magnificent palace there. But his self-imposed task of
pacification was still incomplete when he was murdered in 1582
by one of his own captains. It was then that Hideyoshi stepped
into the breach and undertook this task himself. His military
victories owed as much to his carefully conceived plans for
obtaining intelligence on his prospective enemies as to his strategy in the field. He, too, followed the precepts of Sun Tzu,
though he adapted these in the most original and cunning manner. Employing a huge army of spies, he insisted on their
travelling the length and breadth of the country so that he was
kept informed of what was happening in each area. These spies
were told to keep on the move and their journeys were planned
in strict rotation so that the reports of one group could be

checked against those who came after them. When planning a campaign he always sent out special agents long beforehand to send him back detailed reports.

For example, when in 1587 Hideyoshi was plotting to subdue the island of Kyushu in the southernmost part of the Japanese empire, he delayed his invasion for more than a year simply because he wanted his secret agents not only to gain more information, but to conduct a propaganda campaign to subvert the people. He asked for and got detailed sketches and maps of the terrain, news of harvests, food supplies and transports as well as reports on the relations of the warlords with their troops. It was by this time a deliberate ploy of Hideyoshi to destroy or win over to his side all who opposed him. As a long-term measure he preferred to win allies. In achieving this latter aim he showed both patience and forbearance. He had a tendency to despise convention and the proprieties of life and often seemed to revel in his proletarian background. Once, when one of his aides dared to make a mild rebuke about his apparent lack of dignity, Hideyoshi replied: "Don't worry about that. There is no one in the country greater than I am, so nobody will rebel."

But though he might often appear arrogant, he knew exactly when to be conciliatory and contrite. It was his deep, instinctive psychological understanding of people that made Hideyoshi such an outstanding leader. His overtures to his enemies, usually made only when the *Taiko* himself had carefully studied the reports of his spies, were superbly timed. The warlord Iyeyasu held out against Hideyoshi for some time, but then offered to surrender. His offer was accepted and Iyeyasu was taken to the *Taiko* who suggested that his rival should try to persuade two other chieftains, Yoshihisa and Yoshihiro, to lay down their arms. Iyeyasu failed in this mission and returned to Hideyoshi's camp. The latter's generals argued vehemently that Iyeyasu was playing a double game and simply trying to regain his power. Hideyoshi, however, took an opposite view: he believed that Iyeyasu could be trusted as an ally.

The power of Shimazu Yoshihisa at that time was immense. He had total control of the three provinces of Hyuga, Osumi and Satsuma. People belonging to other provinces were not allowed to enter Shimazu's domains even for trade and it was impossible to find anyone of another clan who knew these territories. So Hideyoshi organised a special Intelligence Department solely to overcome this problem a year before he sent his armies to Kyushu. He had ascertained that Yoshihisa was a devout Buddhist so he arranged for some half dozen of his spies to be infiltrated into the service of a high-ranking priest named Kennyo who was setting out on a special mission to see Yoshihisa. Among these spies were two of his ablest warriors, Kasuya Takemori and Hirano Nagayusu. It has been a striking feature of Japanese intelligence work down the centuries that even the most aristocratic or high-ranking persons will willingly accept the disguises of the lowest type of worker in order to carry out espionage assignments. Even in modern times there have been instances of colonels posing as coolies and naval commanders as fishermen.

Kennyo had previously been Yoshihisa's teacher and not only was he treated with great deference by Yoshihisa, but he and his servants were allowed to travel far and wide in the provinces. Among the places they visited was Shishijima, a famous Buddhist centre of learning, where Hideyoshi's spies learned a great deal of intelligence. At this stage Hideyoshi moved his army to the bank of the Sendai-gawa and set up his headquarters in a temple called Taiheiki. When the priest Kennyo heard that Hideyoshi was not far away and that war was imminent, he told Yoshihisa that he did not wish to be a burden on the community at such a time and felt he should leave. Kennyo was then given guides who led his party out of Yoshihisa's domains by an infrequented route which brought them close to Hideyoshi's camp. The spies were able to give Hideyoshi an immense amount of information as well as to act as guides for his 50,000-strong army marching on Shishijima.

Yet even then Hideyoshi's whole policy was conciliatory rather than aggressive. If he could achieve what he wanted without fighting, he regarded this as statesmanlike generalship. His generals wanted an immediate advance on the one remaining stronghold in the enemy's territory, but Hideyoshi stayed his hand and waited for three days to open negotiations. "Even to those who have been able to trace the spirit in which Hideyoshi conducted the campaign from the first, his liberality will appear surprising," wrote J. H. Gubbins in his scholarly paper on Hideyoshi and the Satsuma clan.[3] "To advance so far and yet not enter the rebel capital; to have his enemy within his grasp and yet not to crush him; to hold back a victorious army in the hour of victory: all this argues a forbearance and strength of will which few generals in those days possessed." Eventually Iyeyasu sent his head priest to the Satsuma capital to urge surrender. Yoshihisa accepted the terms. Thus Hideyoshi achieved his ends with the minimum of bloodshed and more lasting goodwill than he could otherwise have expected. By 1590 he had succeeded in fulfilling his task and unifying the whole of Japan. It transpired that not only had Hideyoshi infiltrated his spies into the ranks of the priest Kennyo, but that the priest himself had been used as an agent. Kennyo had guessed Hideyoshi's purpose and offered his services in helping to organise intelligence. He was rewarded with a considerable sum of money which he used to build the Nishi Hongwanji Temple which became one of the architectural marvels of Japan. Hideyoshi also ordered the building of the Samboin Temple as well as planning and designing the garden beside the Juraka Palace.

Having come to terms with Iyeyasu, Hideyoshi turned his attention overseas. He began licensing Japan's shipping to Vietnam, Manila and Siam. Initially he encouraged the Christian missionaries who had first come to Japan in 1549 and had by the end of the century won some 750,000 converts among the people. Hideyoshi's attitude towards the Christians was somewhat cynical. Perhaps he felt they might either be persuaded to assist him, or that he could play them off against the Buddhists about whom he was equally cynical. But he insisted that Japan "must not become a battleground for rival Christian creeds." The missionaries failed to realise that Hideyoshi was not a leader to be disobeyed. They proved to be just as hungry for power as some of the warlords and the Franciscans ignored the *Taiko*'s insistence that they had the status only of ambassadors and must not indulge in religious propaganda. Then one of Hideyoshi's spies learned from a foreign seaman that the Spanish empire overseas had been built up by using missionaries as agents. The information was passed back to the *Taiko* and he acted swiftly. In 1597 he introduced his anti-Christian decrees without warning and immediately enforced them, executing six European missionaries and twenty Japanese converts. Yet even after this he allowed merchants from Christian countries to do business in Nagasaki and made full use of Christian Japanese officers, two of whom were actually his generals—Kuroda Yoshitaka and Konishi Yukinaga.

Only once, towards the end of his life, did Hideyoshi blunder. Until 1592 Japan had hardly ever indulged in aggression against other territories and peoples. Then, on Hideyoshi's orders an invasion attempt was made on Korea. This lengthy campaign was a disastrous failure. By 1597 he had come to realise that he had made the greatest mistake of his career and shortly before his death he expressed regret that he should have caused the loss of so many of his countrymen's lives in a foreign land. Almost his last order was that Iyeyasu, his successor, should recall the troops from Korea.

Even in his old age Hideyoshi still had a genius for playing tricks on the enemy. There is still extant a record of a dialogue between the *Taiko* and Asana Nagamasa, who was in control of the *Taiko's* finances at a time when Hideyoshi was planning to send 100,000 men to Korea:

"Nagamasa: What commissariat plans must be made?

"Hideyoshi: You should prepare three million *koku* of rice.

"Nagamasa: What is to be done with the rice?

"Hideyoshi: Use every transport you can lay your hands on and send it over to Fusan.

"Nagamasa: After landing, how are we to protect it?

"Hideyoshi: Don't protect it. Just see what happens.

"Nagamasa: If we don't protect it, the Koreans will capture it all.

"Hideyoshi: Isn't that what we want?

"Nagamasa (puzzled): But if we lose our provisions, we shall be in trouble.

"Hideyoshi: It is a case of 3 million *koku*. Such a huge quantity of rice cannot be carried off in a hurry, nor can it be eaten in a short time.

"Nagamasa: But the Koreans will carry it inland.

"Hideyoshi: If they do that, nothing could suit us better. To get the enemy to do your transport service for you for the amount of rice that can be consumed on the road is good enough. By adopting this plan, our troops will always find provisions waiting for them as they advance."[4]

What Hideyoshi predicted in due course came to pass. The rice was captured and carried off by the Koreans and was repeatedly recaptured by the Japanese as they moved further inland. In the early stages of this campaign the Koreans suffered enormous losses not only in human life, but in goods and chattels. But the campaign dragged on too long, the Chinese intervened and in the long run food shortages proved to be a major cause of Japan's inability to follow up her early victories.

Hideyoshi not only became a legend in his own lifetime, but the one great statesman figure of sixteenth century Japan who has served as an example into modern times. Hideyoshi became to Japanese planners and directors of intelligence what Sun Tzu had been centuries before—the supreme example of a successful spymaster. This example was certainly followed in later centuries by the Japanese themselves, but Hideyoshi himself has been lavishly praised by many Western historians. "The greatest statesman of his century, whether in Japan or Europe,"[5] is how Professor James Murdoch described him, while that brilliant military commentator, Captain Liddell Hart, rated him as a better general than Napoléon Bonaparte.

3

The Agent From England

"The lowly-born William Adams, when cast in wretchedness on the shores of Japan, was not, indeed, received as a prince; yet this man . . . eventually attained rank and acquired possessions in the [Japanese] empire equal to those of a prince"

Thomas Rundle, *Memorials of the Empire of Japan in the 16th. & 17th. Centuries*

WHEN HIDEYOSHI DIED in 1598 his last wish was that Iyeyasu should succeed him until such time as his seven-year-old son, Hideyori, could assume office. But Iyeyasu soon found that the transitional period put great strains on the unity of imperial government. After so strong a character as Hideyoshi it was perhaps inevitable that some chieftains should once again attempt empire-building on their own.

The chieftains' methods of undermining Iyeyasu's authority were to make mischief by means of a whispering campaign and the exploitation of forged documents. So seriously was his position threatened that during the first two years of his rule he must often have wished for the sudden appearance of a genuine ally in no way associated with any of the scheming warlords of his own country.

In April, 1600, this unspoken and probably subconscious wish was granted to him in a surprising manner.

Sailing from the Netherlands island of Texel in 1598, a fleet of Dutch ships seeking new lands with which to trade crossed

the Atlantic Ocean and passed through the Straits of Magellan
to Chile. Storms, depleted food supplies and sickness had played
havoc with this fleet which was much depleted by the time it
left Chile. Their captains knew nothing of Japan, but they had
been told there was a great demand there for woollen cloths.
During February, 1600, one of the ships was parted from the
remainder of the fleet and, death and sickness having taken
their toll, eventually only had two of the ship's company fit
to carry on working, one of whom was the pilot, Will Adams,
who hailed from Gillingham in Kent.

Adverse winds buffeted the ship and caused considerable
damage and in due course she drifted down on the Japanese
coast. To save the craft from being dashed against the rocky
headlands, Adams ordered anchors to be dropped. Within an
hour Japanese fishing craft, skulled by eight men each, came
out to greet them. The crew of the Dutch ship were treated
quite courteously, but it was soon abundantly clear that they
would in effect be prisoners, albeit with the status of something
approaching honoured guests. Lack of a common language was
naturally a serious barrier and communication at first could
only be made by signs. Adams was the only member of the
ship's company to appreciate the difficulties of their position
and to realise that the best way to cope with it was by making
sure that they had something worth offering to the Japanese.
Clearly the latter were intensely curious about their strange
visitors and desperately anxious to learn all about their ship,
how it was worked and especially their methods of navigation.
Quickly grasping that the Japanese had brought with them a
Portuguese in the hope that he could interpret for them, Adams
presented him to the one member of their crew who had a
smattering of that language.

After a while the crew were ferried ashore and given accommodation in "a house only two stories high and built of
wood and plaster, the outside being whitewashed to look exactly like stone . . . two rooms, one above and another below;
the latter was divided into three compartments, the first for the
sick men, the second for the captain and the last for Master
Adams and one other, Melichor van Santvoort." This much
was gleaned from a letter written by van Santvoort who was
still living in Nagasaki twenty-six years later.[1]

They were treated quite well, being fed at regular intervals
and provided with baths. A few days later a Jesuit priest was
produced by the Japanese and it soon became evident to the

Europeans that he understood English as well as actually speaking Dutch and Portuguese. He paid more attention to Will Adams than to any of the others, including the sick captain. Clearly, he regarded him as the most knowledgeable of the crew and their best spokesman. Adams was then able to put forward a plea that in exchange for woollen clothes the Japanese would supply sufficient food and other stores to enable them to make the voyage home after repairs had been carried out to the ship.

But the last thing the small number of Spanish and Portuguese traders in Japan wanted was to see any of their own strictly limited commerce lost to the Dutch or the English. Both the latter races were looked upon as enemies of Spain and Portugal and despised Protestants. No doubt, too, the Jesuit priest was equally determined to resist any attempts to infiltrate Japan with non-Catholic forms of Christianity. He made it clear to Adams that any request for a trading deal with the Japanese must be made through the Portuguese envoy. From all accounts Adams was equally emphatic that he had no intention of dealing with anyone but the Japanese.

The priest was furious and reported back to the Portuguese and Spanish envoys the gist of Adams' comments. They decided to urge the Japanese to have the crew of the Dutch ship executed on the grounds that they were no better than pirates. But Iyeyasu had learned much from Hideyoshi about the psychology of foreigners and how very often their apparent honesty marked devious purposes and selfish aims. He possessed to a high degree that Japanese characteristic of being eager to learn something new and to him these visitors from the Netherlands and the single Englishman were from another world. Logically, he argued that if he had them executed he would never learn whatever secrets or knowledge they might offer. At the same time he was astute enough to realise that the Spaniards and Portuguese were only thinking of their own interests in wishing to have the captured crew put to death.

However, at that time Iyeyasu was busily involved in putting down rebellion in his own domains. So he gave orders that no action was to be taken against the imprisoned crew until he had time to interview them. There was an interval of eight months in which period Adams learned sufficient of the Japanese language to make himself understood, thus increasingly becoming the spokesman for the whole crew. Iyeyasu in the meantime had shown that he possessed something of the skill and generalship of Hideyoshi, for he managed to rout the forces of his rivals despite the fact that he was outnumbered almost two to one. Thus he returned to his palace in an excellent humour.

When the crew of the Dutch ship were brought before Iyeyasu the Spaniards and Portuguese repeated their demands that the men should be executed or banished from the country. But Iyeyasu disliked the peremptory tone of these demands; he felt it was an impertinence for foreigners to tell him what he should do in his own territory. He also sensed that the Spaniards and Portuguese were afraid that the newcomers, if allowed to remain in Japan, would prove themselves to be more accomplished and acceptable advisers. Iyeyasu then insisted that no decision would be made until he had interrogated the crew himself.

He soon found that Adams was the most intelligent and, with some help in interpreting from another and friendlier Catholic priest, the Englishman was plied with many searching questions. The more they talked the more Iyeyasu took a liking to Adams. Soon it was apparent that the Japanese chieftain had no intention of executing the crew and that, though he might insist upon their remaining in Japan for some time, they would be taken into his service and not be confined to their house-prison any longer. Later the crew were ordered to go to Edo where, in 1603, Iyeyasu established his capital and set up Shogunate rule with himself as the Shogun.

"In the ende of five yeeres," wrote Adams in a letter he sent to England, "I made supplication to the King to goe out of this land, desiring to see my poore wife and children ... with which request the Emperour was not well pleased, and would not let me goe any more for my countrey, but to byde in his land."[2] In this letter Adams made it clear that he wanted his wife to have news of him. The English pilot had been born in Gillingham and had left a wife behind in that town. It was undoubtedly a blow to him when Iyeyasu announced that he would never be permitted to leave Japan.

Yet on all other counts he was treated generously by the Shogun, who had been enormously impressed by his experience. Adams had not only served as master and pilot in the navy of Queen Elizabeth, but had been in the service of the Company of Barbary Merchants before joining the Dutch merchant fleet. Iyeyasu gave him a considerable sum of money to share out with the rest of the crew and stressed that he looked upon him as "my most honoured adviser and Intelligencer."

Referring to letters and documents of this period (including six letters actually written by Adams), Thomas Rundle wrote that they threw some light on the "early intercourse between the empire of Japan and the states of the West". He added that "the government of Japan is exhibited in a most favourable light. It was distinguished at that period by high-bred courtesy, combined with refined liberality in principle and generous hospitality in practice... In the instance of a Governor of the Philippines, although shipwrecked and destitute, the claims of rank were admitted. He was received with the honours due to a prince; while he sojourned in the land, similar honours were paid to him, and, to facilitate his departure, he was furnished with all the means generosity could dictate. The lowly-born William Adams, when cast in wretchedness on the shores of Japan, was not, indeed, received as a prince; yet this man, commencing life in the capacity of 'apprentice to Master Nicolas Diggines, of Limehouse', eventually attained rank and acquired possessions in the empire equal to those of a prince. With no claims to consideration but talent and good conduct, he became the esteemed councillor of the sagacious and powerful monarch by whom the land that had afforded him shelter was ruled."[3]

That Adams soon became a valued intelligence agent in an old-fashioned sense is shown in many ways. He swiftly made himself indispensable in a variety of ways and, being extremely well housed and treated, was able to take a philosophical view of not being able to see his native land again. He was employed as personal instructor to the Shogun in all navigational and nautical matters as well as in mathematics. When Iyeyasu wanted to know anything about the outside world, it was to Adams he turned, not the Portuguese or Spaniards. Again, when the Shogun wished to know what these foreign merchants were plotting or thinking, Adams was asked to discover this, using the crew of the Dutch ship as his spies as well as some of the Japanese. As the influence of the other Europeans decreased so that of Adams was enhanced. The Shogun insisted that if the Spaniards and Portuguese had any favours to ask or requests to put to him, these should be made through Adams. At one stage Adams was even required to spy upon some of the ladies at court and to report on their movements and conversation to the Shogun.

Later Iyeyasu ordered that Adams' salary should be increased and that he should have a permanent home in the palace grounds. In return he requested that Adams should supervise the building of a ship which would incorporate in it the latest navigational aids and modern guns. At the same time the Shogun promised that Adams could arrange a trading treaty between Japan and the Netherlands and Britain. It was part of this bargain that Adams should organise "suche intelligence as might be of use to the Emperour from distante parts of the world and especially suche matters touching on the designs of foreign nacions". In letters home Adams described his standard of living in Japan: "the Emperour has given me a living like unto a lordship in England, with eighty or ninety husbandmen that be as my slaves or servents".[4]

In 1613 Captain Richard Cocks, who had arrived to establish a British trading station, revealed something of Adams' close relations with the Shogun in this letter back to England: "The truth is that the Emperor esteemeth hym much, and he may goe in and speake with hym at all tymes, when kinges and princes are kept without."[5]

Adams was able to demonstrate to the Shogun that the arrival of the Dutch and English to trade with Japan had prevented the Portuguese and Spaniards from monopolising this commerce. He had also assisted the Shogun by supervising the building of cargo vessels capable of making long voyages. Above all Adams kept Iyeyasu exceptionally well informed on latest news from the outside world by interrogating closely all visiting ships' masters and compiling reports for the Shogun. To some extent he may have aided and abetted the campaign of persecution waged against the Spaniards and Portuguese and the increasing restrictions on practising Christians.

About this time Adams discovered that some of the Japanese Christians were rallying around Hideyoshi's son, Hideyori, who had not had the chance to become Shogun as he had anticipated. Hideyori lived in a fortress at Osaka and when Iyeyasu heard of the plot to support Hideyoshi's son against him, he sent a force to attack the fortress before Hideyori could make any move. Hideyori and his mother killed themselves rather than surrender and so at length Iyeyasu was the unchallenged ruler of his country.

In 1616 Iyeyasu died and from then onwards the campaign against foreigners was stepped up even though Adams apparently had as much influence with the new Shogun as with Iyeyasu. There was considerable agitation against the Portuguese and Spaniards, but it was not Adams' fault that the English trading station was closed after ten years on account of mismanagement. It would seem that the "English disease" was just as prevalent among British traders in that era as it is today. The Dutch station was permitted to remain open even after the expulsion of foreigners and the missionaries in 1638–9, and this remained Japan's sole link with the outside world for a very long time. Iyemitsu, the new Shogun, was much more hostile to foreigners than Iyeyasu had ever been. Iyeyasu had encouraged "independence of thought"—his own phrase—but his death became a signal for a system of despotism and intolerance. Thus began the era of Japan's isolation from the rest of the world. Yet, despite this, it was a period in which culturally Japan made great progress in all the arts, and the national character seems to have been strengthened rather than weakened in the process. Out of this isolation there developed a feeling of sturdy independence, self-reliance and self-discipline.

It was unquestionably the influence of Adams and the knowledge of his usefulness which permitted the Dutch trading station to be kept open so long. Adams himself was raised to the rank of a samurai and given the privilege of wearing two swords. He assumed the Japanese name of Anjin Miura (*Anjin* meaning the "needle, or compass watcher") and took a Japanese wife by the name of Kadenoyu Magone who gave him a son, Joseph, and a daughter, Susan. One account of his estate is that "the house itself was of vast size, moated after the fashion of a castle, magnificently decorated and strongly built, surrounded by beautiful gardens, wrought after the Japan fashion into hill and dale, mountain with valley, with rocks, fountains, rivulets, flowering-shrubs, rare trees."[6] Adams died in 1626 and was buried with full honours at Hemi, which overlooks the former naval base of Yokosuka. Later his wife was buried beside him and even in modern times the graves have been venerated by the Japanese. The fame of Adams, the "great English Intelligencer", was honoured down the centuries. A street in Edo was named after him and in 1926 the Japanese Government erected a statue in Tokyo to mark the three hundredth anniversary of his death. That anniversary is still celebrated by some Japanese.

In the next hundred years there was much less demand either for internal or external espionage. Shogunate rule was consolidated and, generally speaking, none came into the country and none left it. But the Japanese were not entirely without intelligence from the outside world. A specially selected team of agents were requested to learn Dutch in order to interrogate the Nagasaki Dutch traders who were allowed to remain. This was the sole link with Europe for very many years.

Similarly the Western nations lacked knowledge of Japan. A typical example of this ignorance was the ease with which George Psalmanazar was able to fool British society when he arrived in London in 1703 with the story that he was a Formosan who had been converted to Christianity. Archibishop Tennison was so impressed by the young man that he persauded him to write a book entitled *An Historical and Geographical Description of Formosa, an island subject to the Emperor of Japan*, dedicated to the Bishop of London. It told how the Japanese had invaded Formosa and occupied the country, despite the fact that the island was then a dependency of China and was not formally ceded to Japan until 1895. Psalmanazar's imposture remained undetected for a long time. He had in fact been born in the north of France, but had acquired a working knowledge of a number of languages from which he had concocted a bogus "Formosan".

In the 1790s a castaway named Kodaya returned to Japan after having spent a year in St. Petersburg, and in the process becoming "a living encylopedia on the strange, huge and unpredictable nation to the north."[7] There followed an eleven-volume report on Russia, entitled *Summary Report of a Raft Drifting in the Northern Seas*, compiled mainly from information supplied by Kodaya, but supplemented by some rather less professional accounts collected from Japanese fishermen who had been shipwrecked and landed on Russian territory.

The compilation of these reports marked the first serious and concerted efforts by the Japanese to acquire intelligence about Russia. Their interest in that country had first been aroused when, unexpectedly, a Bering Straits expedition manned by Russians arrived in Japanese waters in 1739. The Japanese may have been building up their intelligence on the slenderest material from chance castaways and shipwrecked fishermen, but at least they never neglected any opportunity of learning more about the outside world. It is eloquent testimony of the powers of observation of even the humblest of their people that a castaway, patiently interviewed and questioned, could produce information for eleven volumes!

Some years later, taking full advantage of earlier reports, a team of fishermen was sent to explore the islands in the Gulf of Alaska. They reported back that though most of these islands were uninhabited and uninhabitable, others had such high rainfall throughout the year that almost any fruit or vegetable could be grown there as a result of the warm Japanese Current.

4

Secret Societies as an Aid to Intelligence

> "Knowledge shall be sought throughout the world so as to strengthen the foundations of Imperial Rule"
>
> one of the Japanese Five
> Articles Oath of 1868

SOME COLLISIONS WITH British and Russian warships in the early part of the nineteenth century revealed the weaknesses of the Japanese fleet as well as the lack of organisation in the nation's military power. By this time intelligence reports indicated that a power such as Russia could very easily play havoc with Japan if she should have aggressive designs in that part of the world.

At the same time the team of Dutch-speaking students, who continued to benefit Japan by acquiring knowledge of military developments in the West, impressed on the Shogunate the need for stepping up Japan's defences. The northern defences, especially those in Hokkaido, had already been strengthened in case the Russians attempted to invade. No doubt such fears were engendered as much through a realisation of Japanese isolation from the outside world and a lack of allies as from anything positive in their intelligence reports. All these trends helped to push Japan relentlessly and speedily into an escape from feudalism. Gradually it dawned on the nation's leaders that if some changes were not introduced some of the more impatient of the Western countries would not wait if Japan persisted in refusing to open up her ports for trade. In other words, if Japan did not comply, force might be used against her. In the early part of the century various peaceful attempts were made, first by Russia, then by America, to set up commercial relations with Japan. These overtures were politely rejected. Later the Shogunate gave orders that any attempt by unauthorised foreign ships to enter Japanese harbours was to be repelled by force. Even the favoured Dutch, who had a unique position, were not permitted to mediate.

The situation did not really change until 1853 when the American Commodore Perry arrived in the Bay of Yedo in command of four warships, bearing with him a letter from the President of the United States in which was proposed the setting up of a commercial relationship between the two countries. During the same year a Russian ship arrived at Nagasaki with a similar message. This time there was no outright rejection of the requests, but merely a delay in replying. When Commodore Perry arrived a second time with a larger force the Japanese reluctantly agreed to sign a treaty which opened up her various ports to commerce with foreign traders. These treaties did not come fully into effect until 1859.

From then onwards it was only a question of time before Shogunate rule was overthrown. After the signing of the treaty there was widespread criticism that the Shogun had yielded too easily to the demands of the Western nations and especially the United States. For a while the anti-foreigner school of Japanese politicians and soldiers held sway. The extremists of this school of thought were all for waging a preventive war against the Westerners. But the moderates, while disliking the prospect of allowing the foreigners into their ports, were perhaps even more anxious to learn from them and to understand the secrets of their power. In the end curiosity prevailed, while honour was satisfied by abolishing Tokugawa rule and the system of Shogunate government. This did not come about smoothly, however: for some years there was bloodshed, murder and civil war. The only solution seemed to be to restore administrative authority to the Imperial Family.

This was the beginning of the Meiji period. In 1867, with the ending of the Shogunate, the fifteen-year-old Mutsuhito became the Emperor Meiji, and eventually the symbol of Japan's bold step forward towards the twentieth century long before the nineteenth had ended. This was not only the beginning of Japan's modernisation, but of parliamentary government as well.

This diversion into the political history of the era is essential

if the development of Japan's Secret Service is to be understood. From the end of the 1860s onwards the emphasis was
placed on intelligence-gathering in almost every sphere of Japanese life—army, navy, civil service, education and industry.
Never perhaps in the history of the world has one nation set
out upon so comprehensive and broad-based a system of
intelligence-collection. Nothing was neglected, nothing was
allowed to be done haphazardly. The information gleaned was
all obtained systematically, some of it openly, but the greater
part as unobtrusively and secretly as possible. It has frequently
been suggested that Japan over the next hundred years acquired
more intelligence than she could absorb, that much of it was
irrelevant, while much time was wasted in acquiring useless
material. This is nonsense. Japan was largely starting her external intelligence system from scratch. She had so much to
learn that it was only by aiming to obtain every scrap of information that she could possibly be in a position to assess
what was, or was not, important. It must also be remembered
that for Japan to acquire an up-to-date army and navy she
needed an enormous and lengthy intelligence drive before she
could even begin to achieve these things.

Nor was the dislike of foreigners entirely paranoiac: the
Western nations and Russia must take a great deal of the blame.
When nations bring threats of force to back up their demands
for trade, there must inevitably be a fear of imperialistic aggression on the part of the victim nation. Japan had to face threats
of one kind and another from America, Britain, Russia and
France. The truth is that if Japan had not shown some signs of
sturdy independence and resistance to the foreigners, she might
well have been forcibly colonised as was China, Indo-China,
Malaya and India. The murder of an Englishman named Rich-
ardson on the Tokaido highway in 1862 led to the bombardment
and burning of Kagoshima by a British fleet. In 1864 a squadron
of American, British, Dutch and French warships attacked Shi-
monoseki and went ashore to dismantle the gun defences. There
were many other similar incidents of aggression.

The first major attempt to establish serious official contact
with Europe was made in 1862 when a mission of thirty-five
was dispatched to various capitals. But prior to the restoration
of powers to the Emperor the Tokugawa Council had established a bureau for the translation of foreign books in 1855.
Five years later the first team of students was sent overseas
ostensibly to study, but in effect to acquire intelligence as they

were all attached to diplomatic missions. Sometimes this could be done openly, as with the United States, but in other cases in secret and illegally. It was at this time that even greater attention was paid to acquiring intelligence from Russia. In 1855 the Treaty of Shimoda had been signed, dividing the Kurile Islands between Japan and Russia. Twenty years later all of Sakhalin, north of Hokkaido, was made Russian territory, while all the Kurile Islands were ceded to Japan. It was at this time that the imperial slogan became "National Prosperity through Military Strength". Edo was renamed Tokyo when the Emperor and his court left Kyoto to reside in the capital.

The British gradually came into favour despite their earlier show of aggressive force against Japan. This was chiefly because in 1865 they had supported the pro-royalist factions against the Shogun, whereas the French had mistakenly backed the losers. The Japanese had also quickly decided that military power was useless to an island nation like themselves unless it was guarded by a strong navy. So they decided to acquire the intelligence to create one and the model they took was that of the most powerful fleet in the world at that time, the Royal Navy of Britain. Similarly, to improve their army they aimed to model it on that of Germany. Astonishing strides were made between 1860 and 1870 so that by the latter date Japan had highly specialised teams of men trained in Western military and naval skills as well as the industrial techniques to produce armaments. They had established various military factories and ship-building combines on Western lines, including the Saga Cannon Foundry. Educational establishments were reorganised to ensure that the nation had the technology to compete with the West; priority was given to a navigation school, and the first of various foreign language schools was set up purposely to equip secret agents for fact-finding missions abroad. There has never been so highly efficient, smooth and speedy a radical revolution anywhere in the world to compare with the great Japanese experiment in the twenty years between 1865 and 1885. Everything was planned in great detail so that all intelligence received was acted upon as soon as it was received. For example, one astute agent reported from London in 1872 that "the most important lesson to be learned in European countries is that their arms producing factories are not efficiently geared to the national effort. Some firms put their own profits before national requirements, while in many factories production is slowed up through incompetent direction of labour and work which requires 100 or 200 men in Britain and France could be accomplished with a third or less of these numbers in Japan. Yet in Russia, it would seem, the situation is worse: the ratio there would be 4 or 5 Russians to one Japanese. I understand that Commodore Matthew C. Perry was dispatched to Europe as long ago as 1838 to collect intelligence on armed steamers and other matters. From this one must assume that his voyage to Japan was not merely to seek trade, but to find out our strengths and weaknesses. We need to step up our own intelligence in Europe just as the Americans are doing. They have not yet set up a properly constituted naval intelligence department, but even now they have an ordnance mission over here under commander Edward Simpson. I find that British Army officers are more forthcoming in information than those of the Royal Navy."[1]

No doubt bearing this lesson in mind, the Japanese Government kept all industries handling military contracts or undertaking any work which might be concerned with national security or military strategy under very tight control. The telegraph and telephone systems, as they were introduced, were made government monopolies. This was not nationalisation for the worker's or the consumer's sake, but to ensure that such industries were all geared to the requirements of national strategy. The Meiji leaders had not only insisted that, if imperial rule was to be enhanced, it must develop a modern educational system, but had introduced the Five Articles Oath of 1868 which stated that "knowledge shall be sought throughout the world so as to strengthen the foundations of Imperial Rule."

Among the early students sent to the Netherlands was Takeaki Enomoto who had sided with the Shogunate during the civil war which preceded the return of imperial rule. This was intended as providing him with a generous opportunity to make his peace with the new regime, for he was informed that he was expected to bring back a great deal of intelligence, especially on naval and shipbuilding matters. Enomoto was so highly regarded for his work on this mission and his subsequent advice that in 1874 he was promoted to vice-admiral in the new Imperial Navy. The Japanese Government decided to spend huge sums of money to finance the sending of students abroad and the numbers of these were expanded year by year. Women as well as men were included in the teams of students sent to the U.S.A. and Europe, though the males predominated. A particularly important diplomatic mission was that led to the U.S.A.

and Europe in 1871 by Prince Iwakura, the Emperor's Minister of State, and it included fifty-four students employed solely as intelligence-gatherers.

The oriental approach to intelligence work has always tended to be more direct and straightforward than that of the Western powers. The statement cited about the report of the agent in London in 1872 shows that sometimes information would be sought quite openly from officers of foreign armies and navies. Obviously on very many occasions bribery and illegal methods have been employed by Japanese in collecting intelligence, just as by the secret services of other nations. But they have never believed in using devious methods when purely legal and straightforward means are just as effective. Nor have they taken a narrow view as to what a national espionage organisation should concentrate on, but regarded it as embracing all kinds of knowledge. Thus most of their early intelligence was acquired by legal methods and ultra-conscientious powers of observation. No doubt some surreptitious notes were made when visiting dockyards and arsenals in the West when on specially conducted tours, but it must be remembered that the Japanese could never easily disguise their nationality in Europe or America. To a large extent they were compelled to acquire intelligence openly. But how many American or British naval or military intelligence officers would take a sufficiently broad view of their task as to ascertain how many men it took to build this gun or that ship, and whether his own countrymen could do this with less manpower?

On the military intelligence front Japan was greatly helped by a Major Meckel, who headed a German military mission to Tokyo in 1885. Meckel had been a pupil of the great strategist, Count Helmuth von Moltke, who had been chief of staff to the Prussian Army, and he was able to inculcate the need for method and organisation in Japanese military intelligence. He remained in Japan until 1894. His value as an instructor in the arts of intelligence may be gauged by the fact that after the Battle of the Yalu River in 1904, the Japanese General Kodama telegraphed Meckel and said victory was due to the latter's teaching.

Western Secret Services have often been in too much of a hurry. Often it is for this reason alone that they not only use illegal tactics to try to get quick results, but fail to obtain that extra intelligence which can be all-important. The oriental is much more likely to argue that such impatience could merely lead to being caught out. Similarly the Japanese Secret Service has rarely wasted money. In all its branches the motto has been to rely on patriotism rather than bribery. This emphasis on patriotism as a motive in espionage was something not to be paralleled in the Anglo-Saxon nations of this period. Both in America and Britain secret service work was regarded as something rather disreputable and never officially to be acknowledged. This failure to admit they indulged in such tactics was not so much a desire to be discreet and to cover up as sheer hypocrisy and a feeling that spying was all rather caddish. It was an attitude which was to cost both countries dearly in the years to come. The Americans and British will never admit when one of their own spies is caught except when forced to do so by incontrovertible evidence. The Japanese have always made the most vigorous diplomatic protests (and sometimes even a show of force) if one of their own spies is arrested. But where the Japanese scored over the West was in seeking quite deliberately to give spying the status of a noble and patriotic duty, something on a par with that of the soldier in battle. To spy for one's country was as great an honour as to compete in the Olympics and possibly even greater than serving in the armed forces because, it was argued, victories could not be won without intelligence to pave the way.

The Japanese achieved this special status relationship in their secret service by avoiding bureaucratic recruitment, while creating various secret societies whose recruits were sworn to gather intelligence for the honour of Japan. Such a policy had much to commend it. First of all, it harnessed patriotism to secret work of national importance, while at the same time inculcating a strong nationalist sense and patriotic fervour in young men who had previously not raised their sights above their own national boundaries. It encouraged them to travel, to see other countries. Secondly, these societies were able to supply intelligence to the Japanese Foreign Office, the Army and the Navy at very little cost, as the members of these societies gave their services freely, even though some of their missions needed to be subsidised. The societies were privately financed to a considerable extent by wealthy citizens, and so there was not a great drain on state coffers. As the scope for such espionage was increased, however, and results were encouraging, so the Army supplied secret funds to help the societies, though this does not appear to have been the case with the Navy. The main financial support in those early years at least came from the leaders and founders of the secret societies. The amounts supplied by army and government were modest in comparison with the huge sums then being spent by Germany and Russia in organising their own intelligence networks.

The first real external branch of Japanese undercover espionage was that of the *Genyosha*, or Black Ocean Society, which took its name from the strip of water called the *Genkai nada* which separates Kyushu from the mainland of Korea. This was founded in 1881 by Kotaro Hiraoka, a wealthy *samurai* (nobleman) who was also a mine-owner and interested in mining developments in Manchuria. The society was originally very much confined to the Kyushu province of Japan and, outwardly at any rate, was intensely nationalistic and highly respectable. Its declared aims were "to honour the Imperial Family", "respect the Empire" and "to guard the rights of the people". But these sentiments, which might admirably have fitted the Primrose League in Britain, tended to disguise the real purpose of the society which was to expand Japanese influence overseas and to acquire intelligence from China, Korea, Manchuria and, to a lesser extent, Russia.

"The *Genyosha* was a terrorist organisation and a school for spies,"[2] wrote Professor G. R. Storry, who has made a study of the ideas and activities of Japanese nationalist associations. In support of this statement he cited the fact that the leaders of the society were assured by the Matsuka Cabinet in 1892 that the government would pursue a strong foreign policy. So the *Genyosha*, which had already aided the government with a stream of intelligence reports, organised a campaign of terror against all anti-Government candidates at the general elections. Despite this, the oppostion parties won more seats. Nevertheless, the Black Ocean Society started a trend and within a few years other secret societies with similar aims were founded. Most of these amalgamated in 1898 to become the East Asia One Culture Society. Later this organisation was to set up the Tung Wen College in Shanghai to train its members for espionage work in China. In the early part of the twentieth century it had three hundred students and in due course was nicknamed the Japanese Spy College by some sophisticated and knowledgeable Chinese.

The introduction of compulsory education in Japan in 1872 had given a fillip to the secret societies in that the new wave of students were enthusiastic about studying abroad. One of the lesser known aims of these secret societies in the early days (and this particularly applied to the Black Ocean) was to infiltrate the many Chinese secret societies, some of which were hostile to Japan. In 1882 Mitsuru Toyama, one of the leading figures of the Black Ocean Society, had sent one hundred men to China to collect intelligence. This operation proved so highly productive that within a few years he was in a position to arrange with Army Intelligence not only to supply them with information, but to carry out assignments for the Army in China.

Between 1878 and 1882 there had been two developments which speeded up the creation of an all-embracing Japanese Secret Service. The establishment of a Japanese Army General Staff in 1878 led to the formation of an organised Army Intelligence Service. Three years later the *Kempei tai*, or military police, were formed. They evolved into something very different from the military police of most nations, eventually becoming what could perhaps best be described as a combination of the functions of the British counter-intelligence service (M.I.5), the Special Branch of the Police and the French D.S.T. (Internal Intelligence). The Intelligence Branch of the Japanese Army had liaison with the *Kempei tai*, but in due course the latter became very much a power in its own right, much more powerful in relation to its own army than, for example, the military police of most Western democracies.

How effectively the Chinese secret societies were infiltrated by Japanese agents is perhaps shown best by the first real history ever written about the Chinese Triads and similar bodies. It was compiled by a Japanese secret agent and radical intellectual named Hiraya Amane. In his travels he had established contact with various Chinese revolutionaries and discovered a great deal about the rituals, sign language and activities of Chinese secret societies. His history of them, *Zhong-guo Bi-mi She-hui Shi*, was not allowed to be published until many years later, as he had been one of the prime sources for intelligence out of China. It was Amane who, by patient observation in tea houses and restaurants and other places, managed to puzzle out the rituals and secret sign language of the Triad. He soon found that the secret societies had been distorted by radicals into something akin to class warfare: it was not merely a question of "Let us overthrow the Ch'ing and restore the Ming", but "let us strike at the rich and aid the poor".

The secret language was frequently employed in a complex arrangement of tea-cups and teapots on a table, or a tray. Amane made sketches of each different arrangement he noted and then watched to see how a newcomer to the tea house would change the cups around. Under copious sketches of these tea-party arrangements he wrote what he conceived to be the meaning of each laying out of cups and what the visitor should do when he arrived at the table. For example, if a single filled cup of tea was placed alongside a teapot, this meant "... an invitation to rescue a fellow-member from a dangerous situation ... if the newcomer is able to effect a rescue, he drinks the cup of tea; if not, he throws away the tea and then refills the cup and drinks."[3]

Sometimes the newcomer, if a genuine member of the Triad, was expected to recite a certain verse as well. If confronted with four cups of tea and a teapot, this implied that assistance of some kind was desired. If unable to assist, the member was supposed to change the position of the four cups and then drink. If he was willing to help, he had to recite:

> "Han Peng was born at Shanyu,
> On whom did Han Fuh rely?
> Cheng Tien thought revenge his due,
> Why are Chang Kuo's eyes ne'er dry?"

There is even some evidence that agents of the Black Ocean Society were engaged in manipulating the leaders of some of the Chinese secret societies. This was not as difficult as it might seem. Some of these triads were at war with each other, or working against some of their nation's political leaders. K'ang Yu-wei and Liang Ch'i-ch'ao, having failed to advance their political cause in China, went into exile in Tokyo towards the end of the nineteenth century, but kept in touch with various secret societies from the Japanese capital. All their moves were watched. Leading members of the Black Ocean Society set up bordellos both in Japan and inside China with the object of luring some of the triad bosses into what they picturesquely called Halls of Celestial Delights.

These sybaritic institutions, controlled by the Black Ocean agents, set out to ensnare the paymasters of the Chinese secret societies and obtain intelligence from them. By encouraging them to spend huge sums of money on whoring and drinking, they drained the societies' funds and helped at the same time to subsidise the Black Ocean. The training school for the Japanese agents employed on this kind of work was at Sappiro in the north of Japan and, after a period spent there, they were sent on to Hankow, where the Black Ocean had its Chinese headquarters. Bordellos were established at Hankow, Shanghai, Tientsin and Pusan in Korea. Intelligence was obtained partly by blackmail, sometimes by bribery and, more often, by employing prostitutes highly skilled in extracting information from their clients. These bordellos were vastly superior to anything which the Chinese had to offer: they pandered to those who loved luxurious surroundings and had unusual sexual proclivities. The agents who controlled the bordellos patiently studied the weaknesses and vices of their more important clients and used this knowledge to extract the information they desired.

A wealth of intelligence was obtained in this manner both from China and Korea and much of it paved the way for the successful conclusion of Japan's war against China in 1894–5. Professor Jean Chesneaux of the Sorbonne, a specialist in modern Far Eastern history, tells how one of the leading paymasters of a Chinese secret society, Tang Cai-chang, received from a rich Chinese trader in Singapore a large sum (300,000 taels) intended to buy arms for an Elder Brother uprising in the Yangtse region: "he spent most of the money in the pleasure houses of Shanghai, and the planned uprisings could not take place".[4] Some of this money found its way into a Japanese-controlled bordello.

That the Black Ocean Society contributed considerably to the intelligence-gathering prior to the war with China over a long period is clear from various reports, not least those included in the various histories of the *Genyosha*, published and unpublished.[5]

Not all the *Genyosha's* espionage work was conducted in the exotic and titillating atmosphere of bordellos. A great deal of it was tedious and arduous fact-finding in the most uncongenial terrain. This particularly applied to the secret map work and assembling of topographical reports on Korea which some of their members carried out, often in the most severe winter conditions. Most important of all, perhaps, was the task given by Ryohei Uchida, a leading member of the Black Ocean Society, to a specially selected company of fifteen men who formed a subordinate group known as the *Tenyukyo*, or the Society of the Celestial Salvation of the Oppressed. They were instructed to go to Korea and to make contacts with the *Tonghaks*, an eclectic religious cult of what was called "Eastern Learning". It was a society opposed to all forms of Western

teaching. The *Tenyukyo* gave so much support to the *Tonghaks*
that the Korean Government, who were opposed to this sect's
conspiracies, protested to Tokyo. This paved the way for the
eventual intervention by the Japanese in Korea.

Japan's victory over China in 1894–5 was achieved both
speedily and easily. It arose out of the claims of both nations
on Korea. Japan exacted heavy compensation from China for
her war expenditure and obtained the annexation of Formosa
(Taiwan) as well as permission to develop the mines and railways in Manchuria.

The Black Ocean Society and its subsidiary, the *Tenyukyo*,
not only spied in Korea, but used the *Tonghaks* for agitation
and disruption and generally weakening government influence.
Various bomb attacks and murders have been attributed to the
members of the Black Ocean Society, but perhaps the principal
crime in which they seem to have been positively involved was
that of the assassination of Queen Min of Korea in 1895. She
was the daughter-in-law of the Taewongun, an aged Korean
leader brought back to office by the instigation of the Japanese.
This killing was carried out by Black Ocean members with
the apparent connivance of the Japanese Minister in Seoul,
Lieutenant-General Miura.

This was the first occasion following Hideyoshi's abortive
attempts to conquer Korea that Japan had paved the way for a
war by systematic intelligence-gathering. In China it had proved
of crucial value. The Japanese Army chiefs were enormously
impressed by the role played by the Black Ocean Society as
well as by their own Military Intelligence. From then onwards
they gave intelligence as high a priority as armaments. No
other army in the world at the turn of the century put so much
faith in the support of an all-embracing espionage system.

5

Colonel Akashi and The Black Dragon Society

> "The Chinese characters for the River
> Amur, which forms the northern border of
> Manchuria, means Black Dragon River,
> rendered in Japanese as *Kokuryukai*.
> Though generally termed the Black Dragon
> Society in English, the *Kokuryukai*, there-
> fore, really means the Amur Society. It
> was given this name to denote its original
> purpose, which was to expel the Russians
> from Manchuria across the Amur"
>
> Malcolm D. Kennedy in
> *A History of Japan*

THE ABOVE QUOTATION succinctly sums up the real origins of
the Black Dragon Society, or *Kokuryukai*, which was founded
almost as an offshoot of the *Genyosha* in February, 1901.
Though the title "Black Dragon" is somewhat inaccurate, as
Kennedy implies, it is the name by which the society is best
known outside of Japan, so for that reason it is the name which
will be used in this book.

In effect this society took over where the *Genyosha* left off.
It may seem strange that some of the leading members of so
highly successful a society as the Black Ocean should abandon
this in favour of an entirely new secret society. The answer is
that the Black Ocean had been almost too successful. By the
turn of the century news of its activities had filtered through
to the outside world. Not all of that news was favourable to
Japan's image in Western eyes: the assassination of the Korean

queen and the organised terrorism in elections had to some
extent been exploited by its critics. Both Mitsuru Toyama and
Ryohei Uchida, the two most influential figures in the Black
Ocean Society after Hiraoka, saw this only too clearly. Ryohei
Uchida had visited Russia and made a considerable study of
its leading personalities and policies. He was convinced that
only Russia posed a serious threat to Japanese expansion on
the Asian mainland. So it was he who founded the Black Dragon
which became in a short while the most powerful and militant
of the scores of secret societies in Japan.

He had the full support of Mitsuru Toyama, who, while not
joining the new society, gave it every aid from behind the
scenes, especially in suggesting policies. Toyama was a somewhat eccentric and lonely character, part politician and part
mystic. He was an ascetic who enjoyed hours of silent con-
templation and at one time he is said to have lived on a diet
of grass and leaves. Despite this apparent unworldliness and
love of seclusion and even obscurity, Toyama always had access to the highest political and military figures of the day. It
was largely his undoubted influence which ensured that the
Black Dragon took over the work of the Black Ocean Society,
and skilfully turned its attention to Manchuria and Russia. The
clue to its aims lay in its title, the River Amur Society, for the
Amur River formed the boundary between Russia and Manchuria. Toyama remained an adviser of the Black Dragon until
his death in 1944. Latterly he was also a member of the *Taisei
Yokusankai* (Imperial Rule Assistance Association), a right-
wing body which played a part in World War II.

The Black Dragon Society was started in the utmost secrecy
and so it remained for a long time. But gradually, as its numbers
grew and its activities were discovered, its existence was officially recognised. By the 1930s the *Kokuryukai* was mentioned in some Japanese year books.

When it was first formed there seems to have been an attempt
to take care not to recruit some of the thugs and terrorists who
had sometimes been too predominant in the *Genyosha* movement. It was their disregard for the law in a nation which was
by and large essentially law-abiding which brought these members of the Black Ocean into disrepute, especially with some
Army officers. Thus in the early days the Black Dragon Society
had a rather better type of member which commended it to the
Army Intelligence Branch with the result that many Army officers joined it.

In the beginning there was a kind of romantic patriotic aura about joining the Black Dragon and young men were wooed to join it by promises of adventurous careers. However, some of the *soshi*, or "brave knights" as they were called, were in reality unemployed *samurai* who no longer had a role to fulfill after the restoration of the authority of the Emperor. But while in its early years the Black Dragon Society undoubtedly provided such patriotic young men with an outlet for their adventure-loving natures, it also led to a steady growth in the number of rogues and ruffians in membership in later years. Yet from a practical point of view it must be admitted that they were of value to their country and that if they had not been members of the society, they might well have degenerated into unemployed criminals.

Thus membership of the black Dragon eventually ranged from Cabinet Ministers and high-ranking Army officers to professional secret agents, blackmailers and hired killers. They came from all classes of the community and membership increased from a few hundreds at the outset to an estimated 10,000 in 1944. While originally the society's activities were directed almost solely towards obtaining intelligence on Russia and Manchuria, by the end of the 1930s they had been extended to Korea, China, the Philippines, Malaya, Hong Kong, Singapore, India, Afghanistan, Ethiopia, Turkey, Morocco, the United States and many countries in the Caribbean and South America.

One of the Black Dragon's earliest supporters (although he does not appear in the membership lists) was Koki Hirota, who eventually became Prime Minister of Japan. Like Toyama, he kept in the background. Some sources claim that he was a member of the *Kokuryukai*, but the probability is that they have confused the name of this society with that of the *Kokuikai* (the Society for the Maintenance of National Prestige), founded in 1932, of which he was a leading light. Hirota, the son of a stonecutter, was born in 1878, and joined the Diplomatic Service in 1906. In his later years he mellowed considerably and, possibly on account of his diplomatic experience and training, he seems to have had a restraining influence on the Black Dragon Society on occasions. Before becoming Prime Minister he served in various parts of the world and was extremely popular in Washington. His theme in Japanese foreign policy-making was that the world should be divided into three spheres of influence—American, European and Japanese, with the last-named having their own "Asiatic Monroe Doctrine" (his own phrase).

Such a policy, while conforming to the philosophies of the Black Dragon Society, made as much, if not rather more sense, as any other imperialistic plan in the early part of the twentieth century. Japan was in fact only attempting to do in her own part of the world what the Western powers, with far less excuse, had already put into action in China, Indo-China, the East Indies and Java, India and Malaya. The Russians had long had equally greedy designs for colonising parts of East Asia. Long before 1900 the Japanese had good reason to believe that some of these designs not only clashed with their own long-term interests, but actually threatened their national security. It was generally acknowledged in Tokyo at the latter end of the nineteenth century that China and Russia were Japan's two potential enemies. The Germans had done their best to frighten the Japanese with stories of Russian plans to colonise in East Asia and had encouraged them to extend their military espionage to Russia. While the German military mission under Major Meckel had done the Japanese a good turn, they had also sought to make mischief between Japan and Russia, their own potential enemy. It was at the instigation of the Germans that some Japanese students had been sent to Germany to learn some of the principles of Wilhelm Stieber, that notorious spymaster who had stirred up trouble in so many capitals of Europe.

The building of the Trans-Siberian railway, started in 1891, marked the beginning of a Russian push eastwards. Then, following the Japanese victory in the Sino-Japanese War of 1894–5, the Russians, with support from France and Germany, called a halt to the Japanese acquiring a foothold on the Laitong Peninsula. In 1896 General Kuropatkin, well aware of the dangers of Russian expansionist dreams, wrote: "I told Witte that our Czar had grandiose plans in his head: to capture Manchuria for Russia and to annex Korea. He is dreaming also of bringing Tibet under his dominion."[1]

Gradually, despite the warnings of their best generals, Russia seemed to make her designs obvious to all, whether to probe, provoke or out of bravado, it is not easy to say. Sir Reginald Johnston, the British Minister, recalled that about this time British merchants and missionaries in Manchuria regarded the territory as "Russian in all but name".[2] British sympathies were increasingly on the side of Japan whose new navy was largely modelled on that of the British. Possibly the technical aid which the Japanese had had from the British in naval matters also brought their statesmen closer in outlook to that of Britain: they were both island nations. Japan needed at least one strong ally and Britain, at the peak of her imperial strength, seemed the obvious choice. The Japanese were also greatly assisted in having a particularly forceful and astute diplomat in Count Tadasu Hayashi as their first Ambassador to London. He was largely responsible for laying the foundations of the Anglo-Japanese Treaty of Alliance, which was signed in 1902.

A year before this the Black Dragon Society had made one of its first demands on the Japanese War Office. Having decided that Russia was to be the main target for their own espionage activities, they insisted that any military attaché sent to that country from Tokyo must be one of whom they approved. There seems to have been some opposition to this both by the War Office and the Foreign Office. Ryohei Uchida was not only a single-minded person, not easily deterred from achieving what he desired, but tough enough to challenge the War Office. He stressed the enormous assistance given to the military by Goichi Ishikawa, who had been sent to spy inside China prior to the Sino-Japanese War. Prior to his capture by the Chinese Ishikawa had provided the reports upon which the successful Japanese attack on Fengtao had been based. In addition he, too, had urged paying more attention to intelligence moves along the Mongolian border.

Uchida pointed out that it was his society's reports which were invaluable to any military plans and that these could not be properly assessed and acted upon unless there was a Japanese military attaché in Russia who had their confidence. He nominated Colonel Motojiro Akashi as the ideal man for the job. The colonel, who was also a baron, had been attached to Imperial G.H.Q. in the Sino-Japanese War as an aide to General Soruku Kawakami and had already made a considerable reputation as a military adviser and tactical expert. Towards the end of 1900 Akashi was sent to Europe as a roving attaché. Uchida overruled War Office objections to a roving military attaché rather than one permanently stationed in St. Petersburg by explaining that this would enable the Black Dragon's nominee to keep in touch with Russian informants living outside Russia. Uchida's idea was that Colonel Akashi should establish contact with Russian revolutionaries residing in France, Sweden, Germany and Switzerland.

This marked the beginning of a distinguished career for

Colonel Akashi which included posts as C-in-C of the Gendarmerie and Chief of Staff of Japanese Forces in Korea. He was briefed both by the War Office and the Black Dragon. The latter ordered him to offer financial aid to Russian revolutionaries in exchange for information about the Russian Intelligence Services and the strength of their armed forces. It is suggested by some writers that Akashi established links with the notorious Russian double-agent, Ievno Azeff, who not only worked for the *Ochrana*, the Czarist secret police, but also became a clandestine member of one of the revolutionary parties. Azeff was such a devious character that he not only took part in plotting some of the revolutionaries' assassination coups, but betrayed his anarchist and socialist colleagues to the *Ochrana*. Where Azeff was concerned almost anything was possible, but except for the fact that Akashi is said to have met Azeff when the latter was on a visit to Switzerland, there is nothing positive to link these two.

Certainly Colonel Akashi would have been more than a match for Azeff. He had an astonishing talent for spotting an agent who could be "turned" as is shown by his strange relationship with an even more devious double, or treble agent, the incomparable Sidney Reilly. It was Akashi who lured Reilly into working for the Japanese.

The story of Sidney Reilly never fails to surprise any writer who investigates it. The more one delves, the greater the surprises. Such was the versatility of this man that he has appeared in every other secret service history I have written with the sole exception of the Israelis. And that was simply because Reilly was dead before Israel was established!

Reilly was born in South Russia in 1874, his real name being Sigmund Georgievich Rosenblum, the product of an illicit union between a Russian mother and a Jewish doctor from Vienna. But Reilly, who took his Anglicised name after he had joined the British Secret Service, was such a compulsive liar that it is hard to know when he was telling the truth. He insisted to some people that he was the son of an Irish sea captain and gave his birthplace as Tipperary. His own story is that he joined the British Secret Service long before the turn of the century, but Captain Norman Thwaites, a senior S.I.S. man in New York, claimed that he recruited Reilly into the service in 1917.[3] The probable truth is that Reilly was a freelance informant to the British Secret Service back in the 1890s while he was living in Russia and at the same time working for a branch of Russian

Intelligence, but that he was not made a full-time British agent until the First World War.

Reilly was well acquainted with Colonel Akashi and the two men met whenever Akashi was in St. Petersburg. They had some artistic interests in common; Akashi was well known in Japan for his poetry and paintings—an unusual combination for a military intelligence officer—and Reilly was an admirer and collector of his pictures. Quite suddenly Reilly moved to Port Arthur, then an area in which Japanese secret agents were active, and he registered a timber firm in the name of Gruenberg and Reilly. From this it will be seen that Rosenblum was certainly using the name of Reilly long before he officially adopted it. Eventually he became director of another firm, the *Compagnie Est-Asiatique*. It was during this period, when he was under some stress owing to the fact that his British-born wife was drinking heavily and becoming a liability to him, that he agreed to work for Colonel Akashi.

Reilly was in a position to supply full details of Russian defences and naval armaments not only in Port Arthur, but elsewhere. Akashi knew that Reilly was anxious to escape from his domestic problems and that he was temporarily short of cash, so he took a calculated risk making a proposition to the double-agent. Obviously Akashi had ascertained that Reilly also worked for the British with whom Japan was now an ally. The Russians must have had their own suspicions about their agent at this time, as Reilly discovered that a man he had engaged on his staff was an operator in the Russian counter-intelligence service. Reilly found this out when he noticed a cipher-key and a half-finished dispatch in a drawer of the man's desk. But it was Colonel Akashi who tipped him off about the counter-intelligence agent in the first place. Reilly made a quick decision: he sent his wife back to London, and decided to go to Japan and collect a large sum of money which had been promised him. This was one of the few occasions on which the Japanese—in this era at least—actually paid a foreigner for obtaining intelligence for them.[4]

Nevertheless Reilly had no intention of severing his links with either the British or the Russians. It might merely be that the Russians were making a check on him and that they had no positive evidence against him. In this case it was important that his journey to Japan should not appear to be a flight from arrest by the *Ochrana*, or because he believed himself to be under suspicion. So he invented a love affair to throw the

Russians off the scent. A woman with whom he had been casually flirting had expressed a desire to go to Japan and holiday in the interior of that country. Reilly lost no time in making love to her so eloquently and passionately that he had very little difficulty in persuading her to elope with him to Japan the very next day.

In Tokyo Reilly handed over a wealth of intelligence on Russia to a Japanese contact named by Colonel Akashi. But Reilly's activities in Tokyo were just as devious and mysterious as elsewhere. The Japanese were apparently sufficiently satisfied with his information to reward him adequately, but they never really trusted him. They knew he was working for the British, but they also learned that he had not severed his links completely with the Russians. On the other hand Reilly made no attempt to send the Russians intelligence from Japan and he was closely watched all the time. At the end of 1902 he was reporting back to the British Secret Service that "the Manchus are finished. It is only a matter of time before China becomes the playground of the great powers. Their intelligence service, such as it is, for all practical purposes simply does not exist. But I should warn you that in this vacuum which is left a new and much more dangerous Secret Service will eventually spring up. Today it is like a sperm inside the womb. Tomorrow? Perhaps a fully fledged child."[5]

Was Reilly referring to the Japanese Secret Service? At the same time that he was supplying intelligence to the Japanese, he informed London that he wanted leave of absence because he did not wish to be embroiled against Russia in the Russo-Japanese War that was even then imminent. He also made the excuse that he needed to get away from the woman with whom he had fled from Port Arthur. The identity of this woman has never been clearly established, nor for that matter has her nationality, though Reilly swore she was British and that her name was Anne Luke.

Some few years before this another British woman, Mrs. Edith Carew, had been sentenced to death by a British Consular Court in Tokyo for the poisoning and death of her husband. It was considered at the time that there had been a great miscarriage of justice as there was conflicting evidence and rumours of a mysterious "veiled woman in black, named Anne Luke" who had known Walter Carew and had appeared in Yokohama twelve days before his death. Mrs. Carew was saved from the death penalty by the Emperor of Japan who granted an amnesty to native prisoners because of the sudden death of the Dowager Empress. The British Minister, Sir Ernest Satow, without consulting his Yokohama Consul, commuted Mrs. Carew's death sentence to life imprisonment.[6]

Nobody ever discovered what happened to Anne Luke. An offer of a £500 reward was made for evidence leading to her whereabouts, but she was never traced. Could it be that she returned to Japan with Reilly under a false passport and not under her own name?

Reilly disappeared suddenly from Japan and it was several months later that he turned up again in the Chinese province of Shen-si where he lived in a lamaserie. Only at the end of the Russo-Japanese War did he re-establish himself with the British and the Russians. But Reilly's contacts with the Japanese seem to date back even further than his meeting with Akashi, for he was an informant of the Black Ocean Society during an earlier visit to China.

By this time the Black Dragon Society had penetrated deeply into Siberia as well as Manchuria and had even taken over a jiu-jitsu school which the Black Ocean had started in Vladivostock. There is, however, nothing to link Reilly with the Black Dragon, not even as an informant. But he may well have been passing information on activities in Shen-si province to the Japanese as he had shown considerable enthusiasm for a society named the *Dobunkai*, organised by Prince Konoye in 1898 with the aim of encouraging the development of an identical language to be shared between Japanese and Chinese. This society had set up schools in various parts of China.

Meanwhile in Tokyo the Black Dragon Society had sponsored a special college for the study of Russian. One of the most extensive, comprehensive and successful espionage operations ever planned had been fully launched by the end of 1903.

6

The Russo-Japanese War

> "The Japanese accept what their experts
> tell them. But the Anglo-Saxons revolt at
> the very word 'expert'"
> General Sir Ian Hamilton

WHEN THE RUSSO-JAPANESE WAR started on 8 February, 1904, no army or navy in modern history had ever been so superbly backed up with a massive advance intelligence operation. It is no exaggeration to say that it was the most brilliantly conceived and co-ordinated operation of its kind ever planned.

Captain Malcolm D. Kennedy, who once served as a British military attaché in Japan and was also for some years a Reuter resident correspondent in Tokyo, observed that "one of the great features of Japanese strategy and grand tactics in their war with Russia was the secrecy observed and the false information circulated purposely. This, combined with their system of intelligence work, which both before that war and during it, enabled them to have an almost uncanny knowledge of their enemy's doings and potentialities, helped them very considerably to subsequent victory."[1]

General Sir Ian Hamilton, who was attached to the Japanese First Army as a British military observer, bore out what Captain Kennedy asserted, especially on the subject of misinformation. "The Japanese realised the weakness of Russia much better than any American or European observers. The British believed that Russia was in Manchuria to stay. Japan weighed the evidence—superior intelligence—and came to a precisely contrary conclusion . . . The Japanese accept what their experts

53

tell them. But the Anglo-Saxons revolt at the very word 'expert'."[2]

After he had been with the Japanese a few weeks General Hamilton was given a "distribution statement", indicating the actual strength of every Russian unit east of Lake Baikal. "It was for the month of October, 1903, and there was also a supplementary document showing in detail the number of additional men, guns and horses which had arrived on the scene of operations between that period and the end of January, 1904. I was surprised, not only at the masses of professedly precise figures which had been got together, but at the formidable strength of the Russians. There were supposed to be 180 full battalions of infantry, and with cavalry, artillery and engineers, the total Russian forces in Manchuria came approximately to 200,000 men."[3]

Hamilton asked if he could communicate this long statement and was told that he could do so as a very special mark of favour. But he subsequently learned that it was entirely misleading and at that time the Japanese knew full well that the whole mobile army of the Russians would barely amount to 80,000 men by 1 May of that year. Not only did the Japanese know the numbers at General Kuropatkin's disposal, but they had also decided he could not place a large proportion of his troops along the Yalu River because they were satisfied that it would take 3,000 Chinese carts to maintain transport for 30,000 Russians and that these carts had not yet been collected.

Another great advantage which the Japanese had initially in the intelligence game was their language. This involves three systems of writing, quite unlike one another, to express the same verbal sounds. Sometime in the past the key to the written cipher (for that in effect is what it could be) was lost. It does not require a great deal of imagination to see how easy it was to pass on messages which, even if found by a potential enemy, could never be deciphered. Where the Russians were concerned there was hardly any need for ciphers as probably not more than one person in 100,000 could read even printed forms of the language, while those who could read Japanese hand-writing were possibly no more than one in 750,000, apart of course from some Chinese living in Manchuria and elsewhere. Only later when telegraphic codes and ciphers were introduced was this problem slowly solved.

An excellent example of the double meanings which could also creep into Japanese writing is provided by General Sir Ian

Hamilton. He was tremendously impressed by the geishas who acted as hostesses at various dinner parties he attended: "they are essentially young and beautiful hostesses each as anxious to make the entertainment a success as if she herself was the donor... They are delightful company; full of tact and quite smart at repartee. Two nights ago I had a great flirtation during dinner with a young lady called Miss Flourishing Dragon. When I was saying goodnight I confessed to her my deep admiration. She replied that the ideograph expressing her name also meant 'British dominion', and that for all the future she would only use it in the latter sense. I had the curiosity to ask a great Japanese scholar if the ideograph would bear the double meaning and I found that it would do so, subject to a very small stretch of the pen."[4]

The importance of the role which the Black Dragon fulfilled at this time is testified by many sources, not least by the Japanese themselves. An article in the magazine of the Japan Police Society states that the *Kokuryukai* was "active behind the scenes, particularly in the Russo-Japanese War."[5] Through Ryohei Uchida the Black Dragon Society organised Chinese guerrillas to harass the Russians, while *Kokuryukai* volunteers were attached to the Japanese Army as interpreters. No doubt they also played a role in disseminating the disinformation which General Hamilton mentioned.

Colonel Akashi always kept in close touch with some leading members of the Black Dragon when he was in Tokyo, though his name does not appear in any available membership lists. He had a remarkable talent for striking up friendships with foreigners ranging from Sidney Reilly, with whom he remained on excellent terms over some years, to Konni Zilliacus, a Finnish revolutionary, and Abdur Rashid Ibrahim, a Russian Tartar who was frequently consulted by the Russian Government on problems relating to the Muslim population. While this friendship may or may not have helped particularly during the Russo-Japanese War, it certainly bore fruit later. Ibrahim was the prime link in Japanese Intelligence's extensive contacts with Russian Muslims later on.

Akashi, on account of his cosmopolitan sodalities and knowledge of the outside world, became the supreme intelligence officer for Japan in Europe in the 1904–5 campaign against Russia. By this time he had moved to Stockholm where he was busily employed sowing the seeds of dissension among Russian and Finnish revolutionaries in exile. Only a few days

after the Russo-Japanese War had started he was addressing a
secret conference of some of these exiles in Stockholm, urging
them to plan revolts in certain key centres of production inside
Russia and promising them funds for arms and munitions. It
was here that he struck up a relationship with Konni Zilliacus,
whose son became a naturalised Briton and later, a left-wing
Labour M.P. for Gateshead in the days of the Attlee government. The testimony of both Zilliacus and Akashi is that they
met in Stockholm some time in 1905.[6] At that time Zilliacus
was a fervent Finnish patriot only too anxious to see Russian
imperialism overthrown. From both his and Akashi's narratives
it is clear that both men had support from socialists in Sweden
and Britain. One of the latter was Samuel Hobson, a middle-
class Englishman who had already involved himself in the
smuggling of arms to Riga in the 1903–4 period. There is some
indication that certain British officials turned a blind eye on
this illegal arms trafficking from Britain, but whether because
it was aiding the Japanese, as Akashi claimed, or for other
reasons, is not certain.

Akashi had contacts everywhere. He worked in collaboration with the Japanese military attaché in London, Colonel Taro
Utsunomiya, and he employed two agents who travelled backwards and forwards regularly between Stockholm and Irkutsk.
In October, 1904, he was in Paris, and in April, 1905, at a
conference of revolutionaries in Geneva. His own claim, which
there is no reason to doubt, is that by the middle of 1905 he
had seven spies and five assistants working for him on a regular
basis. The network extended to Paris, Zurich, Geneva, Co-
penhagen, Rome, Lisbon and even Warsaw.

When it came to meddling with revolutionaries and actually
financing some of them, the cautious minds in the Japanese
Foreign Office and some at the War Ministry were at first very
worried. It took all Akashi's persuasive powers to convince
them of the wisdom for some of these ploys and to obtain the
cash to finance them. But their fears proved groundless. Akashi
was far too astute to distribute money to revolutionaries freely
and indiscriminately. There is reason to believe that he very
much mistrusted many of the revolutionaries, especially the
extremists, but that he did business chiefly with anarchists and
Finns. The Japanese Foreign Office archives and those of the
Defence Agency show that Akashi scored a great success as
an Army man by winning the Japanese Minister in Stockholm
to his side. Thus he was able to persuade the latter to bargain

with Tokyo for funds for espionage.

The arguments put forward by Akashi for the urgent need for cash were that uprisings were being planned both on the Finnish side and among the Russian revolutionaries and that if these succeeded, Czarist Russia might well agree to sue for peace. Such a prospect suited Japan admirably, but it was not one that would be likely to commend itself to the revolutionaries. For this reason Tokyo was for a long time somewhat sceptical as to the wisdom of Askashi's proposals, even though they were backed by their man in Stockholm. The bargaining for more funds started off with Akashi wanting a million yen and Tokyo talking in terms of an additional 20,000 to be paid in two instalments. But by April, 1905, he had actually been given a million yen.[7]

This money, far from being squandered, actually showed a credit balance at the end of operations, according to the official records. When the war ended nearly a quarter of this sum— 270,000 yen to be exact—had not been spent. How many spymasters in history can show such a record? But there is a record that on one occasion one of his revolutionary agents, Dekansky, was given 40,000 yen to proceed to Odessa to stir up trouble, and in June, 1905, riots occurred in that port.

Valuable intelligence on Russian activities in both Manchuria and Korea was provided by members of the Black Dragon Society. They guided and helped a group of Japanese officers and N.C.O.s in civilian clothes to slip into Manchuria in 1903 to organise meetings with Manchurian bandits. The aim was for them jointly to carry out sabotage against the Russians when war started and to obtain information. One of the bandit chiefs who gave them the greatest assistance at this time was the Chinese warlord, Marshal Chang Tso-lin.

So successful were these Black Dragon agents that it is believed not a single one of them was either caught or lost. Their training in Hokkaido had been extremely thorough. One of them, whose code-name was "Wandering Dragon", went to Vladivostock as early as 1898 in charge of an undercover photographic expedition to bring back pictures and reports on Khabarovsk and Birobidzhan. This was an extraordinarily comprehensive operation, planned to the last detail, not simply gathering military intelligence, but obtaining a wide range of general information as well. Each agent was provided with a different cover, not only regarding his supposed background, but his occupation as well, the idea being that the more varied their alleged occupations, the greater the scope for extending their inquiries. These covers ranged from fishermen to salesmen and to archaeologists and teachers, language students and Buddhist priests. Some were even detailed to become converted to the Muslim religion in order to make a study of it and win friends in areas of Muslim populations inside Russia.

"It is not enough just to make contacts with Muslims," had been Colonel Akashi's dictum: "a diligent intelligence officer will need to understand their religion to know how best to deal with them and not make mistakes. The Europeans do not understand this."

In these pre-war days, although the expenses of these Black Dragon agents were paid, service was regarded as a patriotic duty for which rewards were neither given nor wanted. It was then an élite service in every sense of the word, however much it might have deteriorated in later years when its number increased. Akashi himself received his money direct from the General Staff, not the War Office or Foreign Office, and it is possible that these funds contained a secret contribution from the Black Dragon.

Captain Vincent, a British attaché to the First Japanese Army, spent two months in Korea in 1903–4 prior to joining up with that Army. He got as far as Pingyang and Seoul. Of the latter city he wrote that it was a "hot-bed of intrigue and rumours". Long before the war began he observed that Japanese were "stealing into the Treaty port by each successive junk or peaceful trader, carrying with them in sacks their rifles and military equipment. Even Japanese generals were said to have cleverly disguised themselves as coolies and to be hauling and heaving in the docks until they could emerge at the head of their eager troops."[8]

Every possible chance of finding excuses to infiltrate agents into Korea, Manchuria or Russia was avidly seized upon by the Japanese in the pre-war years. Documents concerning the sale by Mr. James R. Morse, an American citizen, of the Seoul-Fusan railway in 1898 are especially enlightening. This line was the first railway overseas owned by the Japanese. "There occur two exclusive measures," states the document, "that none but Koreans and Japanese may hold shares of the railway capital (Article 15), and that no other foreigners shall reside within lands assigned for the depots (Article 5). Workers engaged on the railway should "as far as possible" be Koreans, but as soon as the Korean finances permitted, the railway might become a common concern between Koreans and Japanese."⁹

Here was ample opportunity for the infiltration of many Japanese agents. It was the same story in Manchuria as in Korea, though in the former country natives had to be recruited to the Japanese cause. In the Russo-Japanese War, states Ronald Seth, "it has been estimated that one in ten of every coolie working for the Russians in Manchuria was a Japanese agent. Not all of them were Japanese. It was found that poor Chinese were quite ready to supplement the starvation wages paid them by the Russians by giving the Japanese snippets of information in return for one or two roubles; and these snippets rapidly built up into a vast mosaic picture of Russian activity."¹⁰

This succinct summary of Japanese infiltration tactics is borne out by most contemporary observers. Both the Russians and the Japanese employed Chinese as spies against each other. It was, of course, economical for them to do so, as such spies were obtained at very low rates of pay. But overall the Japanese were first off the mark in this respect and far more successful than the Russians in doing this. They not only made shrewder use of the Chinese agents, but promised them immunity from arrest on condition that they spied for Japan. Indeed, what the Japanese set out to do once the war had started was to win over to their side those Chinese who had previously served the Russians as spies, but who now feared capture by the men of Nippon and the loss of their homes. Some of these Chinese had actually acquired small properties in disputed territory and wished to stay where they were unmolested. Japanese Intelligence oficers allowed them to do so, but insisted on using them as agents. Others had become unemployed as a result of the war and were only too glad to earn small sums of money.

While there was undoubted pressure from the nationalistic secret societies and some sections of the Army for expansion of Japanese power to the mainland of Asia, there were also moderating influences in the Japanese Foreign Office and among statesmen in the years preceding the Russo-Japanese War. The statesmen had been remarkably conciliatory in negotiations at St. Petersburg on the vexed question of Russian moves in Manchuria and in the border area north of Korea. In 1903 the Russians had sent troops to occupy Yongampo at the mouth of the Yalu River. It was clear that Russia had no intention of keeping her promise of withdrawing troops from Manchuria which she had solemnly given in April, 1902. Then, having made a token withdrawal of a few troops, the Russians promptly re-occupied those areas they had already evacuated. Early in 1904 Russia sent reinforcements of troops and ships to the Far East. Diplomatic relations between the two countries were severed and on 9 February, 1904, the London *Times* reported that "the Japanese Navy has opened the war by an act of daring which is destined to take a place of honour in naval annals. On Monday night February 8th, Japanese torpedo-boats surprised the Russian squadron in the outer roadstead at Port Arthur, and delivered their attack with such good effect that two of the best battleships in the Russian Squadron and a cruiser were disabled."

The Japanese Navy had organised their own system of intelligence and had no contact with the Black Dragon Society, or, as far as is known with any other secret society. Nevertheless although they tended to rely almost entirely on their own sources of information, they had shown initiative and imagination such as no other naval intelligence service anywhere else in the world could then equal. The American Office of Naval Intelligence and the British N.I.D. were both in the kindergarten stage in comparison with the Japanese at that time.

Japanese Naval Intelligence also upheld the code of *bushido* which laid down that spying was an honourable and highly patriotic duty and because of this there was no shortage of volunteers among naval officers to obtain information on the Russian Fleet. In 1908 Colonel Immanuel in a report to the German General Staff attributed the swiftness of the Japanese victory over Russia to "superior intelligence—especially on the naval side".

Two lieutenant-commanders in the Japanese Navy, Seiko Akiyoshi and Kenzo Kamamura, were among the volunteers for espionage some long time before the war. They changed their identities, underwent a lengthy language course in Russian as well as having an intensive indoctrination into all aspects of the Russian way of life. At their training school Russian meals were laid on so that they could accustom themselves to the kind of customs they would be expected to absorb once they got to St. Petersburg. They were even given a thorough instruction in the rituals of the Russian Orthodox Church. Kamamura actually joined the Church in due course. And just as Japanese colonels had willingly posed as coolies to obtain intelligence in Korea, so these two senior naval officers happily and easily accepted the roles of two humble clerks in the St. Petersburg offices of the Potemkin Shipping Company.

The achievement of these two men was all the more remarkable when one considers that it could not have been easy to hide the fact that they were Japanese. But they played on the attitude that Europeans in this era tended to look upon Japanese, Chinese, Thais and other nationalities in the Far East under a somewhat vague blanket description of orientals. Over the years they amassed a wealth of intelligence of all kinds, but mainly of a naval category, which they passed on to the Japanese Embassy in St. Petersburg. They not only gleaned secrets in the shipping offices, but by entering into Russian social life acquired many friends and contacts.

The Japanese had long ago decided that highly technical intelligence could only be obtained and properly assessed by senior officers of either the Army or Navy. So for this type of mission they relied on taking the risk of employing their own nationals. The spirit of patriotism was so strong among these officer agents that they would change their religion for the cause of their country. Right up to September, 1904, Kamamura and Akiyoshi had been supplying the Japanese naval attaché in St. Petersburg with information on Admiral Rozhdjestvanski's Baltic Fleet as well as timetables of all Russian Fleet movements. To consolidate his position Kamamura had arranged to marry a Russian woman and his fellow officer had agreed to act as best man at this ceremony.

Then on the eve of the wedding the two Japanese were arrested by the *Ochrana* and accused of spying. A search of their rooms provided no evidence of this and when the two men indignantly denied the charges it at first seemed likely they would be released. But the *Ochrana* insisted that they had found incriminating documents in the home of the woman Kamamura was to marry, clearly indicating that the two clerks were really Japanese naval officers. Exactly what happened is uncertain. On the Japanese side it was at first thought that the documents had been forged and planted on the Russian woman simply to create an excuse for having the men expelled from the country.

The truth was, however, that the woman was one of the most brilliant counter-intelligence agents employed by Colonel A. V. Gerassimoff, chief of the St. Petersburg branch of the *Ochrana*. He had for some time been disturbed by the revelation that a number of Japanese were marrying Russian women. In the ordinary way this would not have aroused special interest, but for the fact that relations between Japan and Russia were

strained. Also the *Ochrana* had a tip-off from one of their
overseas agents at the Hague that the St. Petersburg Japanese
Embassy was being used as a post office for a network of spies
operating not only inside Russia, but elsewhere in Europe.

Colonel Gerassimoff's female agent not only ensnared the
Japanese clerk and agreed to marry him, but managed to learn
enough of his secrets to implicate him and his colleague. But
the Russian versions of these events, which were not always
consistent, proved to be not entirely correct. It is certain that
Kamamura himself would never have given his wife-to-be any
indication of his real mission, nor would he have left tell-tale
documents lying around. Therefore while Gerassimoff's agent
undoubtedly helped to unmask the pair, possibly by shadowing
them, the real clue to the identity of the clerks probably came
from an *Ochrana* agent elsewhere in Europe, or from the discovery of a cipher-book used by the Japanese Embassy at the
Hague.

While the Japanese language was an admirable and normally
safe cover for hand-borne secret messages, the early codes and
ciphers by telegraph were much more vulnerable. Japan was
not the only power to learn this to her cost. Shortly before the
Russo-Japanese War the Russians were able to read certain
Japanese diplomatic dispatches to which they had gained access. But the Japanese soon discovered the theft and changed
their ciphers. In this sense the arrest of the two clerks was
possibly an unexpected boon for the Japanese. It certainly alerted
the Navy to the fact that the Russians had broken their ciphers.
This alone ensured that when the Japanese Fleet launched their
first attack on the Russians, it came as a total surprise.

For Kamamura and Akiyoshi were only two out of a dozen
naval officers detailed for espionage inside Russia, Holland,
Denmark and Scandinavia. The flow of their intelligence and
the manner in which it was disseminated proved how splendidly
it was all analysed and controlled in Tokyo. From their men
in St. Petersburg and the other European capitals the intelligence was sent first to their embassies or consulates. These
embassies passed a summary of all the messages to Tokyo and,
to save time, to the Japanese Embassy in Berlin, then probably
the most important of all Japan's establishments abroad with
the possible exception of London. The naval attaché at Berlin
was a highly skilled and well-informed intelligence analyst and
able to keep watch on developments in the Baltic and what
was then known as the German Ocean (the North Sea). Thus,

if he had information from either Tokyo or St. Petersburg that a detachment of the Russian Fleet was sailing from a Baltic port, he would alert his agents in Denmark, Holland, Norway and Sweden to check on movements. The Japanese had a team of spies at each key port in Europe and Asia where Russian naval vessels were likely to call for coal and stores on their way to the Far East. In this way Tokyo Naval Headquarters was able to keep track on their movements and plan accordingly. When the Russian ships came within those sea areas in which Japanese fishing vessels operated, the latter kept watch and duly warned Tokyo.

Some of the naval officer spies travelled around the Baltic and as well as making their own observations and reports, acted as couriers for local agents. They usually wore plain clothes and filled the role of holidaymakers; others actually took jobs in the European countries where they were living. On the whole they operated with discretion and efficiency. Kamamura and Akiyoshi would probably never have been suspected in the first place unless the *Ochrana* had had the tip-off from the Hague, backed up by a report from one of their own agents in Denmark. It was the latter who learned that the Danes had arrested a Japanese naval officer at the Skaw, having found he had been sending coded telegrams to his embassy in Berlin.

The result of this intensive naval intelligence-gathering was that the Japanese were able to strike with total efficiency at the outset of the war. The Russians had secured a lease of Port Arthur from China and had tried to get the Chinese to recognise the military occupation of the Amur province. Both the Japanese and the British refused to consider this proposal. At the outset of the war the Japanese Navy attacked Russian fleets at Port Arthur and Chemulpo. By night, having accurate intelligence on the positions of all Russian craft, Admiral Togo's "mosquito" fleet launched a stealthy raid on the ships at anchor off Port Arthur, blowing up the *Cesarevitch*, *Retvisan* and *Poltava*. Later the Vladivostock Squadron was caught by Admiral Kamimura when on its way south to help the Port Arthur Fleet. The Japanese sank the *Rurik*, all but crippled the *Rossia* and the *Gromoboi*, and forced the *Novik* to run herself ashore near Sakhalin.

But perhaps the most mysterious incident of the naval war between the two countries was that which occurred in the North Sea in October, 1904. Orders were given for another Russian fleet to sail to the Far East from Baltic ports via the Mediter-

ranean Sea. Admiral Rozhdestvensky was in command of this
armada which was intended to launch one last devastating attack
on the Japanese Navy. A heavy fog descended as the Russian
ships were drawing near the Dogger Bank and suddenly a
number of small craft were sighted. In a moment of panic, due
to low morale and incompetent leadership, the Russians opened
fire on what turned out to be a British fishing fleet, sinking
some of them. This crass blunder created a critical situation
for Russia with her European neighbours as well as with Britain.
The Russian excuse that they thought the craft were Japanese
torpedo boats seemed at first either to be an example of sheer
stupidity or a downright lie. The British Government demanded
an explanation and reparations, and strained relations between
the two countries seemed almost at breaking point. Eventually
it was agreed that the incident should be investigated by an
international commission of admirals representing the two parties directly concerned, France, the United States and Austria-
Hungary. The following February the commissioners found in
favour of Britain and Russia paid £65,000 in compensation.

Were the Russians somehow fooled by Japanese disinformation into firing on the British fishing vessels? This seems
to be the only possible explanation for their blunder. A good
deal of evidence points this way. Edgar Wallace, the author
and playwright, was at that time a correspondent of the London
Daily Mail. When the Dogger Bank incident occurred he was
sent by his newspaper to Vigo, which was the next port of call
for the Russians, to ascertain exactly what had happened. There
he found two petty officers of the Russian fleet having a quiet
drink ashore. After plying them with further drinks, Wallace
elicited the information that the fog had caused the utmost
confusion, that the fishing vessels had made no response to
signals and that the Russian senior officers had been convinced
from intelligence previously received that a small detachment
of the Japanese fleet was planning deliberately to trap them in
the shallow waters around the Dogger Bank.

Wallace's report of all this was wired to the *Daily Mail*,
whose editor, not surprisingly but perhaps a little unimagina-
tively, felt that the story was rather unconvincing. He wanted
to know much more before printing all the alleged facts. Wallace was told to proceed to Tangier, the next scheduled port
of call for the Russian fleet, to obtain more information. But
when Wallace reached this Moroccan port he learned that the
petty officers had been executed and buried at sea. Apparently

the Russian counter-intelligence officers in Vigo had discovered all about the naval men's talk to Wallace.

Years later Wallace told Colonel Thoroton, R.M., then head of British Intelligence in Gibraltar, that he had discovered that the Russians had been using as an informant a smuggler who operated around the coasts of Spain and who employed agents both in the Channel ports and the Mediterranean. It was this man who had revealed to the Russians that the intelligence they had received about Japanese torpedo boats keeping watch on them around the Dogger Bank had been cleverly planted on them by Japanese Intelligence through a Portuguese smuggler working between Amsterdam and Vigo. Laughingly, Wallace added that the facts were so incredible they could only be used as a short story, which he had written. But the story never appeared, nor (according to Wallace's daughter, Miss Penelope Wallace) can it be found even in manuscript form. It is said that Thoroton vetoed any use being made of the story as one of these two smugglers was also one of his own chief informants and who later kept Gibraltar informed of German submarine movements in World War I. So it is possible that Wallace destroyed the manuscript at Thoroton's request.

Clearly, however, whatever the truth behind this extraordinary story, there is a great deal of substance in it. For on 24 October, 1904, Lord Lansdowne, then the British Foreign Secretary, received from the Russian chargé d'affaires in London the first outline of the explanation which the Russian Government was preparing to cover up this naval blunder. He declared that the Russian Government knew that Japanese agents were visiting England "for the purpose of organising attacks on the Baltic fleet and in these circumstances it was perhaps not unnatural that the captains of the Russian ships should have been alarmed at finding these vessels [the trawlers] in close proximity to the men-of-war".[11]

Later the Russian Ambassador in London stated that "the Russian fleet had acted upon the supposition that these innocent fishermen were Japanese agents in disguise, in spite of the fact that the trawling fleet was upon ground which it habitually frequented and displayed signals required by international regulations". This statement was followed by the astonishing allegation from the Russians that they had positive evidence that two Japanese agents had arrived in Hull shortly before the fishing fleet left that port.

Japanese Naval Intelligence remained highly efficient

throughout the Russo-Japanese War. Even the capturing of the cipher-book used by the Japanese Embassy at the Hague by the Russian agent Manassyevitsh-Manuilov came too late to be of much real help to the Russian Navy. The Japanese changed their ciphers as soon as they learned of the arrest of their two agents in St. Petersburg. Before Admiral Togo made his torpedo attack on Port Arthur he had been supplied with details of the exact positions not only of every Russian ship, but of each searchlight site, too. All searchlights were unerringly put out of action. Admiral Rozhdestvensky's fleet continued on its Far Eastern voyage through the Mediterranean and in February, 1905, was joined by another Russian squadron under Admiral Nebogatov. Then the combined fleet of some forty vessels headed for Vladivostock. Admiral Togo allowed the Russian ships a free passage until, on 27 May, they reached the Straits of Tsushima between Korea and Japan. The Japanese fleet surrounded the Russians and, within twenty-four hours, Admiral Togo had sunk, captured or disabled eight battleships, three coast-defence ships, nine cruisers and nine destroyers. It was a total naval victory from which there was not the slightest chance of recovery by the Russians.

7

Fukushima's Ride to Vladivostock

> "Fukushima was a veritable Don Quixote
> of soldiers. His courage and his drive, his
> exuberant cheerfulness were amazing. For
> a man like this nothing was impossible.
> Tell him something was impossible and he
> would immediately prove you wrong by
> doing it"
>
> General Rafael de Nogales

ONE OF THE most brilliant of Japan's military intelligence officers in this period was Major-General Baron Fukushima, who was born at Matsumoto in Shinano province in 1858, being a member of a *samurai* family. He started life as a drummer-boy, then studied at Tokyo University and spent a year in the Japanese Judicial Department. His quick mind, nimble wit and ability to get along with people caused him to be transferred to the General Staff in 1875. The following year he visited the United States and, on his return home, he was commissioned as a lieutenant in the Army.

During the next few years he travelled extensively, visiting Mongolia in 1879 and being military attaché in Peking from 1882–84. Two years later he was sent on an extensive tour of India.

During his service with the Japanese Army he made a reputation for himself by winning all manner of wagers involving feats of arms or physical strength. Then in 1887 he was promoted to the rank of major and appointed as military attaché in Berlin. An affable, gregarious man, possessed of charm and

67

panache, Fukushima was always eager to accept any challenge put to him. He became immensely popular during his five years' stay in Germany. Fortunately, in the Japanese Army, a challenge made by a foreigner was something which, even if it might appear to be bizarre and conflict with an officer's current duties, was not to be ignored. It was largely a question of prestige and honour. One day, in company with some German officers, the conversation turned to the subject of how far a horse could be ridden day after day at a certain speed. Fukushima, who was a first-rate horseman, declared that his own horse was capable of taking him all the way from Berlin to Vladivostock.

The German officers roared with laughter.

"Nonsense, major, it is impossible," said one.

"Have you taken the trouble to look at the map? The distance you would have to cover would be all of nine thousand miles," another pointed out.

"Of course I know how far it is," replied Fukushima. "What is more I know my horse and what it can do. And I myself am quite equal to the task. I am in fine fettle and used to riding in mountainous terrain."

After a few more drinks the German officers challenged him to carry out this exploit, never expecting him to accept. As a bait, however, they offered a spare horse to be used en route. To their astonishment the Japanese major calmly took up the challenge and obtained permission from his superiors to do so.

This was perhaps the Japanese equivalent of the much publicised feat of that earlier nineteenth century adventurer, Colonel Fred Burnaby, another cavalry officer with whom Fukushima had much in common. Burnaby was in the Sudan in 1874 when he heard that the Russian frontier was closed to foreigners, and he at once made preparations for his celebrated ride to Khiva through Asia Minor. He would have gone further, but for the fact that he was recalled by telegraph by the Duke of Cambridge, then C-in-C of the British Army. The Duke was the archetype of the bone-headed British Army officer of his day, otherwise Burnaby might have obtained quite a lot more useful intelligence. But a far wiser General Staff in Japan made no effort to deter Fukushima.

In terms of human endurance, of course, Fukushima's ride beat all records and was a much greater feat than that of Burnaby. It is interesting to learn that Burnaby was one of Fukushima's greatest heroes and that it was that very ride to Khiva which partially at least inspired his trip to Vladivostock. Burnaby, a man of great strength like Fukushima, had had a varied career as army officer, *Times* war correspondent, explorer, adventurer and, in 1877, as commander of a Turkish brigade in the war with Russia. Fukushima's interest in Burnaby had first been aroused by the fact that both men had spent some years in Germany and that Burnaby had propounded the view that Russia was Britain's chief enemy. As the Japanese major regarded Russia as Japan's greatest potential enemy, he was anxious to read all he could of Burnaby's opinions on this subject.

The gallant Japanese officer set off on his journey across two continents in 1892, arriving in Vladivostock fifteen months later. From Germany he travelled through Russia, Siberia, Mongolia and Manchuria. Anxious to waste no time in returning to his native land, once he had reached Vladivostock, he made the voyage to Tokyo in the same clothes in which he had set out on his fabulous ride, carrying his riding switch with him. It was a bedraggled and ragged figure who eventually reached the Japanese capital where he was duly feted and feasted for some days. The story of his ride made him a national hero. After a public reception held in his honour he was immediately promoted to the rank of lieutenant-colonel. The clothes he had worn and his riding switch were placed in a Japanese museum.

Another story is that Fukushima himself engineered the excuse for this escapade in order to obtain intelligence on Russia during his ride. No doubt when he was given permission to accept the challenge, he was instructed to make a very full report on what he saw and heard en route. Certainly, too, Fukushima had been stressing the need for an intelligence-probe inside Russia by a senior Japanese officer all the time he had been in Berlin: "It is essential for a senior officer to make his own on-the-spot assessment of the reports we have been getting," he argued. But whether this affair was fortuitous, or cunningly plotted, it marked the beginning of Fukushima's career as an intelligence officer. He was fluent in many languages and dialects, including Russian, and this enabled him to obtain considerable valuable information on his ride.

From then onwards Fukushima set out to stamp his personality and originality on the Japanese Army hierarchy. He was made a General Staff officer and sent to Egypt, Turkey, Persia, Caucasia, Arabia, India, Burma, Siam and Turkestan. In 1902 he visited London and not only represented his country at King

Edward VII's coronation, but was prominent in talks behind
the scenes in connection with the Anglo-Japanese Alliance. At
the same time he was created an honorary Knight Commander
of the Order of the Bath.

When General Sir Ian Hamilton led the British military
mission attached to the First Japanese Army, Fukushima was
a major-general and Chief of the Second Section of the General
Staff. Hamilton regarded him as "a very able director of intelligence and obtainer of information" when they first met in
1904. The British officer liked him immensely, despite the fact
that Fukushima's task was to "baffle and thwart in every possible way all the foreigners who have dealings with him, whilst,
to enable him the more effectively to execute this disagreeable
duty, he is officially described as their mentor and assistant".[1]

Hamilton thought he performed this task with charm and
skill. He was enormously impressed not only by the efficiency
of Fukushima's disinformation (which seemed to deceive the
other foreign military observers), but with his highly accurate
information on other matters. He found the Japanese intelligence chief exceptionally well informed on British Indian troops
and their Russian rivals. "The British officer in India," expounded Fukushima, "is more Sikh than the Sikh, more Gurkha
than the Gurkha and more Madrasee than the Madrasee", but
he also criticised in a polite way the self-sufficiency, arrogance
and complacency of the British in India and the way in which
they pushed natives "on and off the trains as if they were
lunatics".[2]

His opinion of the Cossack was terse and to the point: he
had lost all his skill of the past except horsemanship and was
"little better than a yokel living on the Napoleonic legend,
sometimes brave, sometimes not, never disciplined and badly
led".[3]

Under Fukushima, who seemed to be a co-ordinator of intelligence and disinformation, came Colonel Hagino, who was
the titular chief of intelligence of the First Army. Like Fukushima, Hagino was a Russian specialist, and had lived in Russia
for seven years. He was trained in Europe and had a broad and
generous mind which permitted him, even while the war with
Russia was being waged, to tell Hamilton that he liked the
Russians very much and had received great kindness from them
all the time he was in their country.

Hagino was somewhat of a cosmopolitan like Fukushima
and had a European outlook which made him an exceptionally

adroit and skilful interrogator of Russian prisoners. Both he and his deputy intelligence chief, Captain Hikida, spoke Russian fluently, and this allied to their special technique of quiet, persevering questioning paid handsome dividends. A middle-aged man with a greyish beard and regular features, Colonel Hagino was described by Hamilton as "most conscientious, hard-working, considerate . . . a trifle over-careful, ponderous and precise from the military attaché point of view, but obviously upright and reliable in every sense".[4]

Hagino's special talent was for ascertaining how well or how badly trained were the Russian troops. From examining the prisoners he came to the conclusion that the vast majority of the recruits had only had three months' training, while a Russian non-commissioned officer, when asked to read the notebook of one of his own officers who had been killed, failed totally to do so. Yet he claimed he had passed his examination for N.C.O. Hagino was quite satisfied that this was not a pretence of ignorance by other tests he conducted.

One specially interesting point about the Japanese military probes at this time was the close attention paid to the Turkestan troops in the Russian Army. There were two reasons for this: first, interrogation and observation had shown that the Turkestan troops were the best; second, the Japanese had already concluded that it was easiest to make friends with them because they were Muslims. Already Japanese Intelligence had started to look ahead. The men from Turkestan were part of the Asian complex of peoples and it was felt possible that they could in time be detached from Russian imperialist adventurers. This was a theme which was recurringly exploited in the 1920s and 1930s. Two of the chief advocates of this policy were Mitsuri Toyama, who urged that Japanese Intelligence should make as close contacts with Muslims in Asia as they had previously done with Buddhist priests, and Ryohei Uchida, who ventured into Manchuria in the summer of 1900. It was from Uchida and other Japanese agents that confirmation was obtained concerning rumours of new and secret Sino-Russian agreements to give Russia control over all the railways of Manchuria. Another able director of secret service activities in Asia in the years prior to the Russo-Japanese War was Kiyoshi Arao, who died in 1896. He had been attached to the General Staff, but was released to organise the establishment of special information-collecting bureaux on the Asiatic mainland. In 1889 he resigned his Army commisison to launch a project entitled

the Institute for Sino-Japanese Commercial Research and he
set this up in Shanghai, taking with him a team of some 200
students. Here he opened a school largely subsidised by himself
and from private funds. "Graduates of this school were divided
into teams of about twenty to make trips into all parts of China,
Manchuria . . . Later some would be employed as the local agents
of the more enterprising Japanese trading firms; others would
enter the Japanese consular service as specialists in Far Eastern
trade; many became scouts and official interpreters during the
Sino-Japanese War."[5]

Hardship meant nothing to those who ventured to the Far
North. A Japanese consul at Yinkow was astonished one day
in 1897 when two filthy beggars arrived at his office. He was
about to order them away when they revealed that they were
both Japanese agents. One was Heiriku Kogoshi, who had
temporarily had leave from the Navy to spy on any moves
relating to the Russian Navy, while the other, Yoshimasa Ya-
mada, had been captured by the Russians in Manchuria, but
escaped after countless adventures.[6]

The Russians had made efforts to counter the highly successful intelligence drive made by the Japanese in Manchuria
and elsewhere. But they did not realise until it was too late
how intensive this drive was and the large number of people
involved. Their key figure was General Harting, of the overseas
section of the *Ochrana*, who was sent to Manchuria to develop
counter-intelligence. He was provided with carefully selected
agents and large sums of money, but even then it took him a
long time to produce any worthwhile results. The Japanese
espionage machine worked far too smoothly and, by the time
the war had started, they had used the Chinese as spies and
helped them to infiltrate behind the enemy lines. So it was that
Russians and Japanese began to employ Chinese as spies against
each other. Both powers also attempted to use Chinese espionage bureaux in their own interests.

The Chinese were well aware of the infiltration of Japanese
spies among their coolies (it was reckoned that twelve out of
every hundred coolies around Port Arthur were Japanese), so,
being concerned about this as well as Japanese intentions towards China, they tended to favour the Russians. Notwithstanding this, the Japanese still managed to chalk up a number
of successes with Chinese agents.

Espionage bureaux were set up by the Japanese both inside
their own lines and behind those of the enemy. The system by

which information was passed to and fro was admirably worked out, providing each spy with at least three runners to pass messages. This system enabled queries to be put to the spies behind the enemy lines as well as simply relying on what intelligence was sent through. Thus a steady flow of up-to-date information was received from inside Russian-occupied territory from Chinese and Japanese spies. This was how the Japanese learned all about Russian plans for sowing electrically-controlled mines not only in the path of advancing troops, but in harbours and along the coast. Details of these were brought through by the spy network which had even managed to infiltrate the working parties setting up these mines. About one in twelve of those undertaking this work was a Japanese agent. The result was that in the Army headquarters was an ever-changing map showing not only the positions of Russian mines, but the actual detonating points as well. Then, under cover of darkness, men would be sent out to de-activate the mines.

As the war continued so more Chinese were lured to work for the Japanese which proves how skillfully the latter had managed to assuage Chinese doubts about their intentions. The messages they carried were usually in rice-paper balls, but occasionally rather more elaborate methods of communications were employed. Sometimes a ragged mendicant bearing a tray of souvenirs for sale would come into the Japanese lines. The objects on his tray would be set out in such a way as to indicate the movements of enemy battalions. There were so many wandering beggars in Manchuria that this tactic was easier than might seem to be the case.

Within a few months there was hardly anywhere inside the Russian lines where Japanese spies had not penetrated. Both the First Tomsk regiment and the Twenty-Fifth Siberian Rifles were infiltrated and among their mess servants were Chinese agents working for the Japanese. These spies listened in to gossip at dinner tables as well as combing waste-paper baskets for valuable material. Many of the construction workers were also acting as spies. Not all these agents could speak or understand Russian and many of them were of a low standard of intelligence among the Chinese coolies. But this was where numbers proved worthwhile. Out of fifty such people duly questioned, perhaps five would provide useful data.

The Japanese were also among the first in modern warfare to introduce sabotage as a systematic policy. Here again the

work was done by sending agents behind the lines. The special
targets were electrical power stations, searchlights and railways. Early in 1904 two Japanese officers disguised as Mongolians were caught by the Russians while trying to destroy
both the railways and telegraph system in Manchuria. The
surprising aspect of this was that, unless the two Japanese had
admitted their nationality, the Russians might well have thought
the sabotage had been committed by their own people, or by
Manchurians in their employ, which had happened on some
other occasions.

One of the few foreigners employed by the Japanese as a
spy during this war was that celebrated soldier of fortune,
General Rafael de Nogales, who served under many flags,
starting with the Spanish-American War at the age of eighteen.
In a versatile career he worked as a cowboy, miner, explorer
and spy. This Venezuelan adventurer was recruited into the
Japanese Secret Service, according to his own account, by a
man named Evans, described as "an acting secretary of state
of the Korean Empire".[7] Evans, it would seem, was not only
an agent of the Japanese, but a recruiter of spies for them as
well, and actually supervising Japanese espionage in Korea and
the Liaotung Peninsula.

Evans' instructions to Nogales were that he should go to
Port Arthur using the cover of a travelling salesman of Swiss
watches. It was an especially shrewd move because Evans had
discovered that the commander of one Russian garrison in that
area was of Swiss origin, named Stoessel. Nogales' work as
an agent for the Japanese must have been quite extensive for
he seemed to know all about the machinations of Yuan Shi
K'ai, the Chinese warlord who was spying for the Russians
while at the same time conspiring with a Chinese agent of the
Japanese, an old man named Wu-ling. It was Nogales who
patiently coaxed information from Wu-ling by dint of cross-
examination and "tracing and re-tracing, sometimes for hours,
on the dirty mud floor of our room and by the light of a candle,
the outlines of the various entrenchments which we had come
across that day". He told how Wu would "write down and draw
with the help of a magnifying-glass our mental notes and pictures on a diminutive piece of very thin, parchmented tissue
paper, about one-third the size of a cigarette paper. . . . Wu would
roll it into a ball, the size of a pin-head and file it away. He
would pull one of his three or four hollow gold teeth out of
his mouth, place the paper ball into it, shut the empty tooth

with a piece of wax and push it back into its original place."[8]

Wu-ling would then take his messages to the Japanese. He was eventually caught by the Russians, not surprisingly as he had been betrayed by Yuan Shi K'ai. Wu was tortured and had his teeth extracted. Inside were found details of Russian troop movements, camp sites and supplies. He was summarily executed in the most barbaric fashion and his corpse thrown on a bonfire.

A totally different attitude was shown to a captured Russian spy by the Japanese. This incident illustrates perfectly the Japanese tradition, borrowed from Sun Tzu, that the spy is a noble patriot which in that era was in stark contrast to the contempt in which most Western nations held even their own secret agents. A Russian soldier, disguised as a Chinese, found his way into a Japanese camp where he was promptly arrested. Put on trial for espionage, he was sentenced to death. Then, having executed the Russian, the Japanese showed such a high regard for his bravery, dignified bearing and devotion to duty that they sent a report to the Russian Commander-in-Chief, General Kuropatkin, praising his "noble bearing and honesty". This was possibly the very last example of chivalrous generosity in modern warfare. On neither side in the two world wars was there any other incident quite to be compared to this.

No subterfuge was neglected in trying to baffle the Russians. By stressing the importance of intelligence senior Japanese officers had urged the need for constant deception tactics. General Sir Ian Hamilton reported that at Wiju in the region of the Yalu River he came upon an example of such tactics: "the road we were following was open to view from the Russian side of the river and an officer posted there with good field-glasses could have made an accurate computation of what passed into the Yalu Valley during the day. To prevent this the Japanese had called on the forests to assist them. Macbeth could not have been more astonished when he saw Birnam Wood marching on Dunsinane than the Russians when they observed a fine avenue of full-grown fir trees standing one morning on each side of a road where no trees had stood before. The thing was done in style. No scrubby saplings or unsightly gaps, but a handsome, closely planted avenue of forest trees . . . Our avenue led us to our destination for the night—Wiju."[9]

Nogales met Major-General Fukushima later in the war and came to have a very high regard for him. The Japanese intelligence chief asked him many questions about the conduct of the Spanish-American War. Nogales recalled seeing Fukushima and two of his officers at a display of dancing and revelry one night during the war: "this was not, I gathered, a frequent occurrence. The officers had been in conference and studying intelligence reports with every seriousness. Suddenly Fukushima clapped his hands and smiled, saying, 'now we shall celebrate, so come and join us, Nogales.' I was surprised how easily he was able to forget the war for an hour or so."

In the spring of 1904 Nogales had arrived in Fusan, Korea, en route to Japan. A wound he had received during a landing at Pei-tse-wo on the Liaotung Peninsula was apparently causing him some concern, but he did not reveal how he came by it. He was eventually rescued by an American skipper named Johnson, who had made a lot of money "poaching along the forbidden shores of the Czar's Siberian domains".

After Wu-ling's capture as a result of treachery on the part of Yuan Shi K'ai's agents, it became necessary to think up new methods of hiding written intelligence notes. While the enemy were usually unable to decipher the notes, or even read the Japanese or Chinese characters in which they were written, they were able to kill the messengers as they found them. The vast majority of these agents managed to remain undetected, but Nogales thought this was largely due to changing the hiding-places and employing different tactics. Some messages, he intimated, were hidden in a Chinese man's pigtail. Towards the end of the war an effort was made to avoid written communications altogether and to obtain more intelligent runners who could actually memorise messages and only pass them to a Japanese officer verbally. Various colours were used to denote battleships, cruisers and destroyers, or types of armament, and silks in these hues would be sewn into clothes.

Much of the work of the Black Dragon Society which had been so patiently planned some years before came to fruition in this period. There was the case of a specially trained Black Dragon agent named Hajime Hamamoto who left Hokkaido for the north of Manchuria in 1898 and eventually made his way into Russia where he set up a general store in a village not far from a military garrison. Hamamoto kept a small room at the back of his store where he displayed various trinkets, bits of cheap jewellery and inexpensive trifles appealing to women. He would then set out to make himself agreeable to the wives of Russian officers who came to his store and, when he had got to know them better, wait until they made a large purchase and then invite them into his inner sanctum. There, one wife at a time, these women were first of all shown all the wares and then offered to pick out some item which they were given as a present.

To the Russians wives, Hamamoto, who gave himself a Mongolian name, appeared to be just another "oriental", and they had no idea he was Japanese. He had mastered the Russian language sufficiently to be able to recite poetry to them and, within a short span of time, he was the most popular store-keeper in the area with the Russian women. He was said to have ensnared two officers' wives by plying them with an aphrodisiac concoction concealed in small cakes. But whatever the mode of his seductions, the affairs were kept discreetly to the little bedroom which led off the inner display room of his store, so that there would be no opportunity for gossip. He never met the women outside his store at any time and took care that when one was allowed in to his inner sanctum, nobody else would be present in the shop.

For four years Hamamoto sent in regular reports to his superiors through a trusted runner, partly gained by chatting with his mistresses and partly from following up little hints they dropped. All this was passed on to Military Intelligence in Japan via an agent in Vladivostock. One day the people of the village arrived at the store and found it was closed. Hamamoto had fled and shortly afterwards Russian military police began to make inquiries. One of Hamamoto's mistresses had talked indiscreetly. Luckily, she realised her mistake and had warned him there might be trouble. He survived to start a new espionage career in Tientsin.

Everybody had thought that Russia would easily win this war. The Japanese had been quite happy to let people think so. Part of their intelligence plan had been to welcome observers from foreign armies, to feed them skilfully with false infor-mation, but at the same time to go out of their way to be helpful, considerate and to impart a certain amount of accurate information when it would further their cause. This policy, far from alienating the foreign observers, seems in the end to have won their admiration. Thus in referring to Colonel Hagino, the First Army's chief of intelligence, General Hamilton said: "I cannot imagine myself an officer of Colonel Hagino's status in any European army deigning to trouble his head about a party of foreigners; still less can I see him dictating to them a careful little lecture just as a great battle is commencing. . . . I

am certain that in no army in the world would we receive as
much official assistance in carrying out our work as we now
do with Kuroki's command."[10]

Fukushima and Akashi were admirers of one another and,
though not close friends, exchanged views on the long-term
requirements of Japanese Intelligence. Both men were in agreement that in Manchuria, Korea and Mongolia and indeed even
inside Russian territory in the Far East the Japanese prostitute
was a vital asset to those engaged in intelligence-gathering.
Fukushima even composed a poem entitled "From Fallen Petal
to Rising Star" in which he told how a prostitute became a
noble patriot. Makiyo Ishimitsu, who served as an intelligence
officer in Manchuria from 1899 to the beginning of the Russo-
Japanese War, working as an itinerant photographer, enrolled
many of these women as his agents, stating that after they
arrived in Vladivostock in the 1880s, "being gentle, honest and
kind", they were welcomed everywhere and by the turn of the
century they formed a "ready-made intelligence network" all
over the Russian areas of the Far East.[11]

Akashi became a favourite in the *salons* as much because
of his poems and paintings as his military reputation. Promoted
to full General, he was on his way to take up the post of
Governor-General of Formosa when he died in 1919. He left
behind him valuable friends of Japan all over the world and
among some of his Muslim contacts the Black Dragon Society
were enjoying close collaboration in the 1920s, even to the
point of having links with some Muslim secret societies. After
World War I Ibrahim, his friend, visited Tokyo on a number
of occasions and worked closely with the Japanese. Major-
General Fukushima was so highly regarded after the Russo-
Japanese War that in 1912 he was given a rank equivalent to
that of a Governor-General in Kwantung province of China, a
post he held until 1917. He died on 18 February, 1919.

8

China-watching

"Having delayed their entry into the world of espionage until the beginning of the twentieth century, the Japanese grasped two of the basic principles almost at once. One is the need to centralise control, and the other is that any intelligence system must be put out on the ground and made fully operational long before any shooting starts"

Major Jock Haswell in
Spies & Spymasters

VICTORY IN THE Russo-Japanese War had proved to the Japanese the absolute importance of total intelligence. Indeed, as Major-General Fukushima said afterwards, "Sun Tzu would have been proud of this operation. He would have said we had followed his text-book to the very last sentence. But we know that we did better than that. We started a new book where he left off."[1]

Thus, looking to the future, the Japanese decided that something like total espionage was essential if they were to consolidate their position as an emergent world power. The first step was to strengthen their intelligence network on the Asiatic mainland; the second was to extend that network all round the globe, something which would take a long time before it could be fully developed.

To attempt to have a comprehensive intelligence system in every country could only result in a diluted and therefore inefficient network. So they selected their prime targets very

carefully. China and Manchuria, linked to all territories large
and small adjacent to those nations, were the principal targets
for espionage. China-watching had top priority. After that came
Russia and the United States for varying reasons. Japan had
very wisely negotiated an admirably just and even generous
peace settlement with Russia, culminating in the Treaty of
Portsmouth, New Hampshire, where the Americans kept a
watching brief. This settlement angered some of the leaders of
the Black Dragon and other secret societies. But it was fully
realised in Tokyo that the Czar's madcap dreams of acquiring
a vast empire in the East had not been supported by many of
his wisest ministers, especially Count Witte. When the Czar
had annexed the whole of Manchuria he had done so against
ministerial advice. Even so, he could have avoided war if he
had agreed to recognise Japan's sphere of influence in Korea.
When he started to infiltrate his troops into Korea, war became
inevitable. In the end the Japanese had to deal with Witte,
which suited their civilian statesmen admirably, but perturbed
some of the nationalist and expansion-minded generals. Count
Witte ensured that friendly contacts were made with the various
branches of Japanese Intelligence through his own private espionage service, which was mainly concerned with the commercial side. As a result of these secret talks Russian spies
were actually withdrawn from Japan and sent to Shanghai and
Peking, and Witte set about trying to make changes in the
Czarist Secret Service. Russian foreign policy was reversed
overnight.

Similar concessions were made by the Japanese and there
might have been further beneficial developments if Witte had
not been dismissed by the Czar after a relatively brief period
in power. Under the Portsmouth Treaty the Japanese received
from Russia recognition of her interests in Korea, the cession
of the southern half of Saghalien and while Russia was allowed
to retain her rights in North Manchuria, Japan was given virtual
control in the southern half of that country. Eventually Korea
became a Japanese protectorate. Despite all this, there was a
strong body of opinion inside Japan which felt the terms were
far too lenient and that a substantial war indemnity should have
been wrested from Russia. The Black Dragon Society pressed
for a vigilant espionage campaign on the Asiatic mainland in
the vicinity of Russia's borders.

Observers in Tokyo were keenly aware that while Britain
had been sympathetic towards Japan during the Russo-Japanese

War, even though she had not intervened, the German Kaiser had more than once encouraged the Czar's eastern adventures. This marked the beginning of a change in Japanese-German relations. From being exceptionally close in the seventies and eighties this relationship was transformed into a vigilant if polite chilliness in the first decade of the new century. This was to be a deciding factor, if only one of many, when it came to participating in World War I ten years after the Russo-Japanese War. Another factor in bringing Japan in firmly on the side of the Allies was the improved relationship with Russia. Major-General F. S. G. Piggott, who was one of the British officers studying Japanese at that time, commented on how well the Japanese and Russians got on together after their war: ". . . the two countries made friends quickly after the Russo-Japanese war; and one could see the happy results with one's own eyes."[2]

Despite all this outward show of improved relations with Russia, however, the Japanese were still wary of their ex-enemy. Perhaps their attitude—at least that of the military—is best summed up by Colonel Masanobu Tsuji, formerly of the Operations Division of the Imperial General Staff. "Following the Russo-Japanese War, the basic policy had been one of preparing for another war against Russia," he stated.[3] "But after the collapse of Imperial Russia for a period of several years there was no menace from the Soviet Union, and consequently little military planning of importance in Japan. After the Manchurian Incident [the Japanese occupation of Manchuria] we became fully conscious of the Soviet menace to the Far East and our military preparations were expedited."

This may be an oversimplification of the position, but it underlines the fact that an intelligence watch on Russia was still maintained.

From 1900 onwards Japan also increasingly directed her Intelligence Services to take a keener interest in the United States. There were several reasons for this. Curiously, Japan was much more suspicious of the supposedly anti-colonialist United States than of the machinations of Britain as a world imperial power. An American presence in Alaska, in the Philippines and various Pacific Ocean islands was regarded as more of a long-term threat than that of the British in Hong Kong or Singapore. But relations between Japan and the U.S.A. were greatly exacerbated by the harsh treatment and discriminatory policies shown towards Japanese immigrants in some parts of the United States. Countless reports of such behaviour and the failure of the authorities to check it were received in Tokyo. In this period of the early twentieth century many Japanese emigrated to Canada and Mexico and even to South America.

Finally, it was also realised that the United States Navy had begun to conduct an espionage campaign against Japan. True, it was not a particularly effective campaign; on occasions it was so clumsily managed that the Japanese could hardly fail to notice what was happening. American espionage in those days was hopelessly compromised by the disapproval of officers of the armed services for spying in any form. Nevertheless, as far back as 1889, Navy Secretary Whitney was arranging for F. E. Chadwick, the American O.N.I. (Office of Naval Intelligence) chief in London, to buy plans of a cruiser being built in Britain for the Japanese Navy.[4]

The next year efforts were made to obtain details of the new secret torpedoes being used in Japanese warships. A special file was kept in the O.N.I. on all Japanese naval officers visiting America from 1890 onwards. In the Russo-Japanese War Lloyd H. Chandler, U.S.N., was instructed that the Navy Department "wishes to avail itself of your knowledge of torpedo boats and destroyers to make an investigation and report as to the use and influence of these craft by Japan in the present war".[5]

But the emphasis on intelligence by one section of the U.S. Navy was largely disregarded by executive officers. They continued to treat it as of secondary importance and failed to heed its lessons. Thus while the best brains in the U.S. Navy tended to avoid being assigned to intelligence work, because they knew it could be a bar to promotion, the Japanese who succeeded in this field invariably reached the top of their profession.

Japanese Intelligence Services generally were specially concerned at this time with the military and naval installations in Hawaii. In the Library of Congress in Washington there are two sets of Japanese Foreign Office documents entitled *Honoruru Gumbi Chosa*, which contain reports of investigations into the military preparations of Honolulu from 1907–1926, and *Hawaii Rikugi Joho-bu Shuo* (weekly intelligence reports from the Army Intelligence Bureau in Hawaii, 1922–23), amounting in all to some 2,318 pages of print. Such diligence as this far outweighed anything undertaken by the still ridiculously understaffed American O.N.I. But America was then paying the penalty for the orthodox view in her military and naval hierarchies that intelligence work was something underhand and criminal.

From time to time Japanese warships and sometimes fishing vessels carried out extensive surveying, charting and photography off the American Pacific coast. In photographic intelligence work Japan was far ahead of either Britain or America at this time. Indeed, this superiority was maintained right up to World War II. Occasionally there was an "accidental" grounding by one of these vessels. In one such incident in 1908 a number of Japanese officers made this an excuse to wade ashore and explore the whole area. The U.S. Army and Navy seemed to pay little attention to these more or less open probes.

But it was inside China where Japan conducted a really large-scale intelligence-gathering operation. The main purpose of this was to learn about the complexities of Chinese politics and the various secret societies which so often played a part in this sphere. China was rapidly becoming ungovernable and it was apparent that the old order of things in that nation could not last much longer.

Much of the work carried out in this area was handled by the Black Dragon Society which, after 1905, established contacts with the up-and-coming Sun Yat-sen and his aides. This work had been begun by the Black Ocean Society and the history of that organisation claims that a sum of more than 250,000 yen was raised by their members to support Sun Yat-sen's movement prior to 1911.[6]

Both Uchida and Toyama had influence in the highest circles in both State and the Army. These two men encouraged their agents to incite their friends among the young Chinese radicals to rebel against the Peking authorities. It is, if not a mistake, at least a dangerous over-simplification to try to label the leaders of the Japanese secret patriotic societies as being right-wing. Some of them were, others were not, while a few were what Westerners would call on the right on some issues, but strongly leftist on others. Certainly in the early part of this century there was a strong radical streak in most of them. This was particularly marked among the China Lobby of both the Black Ocean and Black Dragon Societies. There were those who believed it was in Japan's best interests for a unified China cooperating with Japan, while others held that Manchuria and part of the northern territories of China should be essentially a Japanese area of influence while retaining Manchu rule. Those who held the latter view were quite happy to see the rest of China governed by Sun.

Thus both parties agreed on the need for supporting the

rising star of Chinese politics, Dr. Sun Yat-sen. By any standards, he was a remarkable man and the Japanese had a talent for spotting potential leaders in other countries. While still young, he had travelled widely, having visited Hawaii and worked as a surgeon in Macao and he had also become an admirer of Japanese skills and innovations. Having tried to launch a campaign to "revive China", as he put it, he started to build up his own intelligence service by utilising the Triad secret societies. By 1894 he had set up a secret society of his own, the Hsing Chung-hui Society, which had branches in Hawaii and Hong Kong as well as in China. Then in 1895 this society plotted to seize the Canton provincial government offices. The plot was discovered and some of Sun's fellow-conspirators were executed. Sun himself escaped to Japan, cut off his pigtail, grew a moustache and adopted Western-style clothes. For a time he passed for a Japanese under the name of Nakayama.

It was in this period that Dr. Sun first sought the cooperation of the Japanese. But leading members of the Black Ocean Society had already learned a great deal about Sun's machinations, not only his setting up of the Hsing Chung-hui, but of the Chung Wo Tong Triad society which he had established in Hong Kong as another base for his intelligence operations. He had used these Triad societies in the hope of manipulating them to overthrow the Imperial Chinese Government.

In October, 1900, a two-week rising was engineered at Waichow, but it had to be broken off when Japanese arms from Taiwan failed to materialise. By this time Sun was getting some wary support from the Japanese and it may well have been that the arms did not arrive because the men in Tokyo had decided the rising was unlikely to be successful. Often the Japanese were more aware of the hazards of his plots than was Sun himself. Later he had increasing support from his secret society contacts inside Japan. His greatest friend among the Japanese was Torazo Miyazaki, the member of a *samurai* family who had been sent to a private school which provided not only a liberal education, but actually encouraged the pupils to evolve their own philosophies and, more important, to propound them in formal talks. The young Miyazaki, following a friendship with a missionary, joined the Congregational Church and actually persuaded his mother and brothers to do so as well.

This conversion was short-lived. Having become enamoured of the economic theories of Henry George (as had the young

Sun Yat-sen), he began to have religious doubts and to mistrust the motives of some of the missionaries. For a while he went to Shanghai to study the Chinese language and he switched his attention to helping to liberate the Chinese people from centuries of bondage. On returning to Japan he had an interview with Ki Inukai, a member of the government, as a result of which he was given funds and a secret assignment to investigate certain societies in China. Inukai fully realised the idealism of this young man and was subtle enough to urge him to undertake some propaganda in the cause of social reform in China.

It was sometime after this that Miyazaki was introduced to Sun Yat-sen. The two men took to each other at once, despite the fact that neither at that time spoke the other's language very well. Within days of their meeting Miyazaki had become a fervent admirer of Sun and a devotee to his cause. They communicated by writing down each other's ideas on scraps of paper, using Chinese characters. Soon Miyazaki was proposing setting up secret bases at Yonaguni, Maku and other islands in the vicinity of Formosa. From these arms supplies could be smuggled over to China by night. Through Miyazaki's enterprise Sun was brought over to Japan as a language teacher. Sun duly impressed not only Inukai, Miyazaki's mentor in these matters, but such men as Hiraoka and Toyama. Consequently Sun began to receive considerable support from his secret society contacts in Japan. Miyazaki also put him in touch with *Huang-hsing* and other of the Hunan secret societies.

Sun himself created the *T'ung-meng hui*, another secret society, which developed swiftly into an international conglomerate with branches in Brussels, Honolulu, San Francisco, Singapore, and Tokyo. Miyazaki provided Sun with funds obtained from Inukai through the Japanese Foreign Office. These were used to enable Sun and his ally, Ch'en Shao-pai, to set up their headquarters in Yokohama as well as to encourage a movement for independence in the Philippines. But while Sun Yat-sen undoubtedly received assistance from such organisations as the East Asian Common Culture Association and the Black Dragon Society, members of the latter certainly infiltrated Sun's circle of friends and even his own secret societies to keep a close watch on his political activities. Miyazaki's motives may have been totally altruistic, but he was certainly manipulated so that his influence should mould Chinese opinion in accordance with Japanese thinking.

Japanese Intelligence has frequently and skilfully used cultural propaganda and literature as a powerful weapon in recruiting allies in other Asian countries. Propaganda has always been regarded as the handmaiden of espionage. There was the case of a nineteen-year-old Chinese student named Tsou Jung, who was provided by the Japanese with a document known as the *Ko-ming chun* ("The Revolutionary Army"). This he had secretly published in China where it became one of the most highly prized of underground revolutionary textbooks, thanks to financial aid from Tokyo. Meanwhile inside China the Black Dragon Society had sponsored a training school for their own agents, including a very few Chinese, in Hankow. This was established under the flamboyant title of the House of Exquisite Pleasures. Apart from training their agents in intelligence techniques, the Japanese also gave them a thorough grounding in how to cope with all manner of sexual techniques, homosexual and heterosexual.

At the same time the Black Dragon Society began to use its influence in India with very similar purposes. One of their agents, Okakura, set up links with Indian terrorists in Calcutta in 1906, while others made common cause with Annamite, Indonesian and Filipino agitators who had taken refuge in Japan. Several of these agitators were recruited as intelligence agents when they returned home to their native lands.

The encouraging of the independence movement in the Philippines was another factor in Japan's attitude to America. When the United States clamped down on the independence movement, however, the Japanese were not willing to push their support for the Filipinos to the point of antagonising the U.S. But their espionage probe in the whole Pacific area was consequently stepped up.

The intrigues, plots and counter-plots which marked this first decade of the twentieth century in Japanese politics tend to present a misleading picture. To understand the situation properly one needs to take into account the spirit of liberalism which developed in Japan in the latter part of the previous century. This liberalism quite genuinely and unselfishly lay behind the wish to help Japan's neighbours in China and elsewhere in the Far East where it was felt they had either been exploited by Western powers or kept in a state of bondage by reactionary feudal regimes, or, as in the case of China, a combination of both. Once this mood spread it was very soon exploited by the nationalists who seized upon the support for independence, radical or revolutionary movements in East Asia

as a means of extending Japanese influence. From there it was
not difficult for the more Machiavellian of the nationalists to
visualise the gradual creation of a Japanese empire overseas.
For a while liberalism and nationalism were in step, but once
the Army and the secret societies launched their own plans for
furthering Japanese influence overseas, liberalism began to lose
ground. In some ways there was a parallel between the secret
societies of Japan and the secret societies set up by the Jacobin
Club in France in the eighteenth century.

For societies similar to the Black Dragon began to multiply.
Ryohei Uchida for example journeyed to Korea in 1906 to
supervise the creation of what he called the Advance Society,
the purpose of which was to help Japanese propaganda in Korea, to spy on Korean nationalists and keep Tokyo informed
of any subversive movements. In all such cases it was usual
for the Japanese to name one or more local inhabitants as titular
leaders. The Advance Society had a Korean leader.

Mitsuru Toyama was still the most powerful figure behind
the scenes in many of these various manoeuvres. When Sun
Yat-sen made a tactless speech in Tokyo in 1907, saying that
if Japan required some territory in northern China as the price
for her help, he would have no objection, Toyama maintained
that this kind of publicity was harmful to Japan's long-term
interests. He believed in achieving his aims by underground
plotting, not by frank talk. Within days the Chinese government
demanded that Sun should be expelled from Japan for making
such a statement. To avoid embarrassment all round, Sun was
privately urged to leave of his own accord. Toyama was the
creator of the *Roninkai* in 1908. This was a subsidiary organisation of the Black Dragon, directed at seeking intelligence in
Mongolia as well as creating a cell of activists in that country.
Shortly after this Toyama launched the *Yurinkai* with the purpose of supporting Sun. It was largely from Tokyo that the
Chinese Revolution of 1911 was planned.

But this revolution was not as well planned as might have
been expected and the Japanese were not fully prepared for it.
A major problem was that Sun was out of Japan at the time.
There was also considerable disagreement within the Japanese
government as to what risks of intervention Tokyo should take.
Some were eager to support Sun Yat-sen, while others had
come to mistrust him. Valuable time was lost in fruitless arguments. Some of the Japanese secret agents inside China felt
that they had been let down by their own government's delaying

tactics. But once the revolution was under way other agents were ordered to get into China as best they could without arousing suspicion or attention. Thus Chochi Kayano, another Japanese supporter of Sun and a *samurai* from Tosa, arrived in Shanghai disguised as a priest.

In 1910 Japan had annexed Korea without any opposition from the outside world. It was a smoothly effected operation, entirely due to a carefully laid plan of intelligence-gathering. Shortly before the annexation Prince Ito, who had been Japan's first Resident-General in Korea, had been assassinated by a Korean while on a visit to Harbin. This provided the excuse which the Japanese needed to justify their intervention.

There was a heavy atmosphere of duplicity and double-dealing in the air in the years immediately prior to the 1911 Revolution. Sun Yat-sen and the Japanese were spying on one another and mistrusting each other's moves. Both on the Japanese and the Chinese side there was some reason for suspicion. The generous, heady liberalism of earlier days had long since evaporated. It was no longer the comradeship of ideals and mutual interest, but each side ruthlessly compelled to safeguard its own requirements. As soon as Sun found he could raise funds for his cause in the Western World, so his ardour for Japanese collaboration cooled. He might, of course, have suspected that some Japanese were using him for their own intelligence-gathering purposes rather than for any zeal to liberate the Chinese people. But some of his actions showed not merely a marked disloyalty to faithful Japanese friends such as Miyazaki, but downright treachery. He took as his military adviser a notoriously anti-Japanese American named Homer Lea. There is evidence, too, that as early as 24 March, 1910, in a letter from Sun to Lea, he was prepared to give Japanese military secrets to the United States, for he clearly asked Lea whether the U.S. War Department would be interested in Japanese War Office documents.[7]

But Japanese Foreign Office documents made available for inspection since World War II reveal that Japanese Intelligence had been watching every movement of Sun for some years before the 1911 Revolution in China. This watch had also been extended to Sun's Japanese acquaintances such as Miyazaki and Chochi Kayano. Mail was intercepted and sometimes the secret police searched the homes of the two Japanese. Some weeks before Sun made what he believed was a secret visit to Japan in 1910 he had written to Huang Hsing, who was in

Tokyo at that time, asking what would happen to him if the Japanese Government discovered he was in their territory. From that moment instructions went to Japanese consuls in various places to report the arrival and departure of Sun, following his movements not only in Hong Kong and South-East Asia, but in Hawaii as well.

The 1911 revolution was largely planned by the secret agents of the Tung Meng Hui and its Japanese allies. The last Manchu Emperor, the boy-king Pu Yi, signed a deed of abdication. But the man who came to power was not then Sun Yat-sen, but the crafty, double-dealing General Yuan Shih-k'ai. The general had control of North China and from this position of strength he was able to start negotiations to bring himself to the presidency. Surprisingly, Sun Yat-sen voluntarily handed over the presidency to Yuan. But China was still in effect hopelessly divided between the various warlords and their allies.

9

World War One

"Suspicion must be cut away, for there is
no cause for it. Japan has won the equal
status of one of the world's Great Powers.
She has been circumspect and restrained,
a mirror of fidelity to her engagements. In
all that pertains to honest diplomacy Japan
can set an example to the whole world"

The London *Observer*,
1918

AS THE SECOND decade of the twentieth century opened Japan
was fast becoming a power to be reckoned with. The Anglo-
Japanese Alliance remained the cornerstone of her links with
the Western World. It had been considerably enhanced by extremely efficient and friendly diplomatic relations on each side.
In 1905 that alliance had been renewed, while in 1907 an
entente with France helped to pave the way for the signing of
a convention with Russia soon afterwards. Thus the foundation
was laid for that quadruple alliance of Britain, France, Japan
and Russia which was to be of paramount importance in 1914.
Lord Grey of Falladon, the British Liberal Foreign Secretary
of those pre-war years, stated in his autobiography that during
the whole of his eleven years in office Japan never exploited
unfairly the advantages she might have claimed from the Alliance and that her government and ambassadors were honourable and loyal.[1]

Yet just as relations between Japan and the European powers
improved, so did friction between Japan and America increase.
Not even the entry of the United States into the world war in

1917 did much to change this situation. Repeatedly, the stepping-up of Japanese immigration to America produced the most tactless responses in some parts of that country. In California there were blatant attempts to boycott Japanese businesses, while Japanese children were segregated in American schools despite the fact that often they were intellectually the equal of and even superior to native-born children. There had been a "Gentleman's Agreement" in 1907 limiting the immigration of Japanese labourers, but the Japanese Exclusion League of California had stridently demanded an end to all such immigration.

The strained relationship between the two countries might have broken down altogether, as in some U.S. naval circles there was an hysterical belief that Japan had become America's number one enemy. There was no evidence to support such a view other than the various intelligence probes which the Japanese had conducted, but these could hardly be construed as making preparations for war at that time. In any event Japan was suffering from an acute strain on her economy as a result of the rapid expansion of her industrialisation programme. She was in no position to indulge in a war of her own making.

An armaments bribery scandal in Tokyo which caused the break-up of the Yamamoto Cabinet in the spring of 1914 also gave rise to American suspicions about Japanese involvement in the international armaments race. It was reported that three directors of Mitsui Bussan Kaisha, the agents of the British firm of Vickers in Japan, were accused of bribing Vice-Admiral Matsumoto with £40,000. It was then stated that "Herr Hermann, the Tokyo manager of the Berlin firm of Messrs. Siemens-Schukert, is charged with having given an indirect bribe of £1,100 in connection with the wireless contract obtained by the German firm, and with the destruction by burning in the German Consulate at Yokohama of evidence in the shape of documents which it was notorious had been stolen".

These revelations led to an inquiry into the allegations against Vickers and their agents in Japan as well as a widespread investigation by Army and Navy Intelligence Officers and the *Kempei tai* into German as well as British machinations in the complex world of armaments trafficking. Later the *Japan Weekly Chronicle*, reporting the inquiry into the allegations against Vickers, stated that ". . . in the evidence of Admiral Fuji it is explicitly stated that the Vickers Company remitted to Admiral Fuji on various occasions in 1911 and 1912 sums reaching the great total of 210,000 yen . . . Whether the money was accepted by Fuji legally or illegally, its payment by Vickers was totally illegal and contrary to the Corrupt Practices Act of 1906 (English Law)."

The sinister mastermind behind these corrupt practices in the armaments industry was Sir Basil Zaharoff, the chief agent of Vickers in negotiating foreign deals. Japanese Intelligence had a considerable dossier on Zaharoff, probably a much more accurate one than had the Americans at this stage. They fully realised how he had made himself a vast fortune from commissions acquired by fomenting wars and selling arms to both sides. Their agents in the U.S.A. and Mexico had long before alerted them as to how Zaharoff had helped to precipitate the Spanish-American War and then set out to make a large profit from Spain and the U.S.A. From that moment they determined not to become one of Zaharoff's pawns on the chessboard of international armaments deals. They dealt with him warily.

When World War I began and Japan joined the Western Allies, despite being in the thralls of a financial crisis, it was a cautious, limited role which she played, but an invaluable one nevertheless. Though Japan had built up her armed forces rapidly since the Russo-Japanese war, there had been much criticism in the country that she was weakening herself by spending too much on arms and defence. Such criticism was particularly vociferous in some commercial and banking circles. But by entering the war Japan became a supplier of cheap goods to the Western Allies and this helped to improve her economy. But when she declared war on Germany under Okuma's premiership in 1914, the Japanese Army had some 250,000 men under arms.

It was at this stage that the nation's long-term Intelligence projects began to bear fruit. A cautious period of limited cooperation with Russia had led to the signing of a series of secret conventions with that country in 1916, amounting almost to a defence pact. But it was in China where Japan was able to make most gains. Operations against the Germans were opened at Tsingtao, which port Germany had acquired as a naval base towards the end of the nineteenth century. This campaign lasted for only two months before the Germans surrendered. For the rest of the war the Japanese Army's role was practically reduced to establishing a firm foothold on the Chinese mainland, while the Navy seized the various German-occupied islands in the Pacific, the Caroline, Marshall, Mariana and Pelew groups as they are today.

Such actions may well have been prompted as much by self-interest as loyalty to her Allies, but at least the Prime Minister, the Marquis Okuma, made no secret of the fact. In November, 1914, he declared that in his opinion the time would come when the world would be "divided up among a few strong nations and governed by them" and that it was "Japan's duty to be ready to become one of these elite few nations".

So it was that in 1915 Japan took over the German-leased territories in Shantung and presented her Twenty-One Demands to the Chinese Government, which included giving her extensive rights in Manchuria and Northern China. The Chinese accepted these demands, but not without demur and outside China many hypocritical voices were raised against Japan. But perhaps the viewpoint of Lord Grey sums up objectively and fairly the Japanese position. "In the Great War," he wrote, "they [the Japanese] took some advantage of the opportunity to strengthen their position with China in East Asia. Europe was prostrated in War; the attention and at last the energy of the United States were absorbed in it. The opportunity for Japan was immense and unique. What Western Nation with a population feeling the need for territorial outlets would have used such an opportunity with more, or even as much restraint?"[2]

Attempts were made by the Germans during this war to put out peace feelers to the Japanese in an effort to detach them from the Allies. The Germans' principal intermediaries for such talks were members of the Mexican Consular staff in Tokyo. Constantine Fitzgibbon tells how "the Germans made the most tempting offers to Tokyo, including the renunciation of Germany's pre-war Asian and Pacific possessions, a free hand in China and Eastern Siberia."[3]

Mexico and Japan were then on excellent terms and the former country had been more benevolent towards Japanese immigrants than had the United States. The Mexicans were said to be particularly enthusiastic about the German secret proposals and this perhaps was understandable in the context of the notorious Zimmermann telegram, the discovery of which caused so much consternation in the Allied camp about this time. This was a coded telegram sent by the German Foreign Minister, Arthur Zimmermann, to his ambassador in Washington; it was intercepted and deciphered by cryptographers in the Naval Intelligence Division in London. The text of this message, dated 16 January, 1916, was as follows:

"Most Secret for Your Excellency's personal information:

We intend to begin on 1 February unrestricted submarine warfare. We shall endeavour in spite of this to keep the United States neutral. In the event of this not succeeding we shall make Mexico a proposal of alliance on the following basis: make war together, make peace together, generous financial support, and an understanding on our part that Mexico is to reconquer the lost territory in Texas, New Mexico and Arizona. The settlement in detail is left to you. You will inform the President, that is President Carranza of Mexico, of the above most secretly as soon as the outbreak of war with the United States is certain, and add the suggestion that he should on his own initiative invite Japan to immediate adherence and at the same time mediate between Japan and ourselves. Please call the President's attention to the fact that the ruthless employment of our submarines offers the prospect of compelling England in a few months to make peace."[4]

Admiral W. R. (later Sir William) Hall, chief of British Naval Intelligence in 1916, had one great worry at the time: how was he going to convince the Americans that Germany's incredibly naive proposal to restore Texas to Mexico was anything other than a hoax, or a faked telegram concocted by the British to try to draw the United States into the war. Hall was an able and outstandingly original chief of Naval Intelligence, but he was often unhelpful to and suspicious of Britain's Allies. Had he cooperated with the Japanese, he could have received ample evidence from them confirming the German proposals. Indeed, better Anglo-Japanese collaboration on the naval intelligence side could have given the British hints of what the Zimmermann proposals would be months before they were made. Naval Intelligence in Tokyo had been asked to give their own assessment of German-American and German-Mexican relations, for while the Japanese Foreign Office remained completely loyal to their Allies, they took the realistic view that from an intelligence viewpoint they needed to know exactly what Germany was planning. Some of the terms suggested in the peace feelers seemed as incredible and impracticable to Japan as to Admiral Hall. So the order went out that, while continuing talks with the Mexicans, the Japanese would mount an intelligence operation in Mexico itself.

During 1915 a small Japanese naval squadron had spent some time in Mexican waters for no apparent reason than a courtesy visit. One excuse for extending the period of this visit was that the warship *Asama* had run aground on a sandbank in the Gulf of Lower California and could not speedily be refloated, as extensive repairs were necessary. The visit was a carefully planned exploratory mission, keeping a watch for any possible German moves in the area while intended as a warning to Mexico to stay neutral. Parties of Japanese naval officers went ashore both in Mexico and California where there were several thousand Japanese immigrants among the population. Some resident Japanese in both California and Mexico who had been acting as informants were contacted. A considerable amount of evidence was amassed which showed that Mexico was not really in any position to provide the kind of help which Germany most needed other than to give them supplies and bases. Not that the Navy had seriously thought that Mexico could aid Germany in any substantial way; it was in Army circles that Tokyo had some suspicions that a German-Mexican axis could be a war-winner for the Germans. Perhaps this aspect of Japanese thinking is best summed up by a comment from the British military attaché in Tokyo just after the war in a report he sent home. This was to the effect that the attitude of some of the senior Army officers in Japan had been "unsatisfactory and disappointing" whereas the Navy had been "wholeheartedly with Britain throughout".[5]

But while Navy Intelligence inquiries in Mexico merely confirmed what they had thought all along, more importantly they learned something from a Mexican who had worked for the Americans that was to prove of immense value to Tokyo. This was the information that the U.S. Navy Cryptographic Bureau had failed to decipher a single code either of the Germans or the Japanese.[6]

It was also discovered that German wireless officers from ships interned in the harbour at Vera Cruz were slipping ashore furtively each night to operate a secret wireless station at Ixtapalpa. Japanese agents not only infiltrated this station with one of their own mechanics who passed for a Mexican, but paid a handsome sum to a Mexican locksmith, safe-breaker and burglar to put the transmission apparatus out of action. What they did not know at the time was that the very same Mexican had been asked by British Naval Intelligence to do the same thing! No doubt the burglar made a worthwhile profit from this operation.

At the same time that the *Asama* was aground on the Mexican sandbank information filtered through to U.S. military intelligence from Indian tribesmen that parties of Japanese servicemen were on some kind of secret exercise in nearby Arizona. Colonel S. Mashbir, then a junior officer in the Arizona Infantry, was detailed to investigate these reports in 1916. Eventually he discovered some "unmistakable Japanese ideographs written in charcoal upon rock walls of passes in the Tinahas Atlas Mountains. They were, he estimated, the notes of column commanders who had gone before for the benefit of those to follow." As a result Colonel Mashbir put in a report to U.S. military intelligence about this secret operation, but the General Staff paid no heed to it.[7]

The Japanese Navy played a vital role in World War I and never received the credit it deserved. Its friendly ties with the British Navy, despite everything, remained almost up to the eve of World War II. The part they played was as effective in the Mediterranean theatre as in the Pacific. Often Japanese warships were engaged in the unpublicised work of protecting trade routes and patrolling for enemy submarines. Though an ally from the beginning of the war, Japan had some cause for feeling she had never been treated as an equal, or fully consulted on all issues. This feeling was aggravated after America came into the war. This unquestionably gave the Army, who had a lesser role in the conflict, a feeling of isolation from events. Consequently the Army tended to take a more detached view of the war and encouraged its intelligence officers sometimes to plough their own secretive furrows.

10

Kawashima: The Manchurian Adventurer

"Firefly, come hither, and you
Shall have water to drink!
Yonder the water is bitter:
Here the water is sweet!
Come, fly this way, to the sweet side!"
Japanese nursery song

THIS CHILDREN'S "firefly song" from the Japanese province of Izumo was adopted by some of the early Japanese-controlled "Manchurian guerrillas" as a signature tune and a code. It was apparently a life-long favourite song of Naniwa Kawashima, the master-mind of these guerrillas. He had it translated into Chinese and Russian, with suitable changes in the phraseology, just sufficient to provide a certain amount of propaganda. But there was to be no doubt which was "the sweet side": that lay with the Japanese.[1]

Kawashima, a member of a *samurai* family who settled in Tokyo after the restoration of the Emperor in 1868, was one of the most outstanding of Japanese secret agents over a period of more than twenty years. Like Miyazaki, he had first been converted to Christianity and then become disillusioned with it. As a result he began to regard the Westerners as hypocritical aggressors, who preached peace on earth while keeping Asia poor and waxing fat on the money they took out of the continent. He had visited China as a young man and had been appalled by the poverty of the masses and the corruption of local government.

An excellent linguist, he served as an interpreter to the Japanese Army during the war with Russia. It was after this service that he found himself drawn into intelligence work, first as chief of police in the Japanese section of Peking, and later as a member of the Black Dragon Society. Kawashima had much clearer ideas than either Miyazaki or Kayano, or any other of the China specialists as to what he wanted to achieve. His dream was of a benevolent Japanese empire, protecting the people on the mainland from Russian aggression, Chinese corruption and the money-grabbing Western powers. He visualised Japan controlling the whole of Manchuria and part of Northern China, though to bring this about he was prepared to accept that the Manchu ruling dynasty would play the role of nominal head of state.

There was in Kawashima's make-up that extraordinary tendency in many Japanese nationalists to be both right-wing and left-wing at the same time, to be Machiavellian and yet still idealistic. It is a quality much more rarely to be found in the Western World. In his early days Kawashima was a strong supporter of Sun Yat-sen and prepared to play along with Sun and encourage the Chinese radical rebels as long as their policies coincided with his own aims. But, unlike Miyazaki, he gradually came to mistrust Sun. To close associates he revealed his suspicions that once Sun achieved power, his professed friendship for Japan would be a mirage. It was for this very reason that he kept clear of the kind of entanglements with Sun to which both Kayano and Miyazaki had committed themselves.

After his service in the police in Peking, Kawashima started a school to train Chinese police on Japanese lines. Such was his skill as a shrewd manipulator that when Peking once again came under complete Chinese control, he somehow managed to infiltrate his own agents into key positions both in the police and elsewhere. Later his influence was felt to be dangerous, not so much by the Chinese as by American and British officials in Peking where he had made a number of enemies. They felt Kawashima was usurping some of their own authority, and he, suddenly constricted in his movements by these intrigues, moved his school to Japan.

It was during this period that Kawashima had begun to set up what he called Manchukuo cells with the aim of having the nucleus of a pro-Japanese organisation in Manchuria when the time was ripe. Soon he came to be better informed on events in China and Manchuria than any other Japanese. He used his school as a recruiting ground for his agents and, even from Japan, managed to get them cunningly placed in posts all over

China. While in Peking, he had made friends with Prince Su Chin Wang, a Manchu supporter who had been appointed head of the Chinese Police Bureau in the Chinese capital. Though Prince Su eventually lost favour in the eyes of the Imperial Court, he was a figure of some importance and in 1901 had been sent as a special envoy to the coronation of King Edward VII. Such was Kawashima's power of persuasion that Prince Su was slowly won over to the former's own views of Sino-Japanese collaboration and the project for a Manchuria under Japanese control but with a nominal Manchu ruler.

Early in 1911 Kawashima's chance came. He had advance information about the plan for the Chinese revolution of that year and he was not only one of the first to advise Tokyo about this, but urged a policy of giving aid to the rebels in Southern China, while backing the Manchus in the north. Devious and contradictory as this policy might seem, it made sense in the light of Kawashima's long-term plans. He expounded his ideas to Hikokichi Ijuin, the Japanese representative in Peking, and there perhaps he made his first mistake. Ijuin listened carefully and appeared to agree with Kawashima. But whether he had a sudden change of mind, or was merely trying to keep all options open, Ijuin later switched his support to the very man who had been called in to suppress the rebellion—Yuan Shih-k'ai.

This new strong man of Chinese politics had already attracted the attention of the Black Dragon Society. As well as having agents inside the ranks of Sun Yat-sen's supporters, the society had also made allies of agents of Yuan Shih-k'ai. Yuan was well aware that Sun had joined forces with some of the Japanese radicals, so he sought to undermine this pact by doing a deal with the Japanese Government. So it was that Japan acquired not only the railway rights in Manchuria, but a promise that the Hanyehping Iron and Steel Works should be made a Sino-Japanese combine. Secret clauses were included in the deal the Japanese made with Yuan Shih-k'ai and these included an agreement that the police departments of China should be jointly administered by Chinese and Japanese officials.

This was, of course, an attempt to obtain intelligence by having joint control of the police. The details of the secret clauses were leaked to Sun Yat-sen by his own agents inside Yuan's ranks and, by exposing this plan, Sun was able to swing opinion against Yuan. Meanwhile Kawashima and Ijuin were playing a cat-and-mouse game with each other, the former collecting evidence of Ijuin's intrigues and the latter having Kawashima's movements watched.

Being a determined and energetic character, Kawashima decided to go ahead and formulate his own policy. It was at this time that he instituted the ritual of the firefly nursery song as the recognition signal for members of his Manchukuo guerrillas. This was sung, or recited quietly, on any occasion when recognition and identification of one member was required by another. As a member of the Black Dragon Society, Kawashima had considerable backing as well as the advantage of being on excellent terms with some of the Chinese warlords, who were never averse to collaboration with the Japanese if it suited their own provincial policies. One of these was General Wu Lu-chen, who had lived in Japan for some few years. Kawashima plotted with Wu to stop Yuan Shih-k'ai from returning to Peking. But in some way this plot was discovered and Yuan had Wu killed before he could put his plans into action.

Later Kawashima was the instigator of a plot to plant a bomb in the train which was to bring Yuan to Peking. Almost certainly this was a Black Dragon operation as, apart from Kawashima himself, two Army officers involved as his agents, Colonel Takayama and Major Taga, were members of that society. But once again the plot was thwarted, possibly by Ijuin himself, as he seems to have kept a constant watch on Kawashima and to have pursued a vendetta against him. There was one last plot to plant a bomb in Yuan's residence, but this failed when he suddenly changed his headquarters without any warning.

Meanwhile Prince Su had stayed in Dairen (now Luta) on the Kwantung Peninsula, faithfully fulfilling his promise to Kawashima to hold himself in readiness to cooperate with him when the opportunity arose. From this time onwards Kawashima concentrated on his Manchurian project and the setting up of Prince Su as a puppet ruler. He created entirely on his own, though with the full approval of Mitsuru Toyama, another secret society known as *Kanzan So* (the Mountain of Sweat Society). No doubt he saw his task as a herculean one, calling for a great deal of sweat and uncomfortable missions in bleak parts of the world, in Mongolia as well as Manchuria. For the aim of the society was to plan secretly for establishing a Manchurian-Mongolian nation which would come under Japanese jurisdiction with Su as the titular head of state. Briefly Prince Su came back to Peking for secret talks, but the Chinese revolutionaries got to hear of this and set out to find and kill him. Su was smuggled out of Peking with the aid of three Black Dragon members.

The prince showed his gratitude for this rescue from summary execution by helping to raise funds for the Manchukuo guerrillas and the Mountain of Sweat Society, even selling some of his family's works of art and jewellery. Kawashima's project seemed about to prosper, as the Okura Trading Company, which had often helped out with funds for secret manoeuvres overseas, contributed some two million yen to the organisation. But the chief impediment to the implementation of the Manchurian plan at this time was a considerable change of mind both in the Japanese Foreign Office and the War Office. The Foreign Office did not matter so much, but it was essential that Kawashima should have full backing from the Army. Many Army officers both in the field and in the War Office were on his side, but important senior officers were highly critical of allowing the secret societies such a free hand. They did much to delay decisions and to take a pessimistic view of *Kanzan So*'s chances.

Kawashima's plans involved not only Prince Su, but two Mongolian "princes" with rather less pretension to royal titles than the prospective Manchu ruler for the new Manchukuo. They were known as K'e-la and Pa-lin who each enjoyed a certain amount of autonomy inside Mongolia. Despite the War Office's lukewarm attitude towards Kawashima's plans, permission was obtained from the headquarters of the Army in Tokyo to allow several officers to assist in this project. An agreement was signed between Kawashima and the Mongolian princes which guaranteed Japanese aid in arms, advisers and agricultural specialists and some supplies and funds, while Japan obtained controlling rights in administration of the country.

This agreement also gave the Japanese special trading facilities and in effect barred Mongolia from making any separate deal with Russia. Nominally, Mongolia belonged to the Chinese empire, while Russia had long considered it one of her own spheres of influence. Bounded by Siberia in the north and by China in the south, while having an eastern boundary with Manchuria, Mongolia was wide open to exploitation. Kawashima played very cleverly with his firefly song in seducing Mongolians to his cause. There were very few rivers in Mongolia, except to the north from which area they flow into and across Siberia ("Yonder the water is bitter"), and on the northeast extremity where some of the headwaters of the Amur

("Here the water is sweet") emanate. There was a close cultural
and religious link with the Japanese in that nearly all Mongolians were Buddhists. At that time almost a third of the
population were Buddhist priests to whom the firefly song was
a particularly attractive theme. For it was almost entirely in
the folk song that what passed for Mongolian literature existed.

The young Emperor of China had abdicated prior to the
coming to power of Yuan Shih-k'ai, but Kawashima visualised
that it might be expedient to keep in touch with the twelve-
year-old ex-monarch. At that time there seemed to be more
promise of Japan establishing herself in East Asia through collaboration with the Manchus than with the revolutionaries. If
Kawashima had been backed more strongly by the Foreign
Office and the Army, probably his aim would have been fully
realised. A major problem, however, was safeguarding the
dispatch of arms into Mongolia and Manchuria. Often this was
undertaken through Korea, but even the Japanese officials encountered en route were not always helpful in letting supplies
through unchallenged. It could be said that officially Japan was
bending over backwards to be as correct as possible in its
actions in China so as not to offend her wartime Allies. The
other hazard which the arms smugglers ran was the risk of
being attacked by bandits. Altogether some fifty or more Japanese agents lost their lives in this dangerous traffic.

Nevertheless some considerable progress was made in this
attempt to take over a country stealthily and simply with the
aid of secret agents. Had it succeeded, while it would have
made very little difference to the outcome of World War I, it
would undoubtedly have curbed Soviet expansionism after that
war and in many other respects changed history. What Kawashima planned and put into operation in this second decade
of the twentieth century was very similar to the tactics adopted
by Hideyoshi hundreds of years earlier. No other nation in
modern times has managed to win some ten thousand square
miles of territory without a war and simply by moving agents
silently into key postions and, what is more, achieving this
without the outside world being aware of what was happening.
True, this represented only a small portion of Manchuria's
363,000 square miles of territory, but it was a formidable
achievement by any standards. Altogether this incursion into
key positions in Manchuria was conducted by some 3,000 agents,
mainly Japanese and always led by Army officers secretly loaned
for the purpose. The intelligence and liaison work was con-

ducted by the Mongolian and Manchurian members of the Manchukuo guerrillas.[2]

Kawashima, believing that his plans were within sight of
being fulfilled, went to Tokyo, confidently expecting to be
congratulated and given full backing. It came as a terrible blow
when he was informed that the Japanese Cabinet had been told
of his plan and did not wish to see it proceed any further. The
truth was that Cabinet, Foreign Office, War Office and even
the Navy were hopelessly divided on this issue. It was not so
much that they were at odds with one another on questions of
policy and principles, but on the methods and expediency of
carrying their policies through.

Kawashima suddenly had a message from the office of the
Army Chief of Staff asking him to go to Tokyo. This he did
with alacrity, fully believing that he would be given details of
military aid. But he was sadly disappointed. It was made clear
to him that in the opinion of the Army hierarchy he had ex-
ceeded his authority in his guerrilla campaign and that he must
bide his time. From the long-term Japanese viewpoint this was
probably an error of judgement, for if a satisfactory Manchurian
settlement could have been made before World War I ended
many of the troubles of the thirties culminating in the inept
intervention of the League of Nations might have been avoided.

But if this first attempt to stage the setting up of a puppet
state in Manchuria failed, Kawashima refused to give up his
aims. He was highly critical of the Japanese Government's
failure to give him full backing, but he never embarrassed that
government by making his strictures public at that time. Strong
though his feelings were, he remained the disciplined and loyal
secret agent. But Japan was now beginning to pay heavily both
for its trust and backing of Sun Yat-sen and its belated flirtation
with Yuan Shih-k'ai. By the mid-summer of 1915 it was apparent that, in dealing with Yuan, Japan had been given little
more than dubious "rights" on paper and that China was as
divided as ever. The only apparent bonus was that the pro-
Japanese faction among the Chinese in Anwei province dominated the Peking Government headed by Tuan Chih-jui.

There is abundant evidence that the Japanese Government
tried scrupulously to keep to agreements made with their allies
in the West and not to do anything to upset these relationships.
When Chochi Kayano approached Shigenobu Okuma, the Prime
Minister, with a request for the release of captured German
arms in Tsingtao for use by pro-Japanese Chinese revolution-

aries, he was given a firm refusal on the grounds that "if we helped the revolutionaries, England, America and France would object".[3]

Secretly and unofficially both Kayano and Kawashima managed to obtain some arms from time to time, but never enough to do all they wished. Kawashima concentrated on developing the small but influential royalist party in Dairen with Prince Su, while the Japanese Foreign Office analysed reports from their own secret agents in various parts of China and produced maps and charts indicating the headquarters, numerical strength and activities of each group of Chinese revolutionaries and attitudes towards the Japanese. But by late in 1916 the Japanese Army began steadily to withdraw even covert support for the Manchurian adventure. There was an attempt by Kawashima's agents to restore Manchu government in Manchuria in 1917, but once again the plot was foiled and the Japanese Government formally absolved themselves of any involvement in it. Black Dragon members were angered at what they regarded as pusillanimous as well as clumsy diplomacy by their own government, and some of them openly condemned the government. From then on the more extreme forces among the Japanese nationalists increased their strength both in membership and influence, and the upholders of liberalism were pushed on to the defensive.

But the Bolshevik revolution in 1917 altered the situation in both China and Japan. Sun Yat-sen had become increasingly hostile to the Western powers and especially to Britain, so he tended to look to the Russian revolutionaries for support. In Chinese eyes Japan became the other "villain", partly because she was allied to Britain: "your country is acting like a marionette on the British string" was how Sun Yat-sen put it. And he added that "it is not to the advantage of Asia, especially of China and Japan, that this war in Europe should end in the crushing defeat of Germany."[4]

Meanwhile America was increasingly tending to favour China rather than Japan not only in public utterances by leading politicians, but in the ranks of government. The U.S. Navy intensified its intelligence interest in Japan, despite the fact that the two countries were allies. The *Nichi Nichi Shimbun* of 12 December, 1918, carried an editorial against the unconditional return of Tsingtao to China, and the United States was not only worried about this, but at Japanese demands that no troops should be withdrawn from Russia until order was restored. The

Japanese Government was firmly on the side of the counter-revolutionaries and the forces of Admiral Koltchak. A letter from the Office of Naval Intelligence in Washington to the State Department in 1919 reported on Japanese plans to gain free port privileges in Vladivostock, the opening of the Sungari and Amur Rivers to traffic and the Japanese purchase of North Saghalien.[5]

There can be no disputing that Japan genuinely attempted to fight communism in Eastern Russia and to see the restoration of a democratic government in that country. Self-interest may have played a great part in this, but Japan was a far more determined supporter of the White Russians from 1918–22 than any of the European Allies. Some historians have suggested that during this period Japan was motivated by anti-semitic prejudices of a virulent kind, a smear which was again made against Japan during World War II and afterwards. This is a total distortion of the facts. Some anti-semitism exists in all countries, but it has always been far less in Japan than in many other countries, not least some Western powers. There was hardly any anti-semitism in Japan prior to World War II partly because there were very few Jews in the country and the Japanese people as a whole neither understood anti-semitism, nor could they identify it.

Indeed, the truth is that in discerning circles in Japan, both among some nationalists of the right and liberals on the left, there was over a very long period a desire to cooperate with the Jews and a desire to understand the nature of Zionism. This dated back to the Russo-Japanese War when Baron Koreikiyo Takahashi of the Bank of Japan was having great difficulties in raising a loan to pay for the heavy cost of the fighting. He found a sympathetic hearing with Jacob Schiff, the Russian Jew who had then become an American citizen. Schiff let him have a loan of £5 millions and explained that he did this because he blamed the Czar for the pogroms against the Jews in Russia. The two men became the closest of associates and when the White Russians launched their vicious propaganda against the Jews in the shape of the forged documents of the Protocols of the Elders of Zion in 1919,[6] the Japanese Secret Service was well aware of the falsity of this material which had been directed towards Nippon troops fighting in Siberia.

Two Japanese officers attached to the staff of the White Russian General Semenov, Norihiro Yasue and Koreshige Inuzuka, studied the Protocols in great detail and when they returned to Tokyo were asked to make lengthy reports for Army and Navy Intelligence and a special Intelligence Section was set up to study the Jewish question. Out of this there grew not an anti-semitic movement, but the nucleus of a plan to make allies of the Jews. But this plan will be examined at a later stage in this book. It belongs to the 1930s rather than the 1920s.

11

A Plan to Rescue the Czar

> "Arrangement completed with Japanese
> special force for removal from House to
> place of full safety"
>
> Coded message from the U.S.
> representative in Ekaterinburg to
> Secretary of State, 15 July, 1918

WHEN WORLD WAR I ended Japan had some cause for feeling
that she had not gained much advantage from it. Indeed, in
some respects, she was at a distinct disadvantage as, even with
fighting on the Western Front over, her troops were extensively
engaged in fighting the Bolsheviks in Siberia. There was an
uneasy presentiment in Tokyo that the other Allies were at best
lukewarm towards the anti-communist cause in Russia and at
worst even hostile to intervening on the side of the counter-
revolutionaries.

Thus a Russian problem had arisen again, but in a new if
not altogether unexpected form. Japan had hoped to finish the
war not only as an equal among allies, but with an established
and acknowledged presence in East Asia as well as being accepted as a powerful naval force in the Pacific. Yet long before
the Peace Conference these hopes seemed liable to be dashed.
Pressure by the Western powers was firmly obstructing any
further moves by Japan to establish her authority on the Asian
mainland. Each European power was interested in maintaining
its own position in China and clinging on to whatever rights it
had in this part of the world. But it became increasingly clear,
much to the dismay of the more liberal of Japanese statesmen,
that there was a distinct and growing hostility by the United

States towards Japan. The U.S. Government, strongly backed
by the U.S. Navy, sought to demand limitations on the growth
of the Japanese Navy.

In 1891 the twenty-three-year-old Czarevitch (later Emperor
Nicholas III of Russia) visited Japan and, while riding in a
rickshaw through Ossu, near Kyoto, was nearly murdered when
attacked by a policeman wielding a sword. An inquiry revealed
that the policeman was a religious fanatic who became enraged
because of some imagined breach of etiquette by the royal
visitor. Curiously, yet not untypically, despite the Russo-Japanese War and the knowledge that Czar Nicholas helped to
perpetrate this catastrophe, the Japanese developed a sense of
guilt about this affair. When in World War I the two countries
became allies, this guilt complex was accentuated. It was almost as though the Japanese felt they owed the Romanovs a
debt of honour. The Japanese Emperor Mutsuhito regarded the
incident as something which required to be propitiated by some
appropriate gesture when the opportunity presented itself. Some
believed that this opportunity occurred when the Russian royal
family were taken prisoner by the revolutionaries and that, if
properly interpreted, it would work in Japan's favour.

The Japanese had maintained an effective, if low-key intelligence organisation inside Russia throughout World War I.
Very little was known about this organisation by any other
powers at the time and not much has been gleaned since. One
thing is certain: the Japanese acquired as much if not more
intelligence on the true position of the captured Romanovs than
any other secret service in 1918. A number of Japanese officers
actually worked in Eastern Russia as barbers, cooks and ordinary domestic servants in order to collect information in this
period. Japan, unlike some of her allies, was in no doubt which
side deserved her support in the civil war between revolutionary
and counter-revolutionary forces. By the terms of her treaty
with Russia she supported the Czarist and loyalist forces who
were still carrying on the war against Germany in 1917–18.
Such support was extended after the armistice of 1918 to the
same forces often in striking contrast to the half-hearted and
always equivocal backing given by the European allies to the
White Russian cause.

It might seem surprising that this was the case. Twenty years
before, Japanese secret agents had been establishing links with
some Russian revolutionaries not only as a means of gaining
intelligence, but in the hope that it would weaken the militarist

forces around the Czar. But this attitude changed markedly after 1906. In any event there was the psychological factor that Japan, like Russia, was a royalist state and royalists tended to form a kind of international trade union of their own. Half way through World War I there was even a secret move, enthusiastically backed by Naniwa Kawashima, to make a secret deal with certain senior Czarist officers to underwrite the Manchurian project. There is a hint of such dealings in a report which William Somerset Maugham, then a British Secret Serviceman in Petrograd, made in September, 1917: "Professor Masaryk insisted on the need for a definite *quid pro quo* for all the money advanced . . . If it were possible to send a Japanese army of at least 300,000 men, these would serve to restore the morale of the Russian troops. Professor Masaryk suggests that Japanese intervention might be paid for, if money would not be accepted, by the cession of a part of Manchuria, which in fact is already under Japanese influence."[1]

It was in this kind of heady atmosphere that some Secret Service executives, members of the Black Dragon Society, the Manchukuo guerrillas and certain senior Army officers visualised a highly favourable outcome to the Siberian campaign. At last, they thought, Japan might be able to win a fairly easy victory. To support, and then perhaps actually rescue, the Russian Imperial Family would clinch their claims for land in North-East Asia. Yet this expedition was never really popular back in Japan and some political leaders doubted its success from the beginning. In this they proved to be correct.

By the middle of 1917 Japan had established a profitable trade through Russia's eastern ports. An increasing number of Japanese firms had opened branch offices in the chief towns of Eastern Siberia and Manchuria, with the result that many Japanese had become semi-permanent residents there.

Altogether the Japanese had two divisions of troops in Siberia as well as a substantial military headquarters staff. By agreement each Allied nation was to send to Vladivostock 7,000 men as a single unit to make up the Siberian expedition and to accomplish the task of ending the war and supporting the loyalist forces. But by November, 1918, Japan had already sent in 73,000 men, and Japanese commanders were even then interpreting their mission as not so much to defeat the Germans (who were not fighting in that area, of course) but to aiding the Czarist forces against the "Reds". Later there were occasions when the Bolshevik forces outnumbered the Japanese in some places by as much as twelve to one.

What worried the Japanese were indications that, as the civil war continued, both the United States and Britain would gradually lose interest in it and, worse, that despite promises to the contrary, Britain would drop its alliance with Japan at the behest of the Americans. Japanese Intelligence was convinced that is what would happen long before it did. They also suspected that there was a Bolshevik plot to discredit Japan and make mischief with her allies. In each instance their fears were justified. For in April, 1919, the *Peking & Tientsin Times* published a story of an alleged secret treaty signed between Germany and Japan back in October, 1918. It was said that the discovery of this treaty was made by a U.S. Army officer, attached to the Siberian Army, who had found the actual document in the Bolshevik archives at Perm after its capture by the White Russian forces.

Almost certainly this story was a piece of Soviet disinformation, cunningly planted on the American officer, as a similar story had been published inside Bolshevik-occupied Russia.[2] The details of this bogus treaty were significant: Japan and Germany were to help the White Russians to defeat the Bolshevik forces; Japan was to support Germany having a free hand in Persia and the Middle East and a privileged position in South China and both countries would not allow further concessions in China to the U.S.A. and Britain. There were implications that Japan would, with German agreement, gain concessions in Manchuria, Northern China, Korea and parts of Siberia. Though there was not an iota of truth in all this, a certain amount of damage was done to Japan, especially when some of the European press copied the story from the Peking newspaper.

This propaganda war, so mysteriously waged that not even today is it easy to arrive at the exact origins of the plot, had been stirring in the chancelleries of the world since the middle of 1918. On the strength of some of these reports Major-General Masatake Nakajima, the Intelligence Chief of the Japanese General Staff and a Russian specialist, was ordered to visit the Far Eastern front. Soon afterwards there was a regular procession of intelligence officers from Tokyo going to Russia, North China, Mongolia and Manchuria and returning with reports. Records of the Japanese War Office in this period "show disbursements being made from secret funds for intelligence purposes for work in the Far East".[3]

Japan's Secret Service at this time (as distinct from the

unofficial branches of intelligence run by the secret societies) came under the advisory and vetting bodies of the *Gensuifu* and *Gunji Sangiin*, comprised of senior Army and Navy officers. They controlled the operations of the Secret Service inside Siberia where there was close contact between the Japanese military headquarters and agents in the field. Some of the latter had established listening posts inside Eastern Russia, including the area around Ekaterinburg (now Sverdlovsk) where the royal family were eventually moved to captivity. Occasionally agents were hidden in "safe" houses in the villages, such as Koptyaka and Bizim-Baievsk, but more often they operated from within Japanese trading posts.

There is an interesting item in the Japanese *Who Was Who* which lists Kenkichi Inoue as follows: "1882–1952. Spy. Born in Nagasaki Prefecture. Saw action in the Russo-Japanese War and then, together with his brother, engaged in espionage in Chula, Siberia, as hotel-keepers (1919–20) and supported General Semenov." This is not an untypical picture of a Japanese spy in Siberia in this period and of the kind of cover he adopted.

In the military agreement between the Japanese and Chinese signed on 16 May, 1918, relating to the fighting in this whole North-East territory, there was this clause: ". . . in the areas in which military operations are taking place, intelligence agencies may be established and the two countries shall exchange intelligence information." This supposedly amicable arrangement did not last long. Within a few years relations with the Chinese had suffered another set-back. In 1924 Kenkichi Inoue, with another agent, Wanisaburo Deguchi, were arrested by the Chinese on unspecified charges. Inoue was, however, released through the intervention of the Japanese Embassy. Afterwards he stayed in Peking, for the purpose, according to Japanese accounts, of "spying on the activities of Ko-manji-kyo, a religious sect in Manchuria".[4]

It is impossible to ascertain who originally put forward the idea of launching a massive rescue plan for the Russian royal family. The United States, Britain, France and Japan were all to some extent involved at various stages, but records of what actually transpired are either incomplete, missing, deliberately held back or even faked. The real problem in ascertaining what happened is to separate fact from fiction, genuine records from bogus documents, as somewhere along the line of communications there have been various attempts to scatter faked and misleading papers all over the place.

Two points need to be made. First, it is now indisputable
that whatever was the exact fate of the Czar and his family at
Ekaterinburg, the version of what happened there as given in
the official inquiry report by Judge Sokolov is inaccurate and
sometimes falsified. There is no adequate proof of the executions having taken place as described in that report. The
second point is that reports circulating on various occasions in
the past fifty years that the royal family were all rescued by
some top-secret Anglo-American-Japanese mission and smuggled to safety and a life of total anonymity are totally without
foundation.

A British Secret Service agent named Robert Wilton retained
the original dossier on which the Sokolov report was based.
The most sensational part of this historic dossier is the evidence
which for some reason Sokolov saw fit to suppress—testimony
that female members of the Imperial royal family were seen
alive at a date later than the alleged executions of all of them.[5]

But what is not to be doubted for a moment is that there
were plans to rescue them—not just one, but at least three or
four—and that the Japanese were concerned in at least one of
these projects, if not more. Of all the countries involved Japan
had most cause to see this plan prosper, if only because the
realisation of the Manchurian, Mongolian and Siberian dreams
would have been likelier if the Romanovs were kept alive and
the Czar restored to power. This at any rate was the fantasy
nourished by the extremer nationalists. It might have worked
for a time, if the Czar had been restored, but Russian military
history suggests that in the long-term Czarists expansionist
policies would have been just as uncompromising as Soviet
imperialism today and equally hostile to Japan.

Nevertheless, the fantasy had some substance. Japan was
in many respects in a better position to bring off a rescue coup
and to make her own terms with the White Russians than any
of her Allies. The Bolsheviks had made fools of many of the
American diplomats and Secret Service agents in Russia: they
had found that the latter were highly susceptible to forged
papers and hoaxes. The British had brilliant agents inside Russia,
but were badly served by a vacillating government under Lloyd
George. The French were well informed, but too realistic to
be drawn into madcap projects. But the Japanese had the forces,
the resident agents in the area and, far more important, through
their ability to penetrate Soviet Intelligence had even obtained

copies of the Bolsheviks' wireless codes. Therefore they knew far more of what was going on than most of their Allies. It was the Japanese military attaché in Warsaw who passed to the Poles the Soviet code in use in Siberia, an action which was invaluable for Poland and enabled them to withstand a Bolshevik attack at a later stage.

It is interesting to note that one of the first rumours of the Romanovs escaping from their prison camp came from Tokyo. The London *Times* of 17 February, 1919, reported from its own correspondent in the Japanese capital: "I learn on trustworthy authority that the Czar is alive and a prisoner in the Kremlin, whither he was conveyed in the guise of a merchant, while his family (including the Czarina) are interned in the monastery of Troitsko-Sergievsky.... The 'death at Ekaterinburg' was elaborately staged."

This news item appeared seven months after the alleged murdering of the Romanovs on 16–17 July, 1918. There was no indication of the source of this information either then or subsequently. But reports were repeatedly circulating in Tokyo in the summer of 1918 that the Japanese were trying to arrange, either by diplomacy or clandestine action, for the release of the Czar and his family. One of the intermediaries was Dmitri Abrikosov, a close friend of the Grand Duke Michael and Czarist *chargé d'affaires* in Tokyo until Japan's eventual recognition of the Soviet regime in 1925. Even then Abrikossov stayed on in Japan as a private individual for another twenty years.

Some fifteen miles outside Ekaterinburg, where the royal family were held, was a walled compound which was supposed to house a Japanese trading mission. It was protected by a small detachment of infantry and, according to contemporary reports, was guarded with exceptional zeal. No Russians, even those of loyalist persuasion, were permitted into the building. A key figure who made frequent visits to this trading station was a mysterious intelligence officer known as Major Chikayochi Kuroki, a nephew of General Tamemoto Kuroki, who served with such distinction in the Russo-Japanese War of 1904–5. Major Kuroki, who was born in 1883, was a military adviser in the Imperial Army, a title which was often used for intelligence officers. He was operating in Siberia as early as the beginning of 1917, acting as a go-between for Japanese Military Intelligence and the White Russians. Later he left the service on account of the Japanese Government's refusal to follow his advice on "an Eastern policy".[6]

It is from this time onwards that his career begins to be wrapped in mystery. He stayed on in Siberia and became an adviser to General Grigori Semenov, a Cossack in the service of the White Russians. A Captain Shinkei Kuroki was also assigned to liaison work with Semenov at this time, but whether he was a relation of Major Kuroki is not absolutely clear. Some sources assert they were father and son. Captain Kuroki made strenuous proposals for Japan to undertake the repairing and operation of the Trans-Baikal Railway, which had been destroyed at several points by Soviet troops.

It was Major Kuroki who was the intelligence officer given the task of planning the rescue of the Czar and his family. To this extent, while leaving the Army, he seems to have continued to work as an intelligence co-ordinator. Talks had continued for several months as to how best to plan the rescue coup, but finally it seems to have been decided to make the effort early in July, 1918. The family were to be taken by truck to the Japanese trade mission and kept there until a joint White Russian-Japanese guard could escort them on to Kungar. At one time there was a suggestion that they could be smuggled out of the country and taken to Japan.

Dmitri Abrikossov gave only one ambiguous hint of the rescue plan in a dispatch to General Semenov, sent via a special courier: "Do your utmost to keep the Colonel [sic] Kuroki informed about all matters touching on routes in and out of Siberia, most especially on the irritating manner in which territories in some areas appear to be held one week by the enemy and another by ourselves. This makes it very confusing to those in Tokyo who are hoping to arrange for the safe transfer of our illustrious Guests-to-be."[7]

This at least seems to be a positive reference to the fact that Abrikossov expected to offer sanctuary to the Czar and his family in the Russian Embassy (Czarist) in Tokyo. But that is about the only factual evidence. I have myself been shown photocopies of documents, some in plain language and others in cipher, purporting to pass between the United States Representative in Ekaterinburg and the Secretary of State in Washington. Repeated inquiries in Washington both at the White House and the State Department have drawn denials that any such documents are in their possession. The Japanese Foreign Office have been equally puzzled by the revelations of what are supposed to be the "Chivers Papers". My own view is that a few of the documents are partially authentic—those referring to a rescue operation—but that faked material has been cleverly introduced, though by whom and for what reason is unclear.

I propose only to quote those items which seem authentic and which refer specifically to Japanese links. One message, dated 10 July, 1918, states: "The plan is now in readiness. Today I visited the chief of staff whose excellent English made my understanding of him simple. He is the equal of a Colonel in the Imperial Army, his name being Kiyaki [sic]."

This clearly looks like a reference to Kuroki, though the sender has got the spelling wrong. The fact that he is referred to as the "equal of a Colonel" makes sense in the light of Kuroki having left the Japanese Army. Another message, dated 15 July, 1918, allegedly from the U.S. Representative in Ekaterinburg to the Secretary of State indicates that "arrangements completed with Japanese special force for removal from House [Ipatiev?] to place of full safety". Yet another message mentioned that money for the escape project had come from "His Imperial Majesty of Japan, about the equal of 75,000 dollars, but this is short and no less than 200,000 dollars will be enough".[8]

Probably the full truth of any attempts to rescue the Czar will never be told. That the Japanese played a part in such a rescue project is not to be doubted and, if it had been brought off, it would have been the Secret Service coup of the century. But the project seems to have been kept so highly secret that it is possible that it was undertaken quite independently of government or army. There is that tantalising reference in the Japanese *Who Was Who* to Major Kuroki—that he left the Army because the government declined to take his advice. Was that advice connected with a plan to rescue the Romanovs? A former Japanese diplomat and historian, Toshikazu Kase, has stated that a certain Vassily Yakovlev "had the special intention of taking the Imperial family further east from Omsk, making contact with the White Army and sending them to Japan".[9]

From this statement there emerges a shadowy picture of links between Major Kuroki and Vassily Yakovlev, but just as the rescue story seems to acquire more substance, another mystery appears to cloud an author's vision. For who was Vassily Yakovlev? There is ample evidence that a Vassily Yakovlev arrived at Tobolsk, some 200 miles from Ekaterinburg in April, 1918, and reported to the local Commissar. But this Yakovlev introduced himself as a Special Commissar sent to Tobolsk on

a very secret mission by Sverdlov, the chairman of the Soviet
Central Executive Committee. It emerged that this "secret mission, was to remove the Romanovs from Tobolsk". Yakovlev
actually succeeded in getting the Romanovs aboard a train
which, he declared, was to go to Moscow, but his plan was
"to reverse back through Tyumen again, with all lights extin-
guished, on the way to Omsk."[10]

But suspicions were aroused and Yakovlev was ordered to
bring the royal family back to Ekaterinburg where he was
accused of treachery and had some difficulty in talking himself
out of trouble. The Soviet version of this extraordinary story
is that Yakovlev was sent as envoy of the Central Committee,
but that he turned traitor. Yet another version is that he was a
German agent according to Sokolov, but there is no evidence
for this. He was also said to be the son of a Lithuanian engineer
called Zarrin, who adopted the name Yakovlev in 1905 when
he deserted from the Russian Navy. There is a hint that he was
sent back to Russia as a British secret agent in 1917. But
perhaps more intriguing is the story that in Canada he was
befriended by some Japanese immigrants on the west coast and
that through their influence he became an agent for Japan in
Manchuria.

Yakovlev, the one man who could clear up some of these
questions, disappeared completely. Nobody knows what happened to him. Curiously, his is one name which does not appear
in any of the copies of the so-called Chivers Papers that I have
seen. As to the faked documents which make such extravagant
claims that the Romanovs were brought safely out of Russia,
there is some indication that the earliest of these forged papers
were planted by Soviet sources as long ago as the early twenties.
By this time the Soviets had established themselves as being
extremely adept in the technique of disinformation. It may well
be that the presence of so many Japanese troops in Eastern
Russia seemed to pose a greater threat to the survival of the
Soviet regime than Britain, France or the U.S.A. Therefore
the propaganda war was directed more against Japan than any
other nation. At the very same time the Russian communists
were seeking to stir up trouble inside Japan. It is possible,
though no one else seems to have realised it, that the disinformation on the rescue of the Romanovs and that on the
German-Japanese secret treaty were both examples of Soviet
deception. In the first place they were ploys against Japan, but
their resurrection in recent times suggests they have been in-

tended to confuse historians and to hope some gullible people would accept that some of the Romanovs were still alive and might even be serving the Soviet cause.

The failure to succeed in their multifarious Russian plans was merely one of a number of blows which the Japanese suffered at this time. They had considerable casualties in Siberia which created an unfavourable impression back in Japan. At the Peace Conference at Versailles both President Woodrow Wilson and Lord Cecil (for Britain) opposed Count Makino's "racial equality" clause which the Japanese wished to have inserted in any final peace settlement. All that Japan got out of this conference was the German mandated islands in the Pacific where eventually they were able to set up air and naval bases. Japanese troops withdrew from Siberia in 1922, two years after the evacuation of American, British and French forces. The final Japanese withdrawal from Vladivostock was not completed until October, 1922. At the same time various independent detachments returned to Japan from Shantung, Hankow, Saghalien and Manchuria.

12

The Cryptographical War

"We had turned a proved friend . . . into a
potential and powerful foe"
                    Admiral of the Fleet
                    Lord Chatfield

AFTER THE PEACE CONFERENCE relations between America and
Japan grew steadily worse and the Anglo-Japanese Alliance
showed all the signs of strain. Kunishige Tanaka (later General
Tanaka and a head of military intelligence), who had been
military attaché in London during the latter part of World War
I, returned to Tokyo and told F. S. G. Piggott (later Major-
General Piggott), the British military attaché, that "in future it
may even be that we shall no longer welcome the mutual exchange of language officers for attachment to units".[1]

Piggott was the Japanese expert in the British military
delegation at the Four-Power Treaty talks when the Anglo-
Japanese Alliance was ended in 1921. It was a tragic business
which in the long run had just as serious repercussions for the
Americans as the British. Yet it was American pressure which
largely contributed to the break-up of the alliance. There was
one lone American voice raised against the U. S. Navy and
the State Department on this disastrous policy of creating a rift
between the two allies. Frederick Moore, who had been Counsellor to the Japanese Government for fourteen years, stated:
"I felt strongly that it was a mistake in foreign policy for the
United States to press the British for a termination of their
alliance with Japan. The alliance could not menace the United

States. The charge that it could was false . . . The Japanese were shocked by its termination . . . This was the beginning of the nation's turn towards independent action . . . It opened the way psychologically for cooperation with Germany . . . Had the alliance been permitted to continue there would have been enough restraint kept upon the [Japanese] Army by civilian and naval influence in Japan to prevent its going to China."[2]

Two former British military attachés in Japan have described reactions to the break-up of the Anglo-Japanese Alliance. Piggott gave a vivid picture of the smiles on American faces, "the British looking glum and the Japanese taut and grim". Captain Malcolm Kennedy recalled how uncomfortable he felt when General Itami, the Japanese military attaché in London, looked in to see him at the War Office a few hours after the Euro-Power Treaty had been announced. "I sought to say how sorry I was that our alliance was to end, but that I was sure our two countries would remain as friendly as ever. Noticing my embarrassment, he checked me. 'I understand your feelings and appreciate them,' he said, patting me on the shoulder in a fatherly manner. Then he added, 'But you British will find how mistaken you have been. You think that the Americans will be so pleased that they will cancel your war debts, but they won't. I am sure they won't, and you will lose far more than you gain by giving up one friend to win the favour of another.'"[3]

General Itami's words proved prophetic. Soon afterwards the British Prime Minister, Lloyd George, tried to persuade the United States to write off the Allies' war debts. He had a sharp rebuff and only succeeded in alienating American opinion. Japan also noted the ridiculously harsh economic terms inflicted on Germany by the victorious Allies, demands for reparations that could not possibly be met. Not unnaturally, Japanese resentment at Anglo-American treatment caused that proud nation to turn once again to Germany, which had done so much to help build up the Japanese Army in the 'seventies and 'eighties of the nineteenth century. How rightly did Admiral of the Fleet Lord Chatfield declare later that the British had turned "a proved friend . . . into a potential and powerful enemy."[4] Even Sir Winston Churchill, writing after the Second World War, stressed that in the first war Japan had always "punctiliously conformed" to the Anglo-Japanese Alliance and that its annulment had caused "a profound impression in Japan and was viewed as the spurning of an Asiatic power by the

Western world. Many links were sundered which might afterwards have proved of decisive value to peace."[5]

The cancellation of the Alliance with Britain certainly caused both General Tanaka and Major-General Matsuo Itami to lose their pro-British leanings and to be swept up into the ranks of the ultra-nationalists. Tanaka was succeeded as Director of Military Intelligence by Itami who left his post as military attaché in London to take up office in 1922. But indisputably the one single incident which did more than anything else to ruin American-Japanese relations irretrievably was the revelation that, during the Washington Naval Conference of 1922 and for some months before this, the Americans had deciphered confidential messages emanating from Tokyo. It was as a result of the information obtained by this action that the Americans were able to gain such favourable terms in this conference.

This secret was tactlessly and crudely revealed when the United States master-mind in the field of cryptography, Herbert O. Yardley, told the whole story in his book, *The American Black Chamber*, published in 1931. Yardley, who had been in charge of the "Black Chamber" (Section 8 of U.S. Military Intelligence) had spent so much time in trying to solve Japanese ciphers that he had set up a special sub-section to cope with this problem alone. His first break-through came during the summer of 1921 when he intercepted a message from the Japanese Ambassador in London to Tokyo. This contained the first hint of a forthcoming conference for naval disarmament. Thus alerted, arrangements were made that during this conference Section 8 would set up a daily courier service to the State Department. The most vital information acquired was a Japanese Foreign Office cipher message to their Ambassador in Washington, stating "It is necessary to avoid any clash with Great Britain and America. You will to the utmost maintain a middle attitude and redouble your efforts to carry out our policy. In case of inevitable necessity you will work to establish your second proposal of 10 to 6.5"[6]

The result of Yardley's probings was that he was able to advise the Americans that, if pressed, the Japanese would yield. The result was that the Japanese, in an attempt to be reasonable, capitulated and accepted the naval tonnage ratio proposed by the U.S.A. which was that of 10–10–6–3.3–3.3 respectively for the U.S.A., Britain, Japan, France and Italy.

It was a short-lived triumph and it certainly contributed towards Japan ultimately denouncing the naval treaties. Yardley, as much as any man, helped to precipitate World War II. The Tokyo newspaper, *Nichi Nichi*, published a long article on his book, stating that "the disclosures of this breach of faith committed by the United States Government will doubtless serve as a valuable lesson for the future of Japan in participating in international conferences." That lesson was certainly learned, for more than 40,000 copies of the Japanese edition were sold.[7]

During this period the U.S. Navy sent Lieutenant-Commander E. M. Zacharias, later one of their ablest intelligence officers, to Japan. Having spent three years in Tokyo, he returned to the O.N.I. Code and Signal Section. U.S. Naval Intelligence records show that he collected considerable information while in Japan. On the other hand during the Great Depression of the late twenties the O.N.I. was reduced to a force of eighteen officers and there appears to have been no system of agents inside Japan.

Japanese Naval Intelligence was not lagging behind in the cryptological war at this time. As a result of important contacts made during the Siberian campaign and in reciprocity for Japanese help in passing Soviet codes to the Poles, a Polish cryptographer, Captain Kowalefsky, revised all their cipher systems as early as 1919. It was an invaluable *quid pro quo* and it was to repay the Japanese even more handsomely later on when Kowalefsky was military attaché in Moscow from 1919–33. Between 1919 and 1925 the Japanese had used eleven different codes and at the end of this period the Imperial Navy had begun its own cipher analysis work. This was undertaken by a very hush-hush *Tokumu Han* (Special Section) in the Fourth or Communications Department of the Naval General Staff. This section had a staff of six and operated in the Navy Ministry building in Tokyo.

Naturally, there were enormous language difficulties encountered in developing Japanese cryptography, apart from the fact that some of the Western powers were far ahead of Japan in this particular field. For example, the Japanese cipher which Yardley solved in 1921 was based on a relatively well-known bigram substitution similar to that composed by Rossignol for Louis XIV. But Captain Kowalefsky was a highly efficient and much appreciated mentor who became the "headmaster" of the section. Soon he found an exceptionally apt pupil who was able to carry on his good work. This was a young naval officer, Hideya Morikawa, a nephew of the Naval Chief of Staff, Admiral Kanji Kato. From the beginning the Japanese concentrated on breaking American diplomatic codes. In this instance the Navy cooperated with the Foreign Ministry's decipherers. The latter had their own small cryptographical analytic section, the *Anpo Kenkyu*, or Code Research Section.

Top priority was given to solving American and British codes. There were some successes and probably an equal number of failures. The American diplomatic codes were fairly speedily broken and this certainly provided evidence for the ultra-nationalists to inveigh against American imperialism. Perhaps it would be more correct to say that it caused the Japanese Foreign Ministry to urge the Americans to be more cautious in their communications. Joseph C. Grew, the U.S. Ambassador to Japan, told how "one of the high officials of the Japanese Government wanted to send a secret message to our government which they did not want the Japanese military [navy?] to see, and in passing this message on they asked me to please put it in our most secret code. I said, of course I would do so."[8]

There is no reason to doubt the sincerity of this appeal by the Japanese Foreign Ministry. It shows that in this instance spying on the other side's communications had led to a rational understanding of problems. The tragedy was that there was not more reciprocity on the American side. On the British side Admiralty records of the period suggest that the Naval Intelligence Division had little comprehension of the extent of Japanese espionage in the years between the wars, or how far Japanese naval intelligence had been developed. In every British colony in the Far East there was a resident director of Japanese naval intelligence of high rank who was able to pin-point weaknesses, thoroughly assess the whole strategic position and at the same time ensure that there was a permanent team of agents to keep such information up to date.

In the late 1920s the Americans, Dutch, Germans and Swedes all produced cipher machines, incorporating cipher wheels, which could be operated by typewriter keyboards. The Japanese bought these machines, adapted and improved upon them, introducing what came to be known as the "Purple Machine". This was swiftly adopted both for Japanese Naval Intelligence and the Foreign Office, but its use was confined to some thirteen embassies overseas. For some years it defied American attempts to crack it and, in the end, the task of solving this enigma was assigned to one William Friedman, son of a Moldavian Jewish family, who had emigrated to the U.S.A.

in the 1890s to escape the pogroms. This was long after Yardley's Black Chamber was decommissioned in 1925 when U.S. Secretary of State, Henry Stimson, ruled that Yardley's tactics were "indefensible".

The Purple Machine consisted of what resembled two electric typewriters, separated by cipher wheels and a plug board, the plain text being typed out on one typewriter and the cipher text automatically reproduced on the other. It had the great advantage of speeding up communications while keeping them in cipher. The secret of the Purple Machine was only broken by the Americans when one of their naval spies smuggled a miniature camera into one of the relatively few Japanese embassies which possessed such cipher apparatus. This operation was then repeated in two other embassies until Naval Intelligence had three different photographs to work on. These photographs were then "blown up" to a scale ten times higher than the actual size of the machine. It was from these photographs that the final deductions were made. The task of breaking the Japanese cipher system was then relatively easy because of the simple fact that, as the Japanese alphabet consists of more than 50 letters and 2,000 hieroglyphics, the Japanese sent their codes in Roman letters.

This break-through by the Americans resulted in a reversion to the Yardley system of making a point of reading all other nations' confidential cables as far as was possible. But some of the claims made by the Americans in their alleged cryptographical victories are not altogether upheld by evidence. Certainly by the end of the 1930s they were reading at least some of the Japanese messages. But to read such ciphers is one thing, to understand what they mean is altogether a different matter. Where the Americans failed abysmally was in their inept and inaccurate interpretation and analysis of such messages. But it is almost certain that the Japanese were aware of this and that on the occasion of really top secret messages they maintained radio silence and employed other methods. Prior to World War II and in the early part of it the Japanese were reading American ciphers rather more effectively than the United States were reading theirs. It is probable that, through their German contacts, they were also reading the ciphers of some other nations.

Occasionally the Japanese would seek to score a point by actually letting the Americans know that they were being kept under observation. Winfried Ludecke told how in the late 1920s an American cruiser and some Japanese battleships happened to be visiting a Chinese harbour at the same time. Officers of the two navies exchanged visits. "One of the Japanese caused the American commander no little amazement by telling him matters which the American had believed only known to a few in his circle. The Japanese picked up a table napkin, threw it over his arm like a waiter to remind the American that he had been in the service of the Americans as an officer's steward when the former was in charge of another ship."[9]

The Eberstadt Report on national security in 1945 gave the United States very low marks for both army and naval intelligence prior to World War II. "Available finds were grossly inadequate and there was considerable duplication of effort... Few Intelligence agents were employed and some of them were of mediocre ability. Evaluation was largely in the hands of officers untrained in Intelligence techniques."[10]

The *Tokumu Han* department of Japanese Naval Intelligence concentrated on finding a way of deciphering Chinese cryptograms in the late 1920s. This they achieved when they discovered that Chinese ciphers were based on a simple commercial codebook which changed the Chinese ideographs to four-digit numbers for telegraphic communication. Hideya Morikawa was dispatched to Shanghai after the Japanese capture of this city and port in 1932. There he was given the task of forming a special deciphering unit attached to the Third Fleet. In this capacity he scored a great success in decoding a Chinese message which indicated that the Chinese Air Force planned to bomb and machine-gun Japanese troops. As a result of quick action following this piece of deciphering the Japanese were able to attack the Chinese Air Force first, destroying most of Chiang Kai-shek's planes on the ground at Hanchow.

China had become the prime target for Japanese espionage in the 1920s, not solely because of the still divided Chinese nation, but the machinations of the great powers in China. Each of these powers continued to grab all they could in China and strengthen their influence in that country, while each had a different reason for intervening in Chinese affairs. The U.S.A. did so for commercial purposes and to use China as a bargaining counter against the growth of Japanese influence. Britain and France saw China as a possible base for operations against Soviet Russia, while other nations simply demanded concessional advantages of a commercial nature. Captain Malcolm Kennedy cites a R.A.F. wing commander in Peking in the inter-war years saying: "We vilify the Japanese for supplying armaments to the two opposing forces, yet we do it ourselves, only that we are such hypocrites that we pretend we don't . . . The more one hears the more convinced one is that half the anti-Japanese propaganda in these parts is simply due to the fact that we and other countries are jealous of Japan's position out here, and if we were in her place, we should do the same."[11]

In the banking world it was the Americans and not the British who now dominated China, but in arms sales there was intensive competition between the U.S.A., Britain and Japan, with France intervening to a lesser extent. Shortly before Sun Yat-sen died he was still beset with the problem of finding out which Western power was selling arms to which warlord. Japan backed Chang Tso-lin, a military dictator of the Fengtien organisation, while the British supported Wu Pei-fu of the Chihli faction. There were, of course, real reasons for some alarm in Western Europe that China was about to be communised, partly because of the anarchical state of the country and the knowledge that Soviet Russia was intervening in Chinese affairs.

Japan had even more reason to be perturbed at the threat of communism in China, particularly as it was Russian-inspired. Vasili Blyukher, who had led the Red armies to victory in the Urals and Siberia, had been appointed chief of the Soviet Military Mission to China in 1924, curiously operating there under the pseudonym of "General Galin". He had certainly achieved a great deal at the Whampoa Military Academy, creating the finest troops in Southern China and developing among them an espionage system designed to weed out malcontents and all those "politically undesirable".

A Sino-Soviet alliance would have posed enormous problems to Japan and in March, 1925, shortly before he died, Sun Yat-sen sent this letter to the Central Executive Committee of the Soviet Union. He wrote that Russia was "a union of free republics" and that he hoped "the day will come when the U.S.S.R. will welcome a friend and ally in a mighty, free China, and that in the great struggle for the liberation of the oppressed peoples of the world, both these allies will go forward to victory hand in hand."[12]

Sun's successor, Chiang Kai-shek, did not have the same starry-eyed view of Soviet Russia. He had discovered from his own private secret service that Borodin, the Soviet adviser to China, had tried to push Sun Yat-sen into a war with northern China in the hope of its failure and the resultant elimination of Sun. So Chiang promptly got rid of Borodin.

In retrospect Japan might have achieved much more by coming to a working arrangement with Chiang Kai-shek after Sun's death than in pursuing an increasingly hostile policy towards China. But the Japanese had perhaps neglected to keep their lines open to Chiang, preferring to maintain links with one or more of the Chinese warlords. Soon, but without much success until the mid-thirties, they were trying to break the Chinese communications ciphers adopted by Chiang.

Eventually the *Tokumu Han* possessed ten staff cryptanalysts and another ten or twelve part-time assistants. Despite this, they failed to break such two-part codes as those used by the American State Department and the U.S. Navy, though later they were able to read the communications of the U.S. naval attaché until America changed its system. Becoming impatient with the slow progress being made, Hideya Morikawa determined to launch a bold initiative of his own. Sometime during 1937 he made arrangements to break into the American Consulate at Kobe in the middle of the night. He had decided this was not only a consulate where he would get results, but that it was also the easiest to tackle without much fear of detection. In many respects this was an operation similar to that undertaken by "Cynthia" for the British Secret Service when she captured the Vichy French ciphers in World War II. Morikawa had obtained a detailed picture of all movements during the night hours at the Consulate and the lay-out of the offices. Entry was made by Morikawa himself together with a locksmith, a photographer and some trained agents who were used to keep watch during the search for the ciphers. As a result Morikawa obtained photographs of the U.S. "Brown" code and the M-138 cipher device which the Japanese had never seen before. Within a remarkably short time the Japanese Navy were able to erect their first major interception station at Owada, a village some fifteen miles from Tokyo. Consequently the Japanese were able to learn much more about American sea traffic and tactics employed during U.S. fleet manoeuvres.

13

The China Wave Men

> "The Wave Men were Super-Patriots and
> China was their hunting ground"
>   Taid O'Conroy

PROFESSOR TAID O'CONROY taught for a while at Keio University in Tokyo and married into an aristocratic Japanese family. He had a genuine affection for the country, but developed a paranoic hatred of Japanese nationalism in all its forms and many Japanese institutions. In his book, *The Menace of Japan*, published in 1933, he gave vent to his dislikes and forgot most of the good things. Thus he is not a reliable witness to all that happened in the interwar years. Nevertheless his description of the "Wave Men" as super-patriots is an apt one, and China was certainly their hunting ground.

"The Wave Men were a feudal relic who became wanderers like waves... they are used as spies," he wrote.[1] The phrase "Wave Men" covered both ultra-nationalist politicians and their agents and members of the growing number of secret societies in Japan, ranging from the Black Dragon and the League of Blood (*Ketsumeidan*) to the Patriotic Government League (*Aikoku Seiji Domei*) and the Society of the Cherry (*Sakurakai*). It was often rather difficult to tell just who were and who were not Wave Men. Ever since the Russo-Japanese War they had been used as spies in China and Manchuria and sometimes Mongolia as well. In this capacity they used a variety of covers, taking jobs as clerks, farmers and even priests and occasionally posing as pilgrims or beggars. They were undoubtedly subsidised from the funds of one or other of the Intelligence Services, but O'Conroy's suggestion that they supplemented their income by trafficking in females and supplying brothels is somewhat far-fetched.

The Black Dragon Society increased numerically, in all-round strength, and in political influence in the 1920s and 1930s. Dominated by Ryohei Uchida, the society laid down its policy as follows: "We shall renovate the present system, foster a foreign policy aiming at expansion overseas, revolutionise domestic politics to increase the happiness of the people and establish a social policy that will settle problems between labour and capital."[2]

Not the language of extremism: the truth is that the ultra-nationalists were extremely clever in propagating their policies and making them sound almost liberal. Where they went seriously wrong was in the dangerous game of mixing espionage and politics overseas. This more than anything else led to mis-understandings, misconceived plots often undertaken without due reference back to the authorities in Tokyo and the acqui-sition of the type of power which inevitably corrupts. There is no adequate parallel in the Western world for this kind of secret society activity in modern times. It was essentially a Japanese conception of how the secret society could devote itself to patriotic causes and the expansion of the national interest in Asia. But it would be inaccurate to equate any of these move-ments of Wave Men or others with either fascism, nazism or the mafiosa.

It is true that there was a tenuous link between the Black Dragon Society and the Nazis through Don Gato, a Nazi press correspondent in Tokyo. He was for some time a close associate of Ryohei Uchida. But there was no common policy between the *Kokuryukai* and the Nazi Party. The Black Dragon Society was in many respects empirical in outlook as well as chauvin-istic. It was just as interested in left-wing revolutionaries as in right-wing reactionaries or muddle-headed liberals, if any of these could be exploited to aid the cause of Japanese expansion. An Indian terrorist who had long campaigned against the British, Rash Behari Bose, fled to Japan in 1915 and was befriended by Mitsuri Toyama. The latter not only helped Bose to become a Japanese citizen, but adopted him into his family when Bose married one of Toyama's followers.

The ex-Indian terrorist became an agent for the Japanese and helped to found the Pan-Asiatic League. This movement was closely linked with the Black Dragon and the Great East Asian Co-Prosperity project. In all these Bose played a considerable role. However, Bose was obviously too old for all the work involved in these organisations and though he worked for the Japanese from Bangkok during World War II, he was eventually succeeded by his namesake, Subhas Chandra Bose, another anti-British Indian the Japanese lured away from Berlin. A similar anti-colonial, pro-Japanese body created by Japanese was the Aryan Army, headed by Raja Mahendra Pratap. This was ultimately taken over by the Indian Independence League of East Asia, which was another of Rash Behari Bose's brainchildren. The latter died early in 1945.

Anti-British feeling became marked in the nationalists' ranks after the break-up of the Anglo-Japanese Alliance. From then on the Black Dragon Society regarded an enemy of Britain as a potential friend of Japan. By skilful manoeuvring they managed to turn a number of such people into active co-conspirators. One such was the quixotic and ambivalent Ignatius Timothy Trebitsch Lincoln, a man of Hungarian-Jewish origin who changed his religion as often as the country he served. He had been born a practising Jew, switched to a nonconformist creed as a youth, joined the Church of England in Canada, became a curate in Appledore in Kent, and later joined up with the Quakers before ultimately taking the saffron-coloured robes of a Buddhist monk. In between these activities he had become a naturalised British subject and elected as Liberal member of Parliament for Darlington.

His political career was cut short when he lost large sums of money (all borrowed from friends) in speculation in the oil fields of Galicia and Rumania. Then at the outbreak of World War I he had volunteered to work for British Naval Intelligence while at the same time he was spying for Germany. Lincoln fled to the U.S.A. to escape arrest in Britain, but was eventually extradited to his adopted country where, surprisingly, he was charged not with espionage, but with forging cheques. After serving a three-year sentence he was deported to his native Hungary. There he found the Bela Kun communist regime irksome and he promptly moved to Germany where he offered his services to a group of right-wingers who were planning a *putsch*. When the putsch failed in 1921, Trebitsch Lincoln established links with the Chinese Government. It was about this time that he became a Buddhist. He joined the staff of the warlord Wu Pei-fu, who was at this very time being covertly supported by the British. This was a very confused situation. According to one version, Lincoln was employed by the Chinese Secret Service to infiltrate the camp of Wu Pei-fu. His biographers, however, suggest that he was actually spying for the Germans in China and that at the same time he offered his services to the British again. It is worth noting that later the Japanese made overtures to Wu Pei-fu to serve as leader of a new political regime in Japanese-occupied China. Lincoln could have had a hand in this, but what is undeniable is that all the time he was double-crossing his various masters.

The Japanese shared the doubts of other nations about Lincoln's real intentions—whether he was anti-British, pro-German, pro-Bolshevik, pro-Japanese, pro-Chinese, or just anti-Westerner. By 1926 he had adopted the name and title of Abbot Chao Kung. During this year his eldest son, a member of the Royal Artillery in Britain, had been sentenced to death for murder. Lincoln immediately tried to re-enter England under his newly adopted name and title. But he was refused permission. The following year Lincoln, admitting his former identity, turned up in Europe again where he was reported to be negotiating a four-million-pound loan for the Chinese Government. By this time there were rumours that Lincoln was hedging his bets between a Bolshevik-Chinese alliance and a German-Japanese pact.

Lincoln had long been watched and even courted by some Japanese secret agents. They were well aware that he was a devious character, but felt he could be exploited in their own cause. Superficially, there was nothing to incriminate Lincoln as far as the Japanese were concerned, but to a close observer there were distinct signs that he was playing a double game. He had recently been in Amsterdam and was known to have close contacts with the Dutch Embassy in Peking. And it was at that embassy that the ex-Chinese Emperor Pu Yi sought shelter before moving to the Japanese concession in Tientsin. Chinese suspicions that Lincoln was moving over to the Japanese side were confirmed in 1927 when he was sent to Europe to pay the first instalment of an arms deal for the Chinese and he kept the money for his own use.

A former member of Chiang Kai-shek's Secret Service told me: "Lincoln was always a modest asset to us even in his old age and when we knew he was backing the Japanese. He had a complicated mind, but we probably understood it better than you Westerners. . . . No doubt you British would have locked him up. But lock up Lincoln and you would learn nothing, let Lincoln free and you might learn a lot.... As far as his links with the Japanese were concerned, we needed to have some kind of hold on someone who was in the Japanese camp, not that Lincoln could provide much worthwhile intelligence on Japan at that period of his life.... We had been fighting the Japanese for years and we realised that a situation might arise when we should need to make a separate peace with Japan and here Lincoln could have been a useful intermediary."

The last reports to be heard of Lincoln were that he was broadcasting Axis propaganda from Tibet in the early years of World War II. In 1943 a Japanese news agency reported that he had died in Shanghai in October of that year. But the "Lincoln Legend" did not die easily. On 5 May, 1947, Reuter News Agency and the *Times of Ceylon* stated that he was still alive, adding that a local journalist in Ceylon had received a letter from him, bearing a Darjeeling-Bengal postmark!

Secret societies actively engaged in intelligence-gathering for their country proliferated throughout the twenties and thirties and made an invaluable contribution to Japan's need for a world-wide network. As these societies took varying forms, it was easy for one or other of them to search out such likely recruits as Trebitsch Lincoln, the two Boses and other malcontents who could be won over to a cleverly painted portrait of a prosperous Asia under Japanese protection and guidance. It has now been seen how thirty years earlier Colonel Akashi had established links with Moslem communities and elsewhere in Asia. A year after his death China Wave men took this a step further by founding the Society of the White Wolf (*Hakurokai*), which had many army officers as members. But what started out as a propaganda body ended up as a terrorist organisation. Later the Turan Society was also founded. Both societies had the aim of keeping in touch with Muslims both in Russia and as far afield as Turkey.

Another, quite independent, Turan Society had been formed several years previously in Budapest when Moslem refugees from Turkestan began to arrive in Hungary. It was known as the Pan-Turan Society. Then in 1920 a leading member of this society went to Japan and made contact with members of the former Black Ocean and the Black Dragon Societies. Out of their talks the White Wolf was formed, taking this name from a superstition among Turkish and Mongolian Muslims that they had descended from the white wolf. Some years later the Turan

Society was founded in Tokyo when some Moslem refugees from Russia arrived in Japan. The two Japanese-controlled societies were linked with the Pan-Turan Society of Budapest and the Grey Wolf Society of Turkey, all of them having close racial and religious ties.

Thus the Japanese were able to exploit both their Muslim-linked societies to obtain intelligence cells in both Turkey and Hungary. Their aims were three-fold: first of all to secure Asian and Middle East Muslim allies against Russia, to ensure a flow of intelligence from Budapest, Istanbul, Ankara and to some extent places inside Moslem Russia and Mongolia, and, finally, to encourage Japanese-Muslim friendship.

The Black Dragon continued not only to spy on, but also to infiltrate secret societies in China. In the inter-war years it went further than this and managed to obtain control of some of these societies. One such society was the Way of Fundamental Unity (*Yi-kuan' tao*), which had originally been formed in Shantung at the end of the previous century. It was a religious organisation with strong Buddhist links, but later gathered strength in North China and in cities such as Tientsin and Nanking. Suddenly this society proclaimed itself openly in support of the Japanese.

Wang Ching-wei, formerly one of Sun Yat-sen's "bright young radicals", having failed to obtain the trust of either Chiang Kai-shek or Mao Tse-tung, had gone over to the Japanese. Becoming head of the puppet government of South China, he relied on various pro-Japanese secret societies operating in his territory. Chief among these was the Hung Society of the Five Continents (*Wu-chow-Hung-men*), which adopted the name of the Hung Triad which had many members among the Chinese immigrants in Japan. This enabled the Japanese to create a fifth column in the British colony of Hong Kong years before World War II. This particular Triad had been all-powerful in Hong Kong for many years, so that when the colony was eventually occupied by the Japanese these Triad leaders emerged as Japanese agents to give full intelligence and cooperation to the invaders.[3]

The word Triad, like the Japanese "Wave", covers a wide range of secret societies. During the inter-war years and throughout the period of World War II, the Triad was divided into three distinct movements. One was linked totally to the Kuomintang and the forces of Chiang Kai-shek, another kept aloof from positive political alignments, but indulged in double-dealing, while the third was a hundred per cent pro-Japanese and in effect a branch of Tokyo's Secret Service.

The Chinese Communists have always been traditionally hostile to the Triads, but even they depended occasionally on secret societies, taking the view that if one could not beat them, one must join them. In the early twenties the Communists relied considerably on the Red Spears for their villages' defence groups, while in July, 1936, Mao Tse-tung issued an appeal to the *Ko Lao Hui*, or Association of Elder Brothers, to help the Chinese Communists to "go and fight together against our common enemies—the Japanese Imperialists and the traitors who are selling out our country."[4]

The dominant figures in the "Waves" in the 1930s were Mitsuru Toyama, Ryohei Uchida, Umpei Ogawa, Yasuguro Sasaki (sometimes known by the nickname of "King of Mongolia") and the fanatical Nissho Inoue. Their chief link in government circles was, of course, Koti Hirota, a Black Dragon member who nevertheless always preserved a tactful diplomatic face to the outside world. It was Hirota who went personally to the British Embassy in Tokyo to express his regret after the shelling of the British Navy ship *Ladybird* in the Yangtse River in 1936.

Nissho Inoue was leader of a society known as the League of Blood, so named because its initiation ceremony was marked by the new member cutting his finger and mixing his blood with that of a fellow member. Born in 1886, Inoue's real name was Akira. He left college without graduating and went to China in 1909 and "became one of the *Shina Ronin*—Japanese experts in China engaged in unofficial activities to bring China under Japanese control."[5] He was said to have adopted the name of Nissho ("Sun-called") when he became a priest of the Nichiren sect of Buddhism, noted for its adherence to the causes of the ultra-nationalists. Inoue had a lengthy history of espionage activities in China and Manchuria, but one of his main self-imposed tasks other than the founding of the League of Blood was the establishment of the Gokokudo School to train right-wing fanatics. His own pupils, under his mentorship, undertook the projected assassination of some twenty leading Japanese politicians in 1932. This plot had nothing whatsoever to do with Japanese Intelligence: it was simply another manifestation of the fanatical lengths to which these ultra-nationalists were prepared to go—a kind of manic patriotism. Included in the list of names were Prince Saionji, Count Makino, Prince Tokugawa, Junnosuke Inoue and Takuma Dan, all men of high repute and devotion to their country. Fortunately, only two out of the twenty were actually murdered, Junnosuke Inoue and Dan. Nissho Inoue with one of his accomplices sought protection in the home of Mitsuru Toyama after the killing, but this did not save them from arrest. Not even the influence of Toyama could impede their prosecution. Inoue was sentenced to life imprisonment, but released by a special amnesty granted to such prisoners in 1940. He survived the war and lived in comparative obscurity until 1954 when he was reported to have organised a nationalist group called the Association for Defence of the Country.

Ryohei Uchida himself was more than once under surveillance by the police for suspected attempts at assassination. Indeed in the early 1930s political murders sponsored by some of the secret societies in league with certain Army officers became a major threat in what was basically a law-abiding society. By this time the fanatical old men of the secret societies were becoming obsessed by their overwhelming desires to liquidate all their opponents. Cliques began to manifest themselves in the Army ranks and these were exploited by some secret society leaders. The culmination of a great deal of ill feeling came in August, 1935, when Lieutenant-Colonel Saburo Aizawa walked into the office of Major-General Nagata, chief of the Military Affairs Bureau, and killed him with his sword.

With the secret societies currently occupied with political assassination as a weapon, and one directed against their own countrymen, not even any potential enemies, intelligence must have suffered in this period. In his last few years Uchida, then an ailing man, founded the *Dai Nippon Seisanto* (Japan Production Party), with Mitsuru Toyama as adviser. This society, like its subsidiary, the *Nippon Seisanto Shokugyo Kumiai Rengakai* (Japan Production Party Amalgamation of Trade Unions), was supposed to be used as a branch of industrial intelligence, but there is little evidence that it acquired much.

Uchida himself died in 1937 and he was succeeded as president of the Black Dragon by Yoshihisa Kuzuo, who was also a member of the Japan Production Party. Kuzuo was also director of the Imperial Rule Assistance Association. Meanwhile the Black Dragon Society maintained its role as a training ground for spies and had two schools in Tokyo alone which held courses in the techniques of the intelligence game, the Nationalists' Training College and the Tokyo & Osaka Foreign Language School.

Koki Hirota was perhaps one of the few Black Dragon members who managed to maintain a mask of tolerance and moderation throughout these years of frenzied nationalism. As an adviser on intelligence matters to the society he was of supreme importance and much more useful than such ageing fanatics as Uchida and Toyama. He had, of course, been ambassador in Moscow for a period and, eighteen months after that term of office ended, he became Foreign Minister. In the latter post he was extremely popular with most of the Western nation ambassadors, some of whom paid high tribute to him. Indeed, possibly Hirota was the one Black Dragon member both Britain and America might have courted more assiduously. He was certainly far more balanced and intelligent than either Toyama, Uchida or Kuzuo. He was an implacable foe of the Soviet Union and this cost him his life. It was the relentless pressure of the Soviet Union that prevented him from having the death penalty waived when he was sentenced as a war criminal in 1947.

14

General Doihara and Yoshiko Kawashima

"His task was to create trouble and then
smooth it over to the advantage of the Japanese . . . His technique was to go into a
disordered area where the political situation was fluid, meet people and get their
confidence"

John Gunther

MAJOR-GENERAL KENJI DOIHARA was one of the most brilliant
of all Japan's spymasters in the years between the two world
wars. The international press corps actually dubbed him the
"Lawrence of Manchuria". That was probably not fair to either
man. Doihara was a far more ruthless character than the in-
trospective Colonel T. E. Lawrence of the campaigns in the
Arabian Desert. But while the legend of Lawrence as a brilliant
secret service operator has been discarded by recent revelations
and he has been shown up as a somewhat pathetic and compulsive liar, Doihara remains as pre-eminently the ablest intelligence officer Japan ever had in Manchuria.

He was, however, very much more than this. As John Gunther
has suggested, Doihara was that rarity among soldiers, an officer with the talents of a diplomat and the flair of a politician.
At the same time he was a highly competent organiser and
administrator and made the fullest practical use of the information which flooded into his headquarters.

Born into a relatively poor family in Okayama in 1883, as
has so often been the case with Japan's leading soldiers, he
found his humble background no deterrent to his military prog-

ress. He showed outstanding ability in all his subjects at military academy and came first in his class. A special talent in languages, particularly in Chinese, which eventually he spoke to perfection, made him a natural candidate for a military intelligence career.

For many years his progress was steady but unspectacular. He was always very much the man behind the scenes, determined to become not merely a Chinese specialist, but thoroughly versed in Manchurian affairs. Manchuria, it could almost be said, was what drove him forward relentlessly. His dearest wish as a very young man was to see this territory part of a great Japanese empire on the Asiatic mainland. He spent many years in China, not only perfecting his Chinese, but learning many of the dialects. Thick-set, stockily built, with a clipped military moustache, he was a jolly, extrovert man who made friends very easily. It was this talent for mixing with all classes and peoples which was so very deceptive.

It was during the Siberian campaign after World War I that Doihara first learned something of the problems confronting an intelligence officer who gets mixed up in politics. It was in this period that he came into close contact with yet another officer-intriguer, Seishiro Itagaki, later promoted to lieutenant-general and eventually Minister for War. A key figure in this political cauldron of the Siberian-Manchurian area, even after the Japanese withdrew from Siberia in 1922, was the Chinese warlord Marshal Chang Tso-lin. He had helped the Japanese against the Russians many years before and it was always the view, at least of the Japanese moderates, that Chang Tso-lin's cooperation was vital to their own interests in Manchuria.

Sir Robert Craigie, one-time British Ambassador in Tokyo, had this to say about Doihara: "What history will clearly establish is that it was the settled policy of the Japanese Army to provoke incidents [in China] and to exploit provocations . . . In all these intrigues, blandishments and threats, one little figure was ceaselessly active on the Japanese side—that of Colonel Doihara . . . His diminutive, though wordy and well-advertised presence in any locality was invariably the precursor of trouble . . . Certainly his methods were skilful and he was usually successful in creating dissension in the Chinese ranks and so smoothing the path of the aggressor."[1]

These comments are, however, not altogether fair. The intrigues and even the provocations were going on all the time in China and Manchuria. The Chinese warlords were constantly plotting against one another, creating instability and uncertainty with their intrigues, now seeking to woo the Japanese, then the Russians. All Doihara did was to exploit such intrigues to the advantage of Japan. If he could have made a deal without involving the nation in war, he would have done so. True, he entered troubled areas, but his aim was constantly to win friends and make a peaceful settlement. There was one occasion when he almost succeeded in detaching the five Northern provinces of China without a single shot being fired, and simply by undercover negotiation. At that time Chiang Kai-shek was too busily engaged in fighting the communists to take any other action.

Kenji Doihara tried hard to coordinate the various Japanese schemes for gaining prestige and extending his country's influence in Manchuria. But his task was not made easier by the fact that many of his countrymen had their own ideas as to how Japanese influence was to be extended and quite often some of them played a lone and dangerous game. Such schemes ranged from plots of assassination and liquidation through black market dealings and bribery of Chinese politicians to winning the support of bandits and even some surprisingly noble projects. There were such China Wave men as Tokuzo Komai, a close associate of Ryohei Uchida, who was sent out to Manchuria as chief of the General Affairs Bureau, a nominee of the Imperial General Staff and whose task was to watch the movements and note the activities of the chiefs of administration on the civil side. Another problem was posed by the formation of a terrorist group known by the somewhat curious title of the Society of the Cry of the Crane (*Kakumeiso*). In fact it was one of those titles of Japanese secret societies which owe their origin to a private and secret joke. In this case the title *Kakumeiso* was used as a pun on the word *kakumei*, meaning revolution. The society was strongly anti-Russian and had an influential branch in Mukden. Its head was a young man of violence named Hajime Suridate and under his direction there was all manner of pressure put on the Chinese, including blackmail and kidnapping. Doihara was strongly opposed to the society as were many Japanese Army officers.

An astonishing plan about which the Western world seemed to know nothing at all was that for settling refugee Jews in Manchuria under Japanese sponsorship. When, during the Siberian campaign, the Japanese realised how virulent was the anti-semitic propaganda launched by their allies, the White

Russians, it was decided to set up a small team to study the whole problem. This was not such an irrelevant departmental exercise as at first sight it might appear. The White Russians were allies of the Japanese, yet some of them had gone to extreme lengths to blacken the Jewish people with the most nauseating propaganda. On the other hand there was the undeniable fact that many of their enemies among the "Red" Russians were Jews. Now, the Japanese had relatively little knowledge of the Jews or their culture, not least because there were very few Jews living in their country. But they had long ago been struck by the fact that the Jews were highly intelligent, and outstanding in the world of art and science, in politics and business. Somehow they felt this was bound up with the Manchurian problem.

A young Army captain, Norihiro Yasue, who had been attached to the Russian General Semenov's staff as a language expert, studied the anti-semitic propaganda together with a Navy officer, Koreshige Inuzuke. But before making their lengthy report on the whole subject they studied intelligence memoranda dating back to the Russo-Japanese War and noted that these contained references to the power of the Jewish socialist organisations to undermine the Czarist war machine in the event of war. The two Japanese officers made a lengthy report on the whole subject, deciding that such publications as the *Protocols of the Elders of Zion* were forgeries. This report was studied both by Army and Navy Intelligence Services and in 1924 it was decided to make a further examination of the records and histories of the Jewish people. The aim was to have a number of Japanese intelligence officers who could be called upon as specialists on all questions concerning the Jews. Yasue was ordered to go to the Middle East to observe them in their Palestinian habitat. He was one of the first to be convinced that the propaganda about an international Jewish conspiracy to dominate the world was nonsense. He had talks with David Ben Gurion and Chaim Weizmann.

A special Jewish Office was set up to coordinate intelligence reports on Jewish activities as gleaned from the various Japanese embassies round the globe. It was noted how very well Chiang Kai-shek had been served by his own Jewish intelligence officer, the London-born Morris Cohen. Out of all this pondering on the Jewish problem there developed another idea which would help Jewish refugees and, concurrently, so it was argued, advance Japan's cause in Manchuria. In brief, the plan was to bring Jewish refugees and capital into Manchuria for Japanese and Jews jointly to develop that country.

This grand design was referred to the highest circles in the Japanese Government which decided it must be kept secret while soundings were taken of American Jewry. There were already some Jews in Manchuria and Captain Yasue thought that they could be won over as allies, if 50,000 of their co-religionists could be brought to the territory to settle. To maintain secrecy this project was called the *"Fugu* Plan", being named after the puffer fish which is edible only after its deadly poison is removed. Captain Inuzuke is said to have devised this ambiguous and somewhat cynically conceived title for the plan on the grounds that if the communists in the Jewish ranks could be weeded out from the prospective immigrants, all danger would be removed and a highly desirable scheme would emerge. It should perhaps be explained that in Japan the *fugu* fish is one highly prized by gourmets, but it must be cooked by licensed chefs who can competently remove the liver and ovaries of the fish because these organs contain a deadly poison, tetrodoxin.[2]

By 1934 the plan was so far advanced that the Japanese Foreign Office actually proposed to bring 50,000 German Jews, refugees from Hitlerism, to Manchukuo, as Manchuria had then been renamed. Yasue, now promoted to the rank of colonel, found negotiations were going slowly. He had persuaded the head of the Jewish community in Manchuria, Abraham Kaufman, to visit Tokyo for talks, and had himself gone to America to discuss settlement sites for Jews, not only in Manchukuo, but in China as well. They were promised total religious freedom and their own educational system, but otherwise they would come under Japanese rule. Yasue appears to have been the most enthusiastic backer of this scheme, even urging that the Jews should have a measure of autonomy, but this the Japanese Army vetoed. It was an imaginative plan and, if it could have been implemented by, say, 1935, probably not just 50,000, but half a million Jews could have been saved from extermination by the Nazis. Certainly the war between Japan and the United States might well have been avoided and Germany and Japan could not have become allies in World War II.

It was shortsightedness on the part of Rabbi Stephen Wise, president of the American Jewish Congress, which destroyed the plan's chances. At the very moment in 1939 when Japan was anxious even to increase the immigrant figure to some hundreds of thousands, he condemned any Jew who supported the Japanese in any way whatsoever. It was a bigoted and stubborn blunder and took no account of the several Jewish leaders who were in favour of the scheme. Wise's opposition was incredibly foolish in that in the summer of 1939 relations between Japan and Germany were strained and this could have been exploited very easily. The Kwantung Japanese Army had been heavily engaged on the borders of Manchuria and Outer Mongolia with Soviet troops five times their number. Yet at that very moment Hitler disregarded the Anti-Comintern Pact which he had concluded with Japan and defiantly made a non-aggression treaty with the Soviet Union, thus violating the Anti-Comintern Pact without warning. Not only could the Jews have taken full advantage of this, but Britain, too, might easily have shown initiative in trying to renew her alliance with Japan when the Hiranuma Cabinet collapsed at the end of August, 1939.

Yasue, a bitterly disappointed man, spent the rest of his career as an adviser to the Government of Manchukuo. He sent his family back to Japan just before the surrender and was himself taken prisoner by the Russians, dying in a labour camp in Siberia in 1950. His intelligence officer friend, Inuzuke, spent the war in Manila, later returning to Japan to form a Japanese-Israeli Friendship League. However, there is some evidence that he was rather less sincere in his support for the Jews than was Yasue. It was discovered that during the war he had actually written some articles attacking the Jews and, though he insisted these were directed against Jewish communists and those who supported the Russians, he was asked to resign from the League. He died in 1965.

Kenji Doihara first made a name for himself when he was assistant military attaché in Peking after World War I. He was in great demand as an expert linguist, as he was reputed to speak nine European languages and four Chinese dialects. Certainly he was fluent in Chinese dialects and this paid off when, in the 1920s, he supported a movement in China called Peace and Joy (*Anfu*). Through this association he was able to persuade members of *Anfu* to sell concessions to the Japanese in Manchuria and elsewhere. There was a public scandal about this and *Anfu* was dissolved. But by this time Doihara had organised a network of renegade Chinese to work for him. Once again the technique of using brothels as listening posts was adopted in Mukden and Harben, linking these with traffic in opium. Doihara organised the development of opium dens as a means of making his Chinese and White Russian informants dependent on the drug. Most of the prostitutes were White Russians: for every six pipes of opium they sold to their clients, they received a free pipe each.

A series of what the Japanese constantly referred to as "grave Manchurian incidents" occurred on June, 1928, and culminated in the Mukden Incident of 18–19 September, 1931. On 3 June, 1928, came the news that Marshal Chang Tso-lin had died after being wounded in a bomb explosion. On the whole this Chinese warlord had been a valuable ally of the Japanese and a stabilising influence in Manchuria. But in some intelligence and Army circles there was also the feeling that he was extending his power, making his own arrangements both with other forces in China and the Russians, and that sometimes these were at the expense of the Japanese. Consequently when somewhat garbled and censored news came through about Chang's death, some suspected that the Kwantung Army had been implicated in a plot to kill him. The view was that with Chang out of the way, there would be ample excuse for further advances in Manchuria.

One of Marshal Chang's secret agents was an Italian named Amleto Vespa, an adventurous mercenary who had seen service in the Mexican Revolutionary Army under General Francisco Madera. Later he had travelled to the Far East and in 1916 became attached to the Allied Intelligence Services following the Japanese Army into Siberia. It was shortly after this that he entered the service of Chang Tso-lin, then governor-general of Manchuria. He changed his citizenship to Chinese after getting into trouble with the Italian authorities. Vespa was convinced that Chang's assassination had been planned by Japanese secret agents: "Explosives had been placed under the steel supports of the bridge and Chinese sentries who had always been on duty at this point had been replaced only a few days before by Japanese soldiers."[3]

In the Tokyo war crimes trials of 1946 evidence confirmed that Chang Tso-lin had been killed by Japanese agents and that the assassination was planned by Colonel Kawamoto, a senior staff officer, without the knowledge of his superior officers.

Chang Tso-lin's son, Chang Hsueh-liang, who succeeded his father, was bitterly opposed to the Japanese and he very soon joined forces with Chiang Kai-shek. From then on tension between the Chinese and Japanese increased. In June, 1931, another "incident" occurred when Captain Nakamura and three of his Japanese companions were shot by Chinese soldiers on the borders of Manchuria and Inner Mongolia. This was promptly followed by more intervention by the Japanese into Manchurian affairs. About this time Doihara had gone to Tokyo to report to the War Office. In September, 1931, he was appointed Mayor of Mukden. During the same month Japanese soldiers received orders to advance on Mukden. On the seventeenth of September there was a bomb explosion on the railway line outside Mukden. A Japanese patrol sent to investigate clashed with a party of Chinese soldiers and there was an exchange of fire. Fighting spread and the next day this new "Manchurian Incident" was seized upon as a pretext for putting Mukden completely under Japanese military government.

When Doihara returned to Manchuria he found it necessary to occupy Harben with Japanese troops. It was in this period that he suddenly became the most powerful and influential man in the whole country. He set up the notorious Special Service Organisation in Mukden (*Tokumu Kikau*), a body which effectively controlled and collated all intelligence operations in the territory. At the age of forty-nine Kenji Doihara was promoted to the rank of general. He threw his whole weight behind the plan for occupying southern Manchuria and in due course creating the puppet state of Manchukuo. It must be admitted that the Japanese undertook the civilian administration of Mukden and Fengtien province with speed and efficiency, largely due to Doihara's excellent intelligence work. He himself headed the Emergency Committee in Mukden as well as taking office as Mayor, making the rounding-up of all Chinese police one of his first tasks.

Commander Charles Drage, a British naval intelligence officer in the Far East at this time, told the author: "The Japanese move into Manchuria was well timed. They knew the ground well and were careful and consistent. Possibly the Japanese chose this time for their move into Manchuria was because of the naval mutiny at Invergordon when the British Home Fleet refused to sail. The Japanese had excellent intelligence on this and they possibly reasoned that the British wouldn't be too keen on sending their main fleet to the Far East just after this episode."[4]

Amleto Vespa, who had been manager of a cinema in Harben at the time of Chang Tso-lin's assassination, has told how on 14 February, 1932, a Japanese lieutenant and sergeant came to his house and said that General Doihara wished to see him. Doihara, who had always shown him a number of courtesies, addressed him in Russian:

"I want you to work for my intelligence agency. I am not inviting you to do so. I am telling you that from now on you are going to work for Japan. This is wartime, Mr. Vespa, and any attempt at flight on your part will be treated as desertion and will be punished with death.

"You speak Russian well, and other languages, too. My aim is to eliminate every organisation or society which is not sincerely friendly to the Japanese."

It soon became clear to Vespa what he was required to do. Doihara knew that Vespa had many acquaintances in the Russian community in Manchukuo. He explained to the Italian with Chinese nationality that, to keep a low profile, the Japanese needed a number of reliable White Russians to act as nominal heads of organisations and departments. "We need Russian names to cover up our activities—men who are not necessarily thinkers . . . It will be part of your job to pick out such individuals from among the Russian refugee organisations . . . When your list is made, bring it to me."[5]

Vespa first had to prepare reports on all the various White Russian organisations in Manchukuo, including such bodies as the Committee of Refugees, the Union of Ex-Servicemen, the Society of Real Estate Owners. A Refugees' Bureau was set up under the control of the Japanese Military Mission, exercising authority not only over all White Russian refugees, but their banks, factories and restaurants as well. The bureau was, of course, a vital instrument of espionage as well and it had branch offices in all the principal towns of Manchukuo. As every White Russian worker who registered with the Bureau had to pay taxes to it, it was indirectly subsidised.

Vespa testified that he was on the whole well treated by the Japanese and one of his closest friends was Colonel Tanaka, chief of Japanese Intelligence in Tientsin. But by 1936 the atmosphere changed and he was warned that his days as a secret service agent were drawing to an end. His family was arrested by the Dairen police and his property in Harben was confiscated. Eventually he got away and published his story in book form. He gave no reason for his dismissal, which makes his narrative somewhat one-sided. On the other hand H. J. Temperley, *Manchester Guardian* correspondent in China at the time, stated in an introductory note to Vespa's book that in 1937 he showed the typescript of this work to "a trusted friend who was a foreign government official and, as such had exceptionally good facilities for testing the truth of Mr. Vespa's statements . . . he was convinced that Mr. Vespa was telling the truth."

While Doihara was earning for himself the press legend of being the "T. E. Lawrence of Manchukuo", a beautiful girl agent also in his service was being described in some newspapers as the "Joan of Arc of Manchuria".[6] As is the case with so many of the more glamorous spies it is difficult to sift fact from fiction when writing of Yoshiko Kawashima. She has inevitably been compared to Mata Hari, but perhaps the nickname of "Joan of Arc of Manchuria" is nearer the mark as she does seem to have had a penchant for dressing in male clothes. Yoshiko, in fact, came from a Manchu Chinese family, being the daughter of the self-styled Prince Su who had collaborated with Naniwa Kawashima. After Su's death she was adopted by Kawashima as his own daughter and so became a Japanese citizen.

From that time onwards she was a fanatical supporter of Japan and one of its most ardent undercover agents in Manchuria. No doubt she had heard stories from Kawashima of how he founded the Mountain of Sweat Society (*Kanzan So*) in 1916 for the purpose of planning a revolt to create a Manchurian-Mongolian empire. One story is that she actually married a guerrilla member of this society and that together they operated as a team. But other information suggests that she acted very much as a lone agent, certainly in the mid-thirties. She was educated in Japan, yet even in those pre-World War II days when women generally were subservient to men in that country, she seemed to act with all the authority and forcefulness of a man. One who knew her said Yoshiko was "strikingly attractive, with a dominating personality, almost a film-drama figure, half tom-boy and half heroine, and with this passion for dressing up as a male. Possibly she did this to impress the men, or so that she could more easily fit into the tightly-knit guerrilla groups without attracting too much attention."

Certainly she seemed to crave for adventure and to tackle the kind of jobs done by men. According to one source she had been working as a secret agent for the Japanese in Shanghai when the Manchurian Incident of 1933 occurred. She had cut her hair and disguised herself as a boy. Then in response to a message from Colonel Doihara she hurried to Tientsin. Henry Pu Yi, the ex-boy Emperor of China, had been given sanctuary by the Japanese authorities in Tientsin after having first been sheltered in the Dutch Embassy through the mediation of Trebitsch Lincoln. Doihara and Pu Yi had been friends ever since 1924 when the Chinese General Feng Yu-hsiang had invaded Peking where Pu Yi was then living. Ironically, the ex-Emperor had first tried to obtain asylum at the British Embassy, but had been turned down. This provided Doihara with just the opportunity he needed. He smuggled Pu Yi out of Peking that very night. It was astonishing that the British should have refused sanctuary to Pu Yi, especially as he had a British tutor, Sir Reginald Johnston, and was himself pro-British. When trouble broke out in Manchuria it was much easier for Doihara and his colleagues to influence the ex-Emperor and groom him for the post of becoming puppet Emperor of Manchukuo.

Disturbances broke out in and around Tientsin shortly after Doihara arrived there in 1931 and it was about this time that Yoshiko Kawashima was ordered to leave Shanghai. Doihara had little difficulty in persuading Pu Yi that he should leave Tientsin for his own safety. It has frequently been suggested that the Japanese kidnapped Pu Yi against his own wishes and this piece of Chinese propaganda (for it was nothing more than that) was even perpetuated at the War Crime Trials in Tokyo in 1946 when some very confused evidence was given on this subject, mainly to blacken Doihara's character. Since then there has been ample reliable refutation of this canard and it is confirmed that Pu Yi was smuggled out of Tientsin under Doihara's personal care of his own volition and taken on a Japanese launch to a seaside resort near Dairen. Pu Yi himself made this abundantly clear in his autobiography, published in 1964 when he was living in Peking, and additional confirmation was provided by his British tutor.[7]

For some reason which is still not apparent, Pu Yi left his consort behind in Tientsin. Obviously it would not be in the Japanese interest if she fell into the hands of Chang Hsueh-liang's forces and a rescue attempt had to be made. Doihara selected Yoshiko as the perfect agent to carry out this assignment. With machine-guns firing in the streets of Tientsin and soldiers interfering with traffic, she disguised herself as a male taxi-driver and calmly drew up at the Empress's home and told her to get into the cab. Then she drove straight to the harbour. Several times on the way she was stopped by Chinese troops, but her resource and coolness, and not least her charm, enabled her to bring the Empress to the safety of a Japanese destroyer.[8]

Many stories are told of Yoshiko Kawashima's activities in Manchuria, some authentic, others rather more legendary. The American *Literary Digest* stated that "whenever a section of the Japanese Army found itself in difficulties, rumour was that Yoshiko was on her way to join them. When her name was mentioned, it invoked victory and inspired the troops."[9]

Rather more apocryphal is the tale that she was also used to help persuade Henry Pu Yi to agree to becoming puppet Emperor of the Japanese-created state of Manchukuo, which came into existence in February, 1932. Certainly Pu Yi, although grateful to the Japanese for his rescue on two occasions, was uncertain as to whether he should accept this post. It was on 29 February that an All-Manchuria convention at Mukden, with a majority of Japanese delegates, passed a resolution designating Pu Yi as head of state of Manchukuo. Six delegates were reported to have gone to Port Arthur to tell him, only to be rebuffed. It was not until mid-March that it was officially announced that Pu Yi was the president of the new state. The Japanese had kept extremely quiet on the subject officially. Even after his rescue and arrival in Manchuria no news about him was released until mid-February. His identity was only hinted at in the press under the reference of a distinguished visitor to Manchukuo, *Maru Maru Sama* (Mr. "X"). It may well have been that the charms of Yoshiko, coupled with the fact that she had brought his consort to safety, made Pu Yi more amenable to her pleas for him to accept the Japanese offer. Yet another story, which smacks of Chinese propaganda fantasy, was that Pu Yi refused her at first, and that she only succeeded in making him change his mind after having scared the ex-Emperor by putting snakes in his bed!

Whatever the full truth of the role played by Yoshiko Kawashima in all these intrigues, Doihara's greatest achievement was undoubtedly the installation of Pu Yi as president of Manchukuo. Having brought off this coup, he very nearly followed it up with another—the creation of an "independent" North China with a government controlled by a pro-Japanese faction. Captain Malcolm Kennedy, who met Doihara when he was received by Pu Yi in Mukden as a Reuter correspondent, asked the intelligence chief whether it was proposed to extend Manchukuo to include North China. Doihara was emphatic that the Japanese wished to keep Manchukuo entirely separate from China.[10]

Doihara was much more of a realist and showed more tact

and diplomacy than some of the senior officers of the Japanese Kwantung Army. On occasions it was Doihara who used his influence to check the bellicosity of some of the generals. On the other hand it is equally true that some steps were taken by Tokyo to ensure that Doihara did not overreach himself. To curb his influence to some extent the authority of his Special Intelligence Bureau in Mukden was excluded from North China by the setting up of another Intelligence Bureau in Peking. Major-General Piggott paid a visit to Manchuria in 1936 and found in Mukden at the "so-called Special Bureau" that it was mainly occupied by intelligence activities, but that it "dabbled in most things". The officer in charge on that occasion was Major-General Miura. Later he discovered another Special Bureau at Peking which was run by a Colonel Matsumuro. Piggott made the rounds of all the various Special Intelligence Bureaux and two years later visited the Shanghai Bureau (then controlled by General Harada), making the comment that its activities "seemed even more widespread than those of the bureaux in Manchuria."[11]

Some time afterwards Piggott saw the Special Bureau in Tientsin, run by Major-General Shibayama. Knowing that Piggott was a life-long admirer of the Japanese, the intelligence officers took him into their map room where he was shown their charts of the British and French concessions in Tientsin, ". . . with the positions of terrorist [Chinese] agencies marked in red: the French Concession had a few red spots, but the British was covered with them, rather like an attack of the measles."[12] The Japanese knew full well that Piggott would pass on to the British authorities their grievance that the British were allowing terrorists to establish nests of resistance inside their Concession.

By this time war between China and Japan had flared up into large-scale activities instead of the purely local engagements that had continued for some years. Once this war had spread across the Asiatic continent there was the real risk for Japan that the Soviet Union might intervene. Doihara set about countering this by trying to win over General Ma Chan-shan, a Chinese general in command of troops on the Russian border. He gave Ma Chan-shan a large sum of money on condition that he would support the Manchukuoan regime. This was one of Doihara's few mistakes. General Ma promised to meet the Japanese intelligence chief, but failed to turn up, making the ridiculous excuse that he had made himself ill by sitting too close to an over-heated stove, a story that somehow leaked to the Chinese press and caused great merriment in the Chiang Kai-shek camp. Ma used the money Doihara had given him to build up his own army against the Japanese. Later, when the latter had sent a force against him, Ma escaped into Russia. But this was one of the rare occasions on which Doihara displayed a faulty judgement.

After he was promoted to major-general Doihara went to Shanghai and from August, 1938, until the middle of 1939 he was operating his *Tokumu Kikan* in China, directing his Chinese puppets. He had succeeded in penetrating Chiang Kai-shek's entourage and thus had spies right in the heart of the Chinese High Command. But his prime prize was the seduction of Chiang's personal assistant, an official of the Central Bank of China named Huang-sen. Doihara had almost made a point of finding out the interests, recreations, hobbies and weaknesses of his prospective victims, or of those he wished to lure into his network. Huang-sen had a passion for goldfish and used to collect every kind of specimen, installing them in tanks in his home. Doihara was an authority on goldfish and he used his special knowledge to give Huang-sen advice and even to find rare fish to add to his collection. Huang-sen's intelligence became invaluable. He told Doihara of a Chinese scheme to trap Japanese ships anchored in the Yangtse River, and it was through the discovery of his treachery on this occasion that he was eventually executed by the Chinese. The fact that Huang-sen had all the time been a spy for the Japanese caused great consternation in Chiang's ranks and a thorough inquiry into this affair revealed that a number of divisional commanders in the Chinese Armies were undercover agents of Doihara.

Later in the war with China Doihara was given the command of a division in the field. He was one of six senior Japanese officers to be hanged as a war criminal at the end of World War II. As to Yoshiko Kawashima, stories of her mysterious activities were heard from time to time and then she disappeared from view. But she worked for Doihara for some years. On 11 November, 1945, a news agency report stated that "a long sought-for beauty in male costume was arrested today in Peking by the Chinese counter-intelligence officers." Shortly afterwards she was executed by the Chinese as a collaborator.[13]

KEMPEI TAI

THE
JAPANESE
SECRET
SERVICE

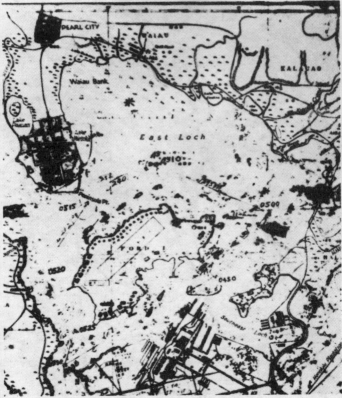

A map of Pearl Harbor discovered by the US Navy in a captured Japanese submarine. Japanese symbols drawn on the chart indicate the anchorage of ships and details of military establishments.

Toyotomi Hideyoshi, the spy-master who unified a nation. (Asahi
Shimbun)

Admiral Isoroku Yamamoto, mastermind behind the drive for intelligence on Hawaii.

Yoshiko Kawashima, nicknamed "the Joan of Arc of Manchuria" for her exploits when disguised as a boy. (Asahi Shimbun)

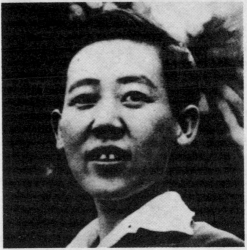

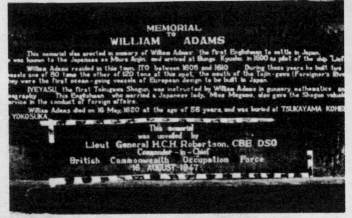

The memorial to Will Adams, the first Englishman to settle in Japan, who became Intelligence Adviser to Iyeyasu, the First Tokugawa Shogun. (Asahi Shimbun)

Japanese surveying Port Arthur by balloon in the Russo-Japanese War of 1904. (Radio Times)

Two Japanese spies executed by the Russians at Harbin in 1904 after being caught trying to blow up a railroad bridge. (Radio Times)

General Kuroki used screens of brushwood to prevent the Russians from estimating the strength of his forces. (Radio Times)

Mitsuru Toyama, a leading figure in the Black
Ocean Society in planning espionage in China.
(Asahi Shimbun)

Ryohei Uchida, founder of the Black Dragon
Society. (Asahi Shimbun)

Kempei Tai officers in their uniform. They formed Japan's most effective counter-espionage organization. (Asahi Shimbun)

Kenji Doihara, an outstanding intelligence officer in Manchuria. (Asahi Shimbun)

ABOVE: The Japanese Purple Machine, used to great effect in the rapid production of encoded messages. BELOW: The Japanese attack on Pearl Harbor. To the left is the moored USS *Helena*, struck by a bomb. (Associated Press)

15

The "Thought Police"

> "At the age of three Comrade Ogilvy refused all toys except a drum, a sub-machine-gun and a model helicopter. At six he had joined the Spies . . . At eleven he denounced his uncle to the Thought Police"
>
> George Orwell

THE ORWELLIAN CONCEPTION of a "Thought Police" as expressed in *Nineteen Eighty-Four* undoubtedly owed more to the O.G.P.U. and the N.K.V.D. of the Soviet Union than any other police force. Certainly Orwell could have known very little about the so-called Thought Police of Japan in the twenties and thirties of this century. There was a marked difference between the fictitious force and that of the Japanese.

Sometimes the *Kempei Tai* have been confused with the Thought Police and referred to by this misleading name. In fact the two sections of the police were separate, though interlocking. But they worked closely together and for that reason it is useful to examine them both in this chapter.

Both government and intelligence circles became seriously concerned in the early twenties by a certain amount of social and industrial unrest in Japan which was mainly the result of revolutionary propaganda from abroad. Some of it came from China and India, but by far the most menacing was that from Soviet Russia which, as the winning side in the civil war, suddenly attracted considerable attention. In July, 1922, a small band of Japanese formed a branch of the Communist Party and

155

accepted Russian aid in doing so. The year 1925 was marked
by increasing communist subversion and evidence of revolutionary Marxist doctrines being spread in the universities, especially at Kyoto. In that year the Communist Party was declared
illegal.

Then in 1927 the Justice Ministry created the Thought Section of the Criminal Affairs Bureau. The purpose of this was
twofold: first, to counter the growth of what was regarded as
subversive radicalism and communism, and, secondly, to make
a serious study of the various new political philosophies and
revolutionary sentiments being propagated. Certainly it could
be said that the aim of this Section was to root out and fight
"dangerous thoughts" and to this extent it could be called illiberal. But it was essentially a Japanese approach to the problem and not to be compared with the Nazis' savage attacks on
all things they considered unAryan. Nor could it be likened to
the crudities and repressive measures of the secret police of
the Soviet Union. In the beginning at least there was a sober
attempt to study the new thinking, to analyse it, to note its
effect on students, workers and civil servants and above all to
discover what was the best means of countering it. To be fair,
there was even an attempt to see whether there were any new
thoughts worth encouraging just as much as to sift out those
to be discouraged.

A staff of thirty-five was created in the Thought Section of
the Criminal Affairs Bureau and periodically they produced
details of their findings in Thought Section Reports. The latter
covered university and school teaching and political parties on
the right as well as the left. In due course prosecutions for
"thought offences" were made. To obtain evidence for such
prosecutions the Thought Police relied on various subsidiary
organisations linked to their own—the Special Higher Police,
which had its book section concerned with censorship, the
Police Research Institute and various independent teams of
spies. All this was achieved quite separately from any help that
might be given by the *Kempei Tai*. There was a system of
espionage in schools and colleges which was active in the early
thirties. Spies in each class were unknown to one another and
each had to report not only on fellow students but teachers and
professors. In some universities the spy system was more powerful than in others. A particularly close watch was kept at
Kyoto University under the prompting of Kyoto's chief of the
Thought Police, Kubota Shan. In Waseda University there was

an active intervention by the *Kempei Tai* who regularly checked on teaching staff as well as the team of student spies.

But the worst feature was perhaps the policy of encouraging the ordinary citizen to spy while building up a vast army of snoopers. In this respect Japan, too, had its Orwellian Comrade Ogilvys. The newspaper *Mainichi* stated in 1930 that quite recently the Metropolitan Authorities in Tokyo "announced that 'henceforth they would welcome secret communications from citizens,' what amounts to a national spying system, of sneaking into each other's houses and reporting them to the police. This system will afford the malignant means to injure others against whom they may happen to have some grudge."

Naturally, the extension of the spy system throughout each province, city and district led to an increase in the bureaucracy of the Thought Police. In the late twenties there were only about fifty Thought Police in Tokyo. By 1932 this number had grown to 380. Similarly the Special Higher Police were enlarged and given special status. Even house-to-house canvassers were used to combine their work with a certain amount of spying. It was relatively easy to try to draw householders in casual conversation and to encourage them to talk indiscreetly.

As World War II approached this internal espionage was stepped up enormously. It reached its height with the creation of the sinister Neighbourhood Association (*Tonari Gumi*). Branches of this association were established in each building, or group of buildings containing ten families. Each branch reported to a larger group which was senior to it and that in turn passed information to the Thought Police. The head of each branch was not only responsible for sending in reports on the families concerned, but was charged with being their mentor and with helping them to eradicate "dangerous thoughts". When Japan came into World War II this system was also used to control rationed goods and to give instructions on air raid precautions and many other things.

When any state has too large a spy network, there is inevitably a deterioration in the standards of detection work as well as abuse of the system and sometimes sheer stupidity. Thus John Gunther, speaking of the spy mania in Japan in the 1930s, said "you could not in Tokyo buy a map of Japan or a plan of Tokyo. Recently the police visited the art shops to confiscate some eighteenth century prints because they portrayed Nagasaki harbour . . . A Danish citizen was arrested because he had some suspicious photographs; they were X-rays of a broken rib."[1]

Possibly some of these narratives of police inefficiency have been exaggerated. Professor Taid O'Conroy reported that one day "a lady of my acquaintance had cause to call at the police station. On the blackboard the orders of the day were, as usual, chalked up. The main feature was '*Kuraberu* Forbes'. *Kuraberu* means 'watch closely, follow every movement of and spy upon.' Mr. Forbes was the ambassador of the U.S.A."[2]

But O'Conroy could not only be biased, but make misjudgements and not all his allegations have been proven. He once made the statement that "India lives in dire misery under Britain's oppressive rule". That rule was easy-going and tolerant in comparison with some of the rule India has endured since independence and it is doubtful whether India was living in any more misery then than today. O'Conroy suggested that a Special Department of the Police kept a close watch on all foreigners in the 1930s and made their lives irksome and often hazardous. Other contemporary foreign observers deny this and in any event there was no such special department as O'Conroy suggests. John Gunther, a critic of the pre-war regime, stated that "spies—most of them highly polite—investigate travellers on all the trains; detectives—who become very friendly and useful as guides—are stationed throughout Manchukuo and Korea".[3]

Sir Robert Craigie, writing of the Japanese secret police, said that "the gendarmerie, with its close Gestapo affiliations, had not yet closed down all association between foreigners and non-official Japanese. . . . Up to the summer of 1940 British and American influence could still be exerted for good in all but extremist circles. To regard Japan as irrevocably committed to the Axis would have been, up to that time, a policy of despair."[4]

On the other hand he viewed the steadily increasing number of police given for their protection with some scepticism. The police "carried out their duties with tact and discretion (the plain clothes police), always anxious to help when they could. They could be brutal, but also extremely kind."

More than one female British resident in Japan during the period between 1935 and 1940 has told the author that Japanese servants told to spy upon them had declined to do so and that some had even asked their mistresses to "tell us something harmless to pass on to the police so that we can keep them happy"!

Much later on, of course, the whole system was tightened

up and there were very many repressive measures. Russell Brines, referring to the World War II period, has alleged that "torture was routine in ordinary prisons and much more highly developed among the *Kempei Tai*."[5] Yet Richard H. Mitchell, of Cornell University, makes the point that "there was nothing comparable in the Japanese experience to Solzhenitsyn's Russian nightmare. The individual was manipulated more by rewards than threats."[6]

Here, in the 1925–40 period at any rate, lies a clue to the more constructive work of the Thought Police. It can be denounced as undemocratic, illiberal, repressive, bureaucratic interference and much else, but what cannot be denied is that there was a positive, tolerant and detached quality about the policies of the Thought Police. Briefly, they fulfilled the role of a somewhat sorrowing priest, or doctor and their motto was that a cure was preferable to punishment. The argument went like this: if you can find out what dangerous thoughts a person has and why he has them, it makes much more sense and is far less wasteful to set out to change them, to eradicate the evil, and to rehabilitate him as an orthodox citizen, than to charge and punish him.

Statistics testify that, broadly speaking, this was the case. According to the *Japan Times*, between 1933 and 1936 the police arrested no fewer than 59,013 people, charged with "dangerous thoughts", which usually amounted to dissent from the prevailing political system, but sometimes meant Marxism or some other form of subversion. But, the newspaper pointed out that less than 5,000 of these persons were actually brought to trial: the rest were set free. Of that 5,000 tried about half of them went to prison. Taking a lengthier look at the whole judicial spectrum, the figures from 1928 to 1941 show that there were still fewer than 5,000 prosecutions for "dangerous thoughts" out of 62,000 suspected cases. Some historians have given a distorted picture by making such statements as that 30,000 students were arrested in the inter-war period, often without the knowledge of their parents. They do not make it clear that in practically all these cases no charges were made.

This is not an attempt to justify the conception of a Thought Police, but it is necessary to correct distortions of the truth. Japan was still an emergent modern state, fighting for a permanent position among the other big powers of the world. Less than a century before this she had been totally cut off from the world. It was not therefore surprising if her ruling classes should fear the end of a dream if nothing was done to check the influx of subversive communism and revolutionary radicalism. The official idea was to use the Thought Police "Think Tank" to analyse the causes for what they regarded as "dangerous thoughts", to think up positive methods of counteracting such views and how best to re-educate those infected. The Thought Police were also given lessons in Marxist tactics and urged to find out what attracted students to this particular political philosophy. Whenever someone was caught propagating, or seeming to harbour, such ideas, the aim was to use the threat of prosecution, but if possible to employ tact and skill to "turn" them to more orthodox causes. Sometimes this took a very short time, occasionally much longer. They used a good deal of propaganda on the subject of the Great East Asia Prosperity Plan and threats were mixed with kindness and even offers of work. The Japanese officials regarded this work as "rehabilitation", the *Kempei Tai* considered it "purging", while some observers would call it brain-washing. But as far as one can tell there was none of the drug treatment, or electrical convulsive therapy which has been used in post-war brainwashing, and certainly no attempt at obtaining forced "confessions".

As to whether these tactics worked, subsequent events suggest that they succeeded far better than prosecutions. Captain Malcolm Kennedy, then a Reuters correspondent in Tokyo, told me that "in the early 1930s many of the former left-wing extremists turned to national socialism and became the most extreme right-wing reactionaries. The *Seisanto*, a body established in November, 1931, and closely connected with the ultra-national Black Dragon Society was composed largely of such elements."

In many respects, of course, the Thought Police contributed considerably to Japanese intelligence-gathering. Through them an enormous amount of intelligence material was provided at a very low cost. But for the military police of the *Kempei Tai* and their counter-espionage operations, the Thought Police might have developed into something far bigger. One of their ablest officers was Ikeda Katso, a Tokyo procurator, who paid special attention to the analysis and collection of intelligence obtained by his officers as well as being a shrewd advocate of the softly-softly approach to offenders and winning them over rather than prosecuting.

In the inter-war years a number of important decisions were taken in intelligence circles and new appointments made. In the Foreign Office Intelligence Service a key man was Kiyoshi Tsutsui, who was chief of the second and third sections of this bureau. He joined the Foreign Office after leaving Tokyo University and served in Belgium before joining the Intelligence Service. Other key figures were General Eini Tojo, Director of Military Intelligence, and Admiral Kiyoshi Noda, Director of Naval Intelligence. But above these, and having control of a number of undercover organisations, was General Jiro Minami, the War Minister since 1931. A few years before World War II occurred Major-General Kiichiro Higuchi was appointed Director of Military Intelligence, a highly significant development.

In 1930, when he was lieutenant-colonel, Higuchi joined some twenty or more Army officers in Tokyo to discuss plans for forming a new secret society. This had as its chief aim the ultimate elimination of all parliamentary political parties. It was named the Society of the Cherry (*Sakurakai*) and many of its members were officers of the *Kempei Tai*.

The *Kempei Tai* had progressed considerably in the interwar years and had become one of the most powerful and certainly the most feared institution in Japan. This had been achieved without changing its very special position inside the Japanese Army, for it remained as a semi-independent unit, commanded by a Provost Marshal-General who was directly responsible to the War Minister. Its links with the Society of the Cherry gave the *Kempei Tai* even greater strength, and though the Minister of Justice had some powers to intervene with the secret military police, these were only occasionally used and rarely pushed against the wishes of the *Kempei Tai*. In only one sphere of Japanese life was this organisation sometimes thwarted—in the Imperial Navy. The Navy disliked both the extreme nationalist wing of the Army and the secret military police and brooked no interference with their own personnel.

Kempei Tai men normally worked in plain clothes, but they were entitled to wear Army uniforms with the special badge of a star surrounded by leaves. By the end of World War II the United States Intelligence teams ascertained that there were nearly 75,000 *Kempei Tai* members, of whom just under a third were officers. It was, however, not altogether clear whether these figures covered all personnel overseas. Naturally the standards and the quality of the men deteriorated during the war when recruits had much less training. But in normal times the selection of personnel was conducted most carefully and sometimes recruits were taken from the Foreign Office on account of language abilities. Otherwise members needed to have six years' military service before they were eligible. There was a year's training at a special college where instruction was given in languages, law, unarmed combat and various espionage techniques. After the training was completed recruits would be given tests such as the penetration of offices and factories while using disguise.

The *Kempei Tai* were responsible for checking on any Army personnel who might be suspected of harbouring "dangerous thoughts" and they could not only arrest soldiers three ranks higher than themselves, but carry out instant punishments on their own initiative. It could hardly be denied that they had excessive power and that this was bound to be abused to some extent. All that is surprising is that the abuses were not as extensive as might be expected. In addition to their normal work of maintaining Army discipline they undertook a certain amount of censorship and a great deal of counter-espionage, as well as assisting the Thought Police.

Their ramifications overseas were considerable. It was a *Kempei Tai* report which accused Colonel Lindbergh and his wife of spying when they landed in the Kurile Islands in 1931. Major-General Piggott found them operating in considerable numbers when he visited Manchukuo in 1931, when the local head of the military police was Lieutenant-General Hideki Tojo. Walter Stennes, who had acted as an adviser and agent to Chiang Kai-shek, had various brushes with them after the Japanese entered the International Settlement at Shanghai. "With the *Kempei Tai*," he said, ". . . if they were suspicious of you, they were like cobras and to be with them at all was like being in a small room with a cobra and the electric light switch off. Your problem was to reach the switch without disturbing the cobra. But in the Army proper one found some fine old soldiers, men who came from good military families and knew how to behave."[7]

Stennes, a former Prussian Army officer, had been living in Shanghai and was forced to go into hiding in the French Concession. He was anxious to meet the local commandant of the *Kempei Tai* to explain that certain interviews he had given to Chinese journalists had been distorted. A dinner party was arranged for the meeting—"good food . . . the geishas were pretty and . . . lots of sake and brandy"—and Stennes was able to convince the *Kempei Tai* chief that printed reports of his interviews had been exaggerated. Stennes, however, could not resist telling the man that he thought Japan would lose the war: "despite this, we parted good friends".[8]

It must have been a strange relationship which Stennes had with the *Kempei Tai* over a long period of the war. They seemed to admire him for his honesty in admitting he had been in Chiang Kai-shek's service and even more for his record as a Prussian officer. His impression was that the higher Japanese officers liked the Germans but detested and mistrusted Hitler. He was told: "It was fortunate for you that you came to see us on your own. Your dossier was two centimetres thick and we had made up our minds that you must be liquidated. . . . When you told us that you were still a monarchist and loyal to the House of Hohenzollern, you touched our hearts. We felt that you had the spirit of the 47 *Ronin* and that you must be protected."

Orders had come from the Führer himself that Stennes was to be executed. But the Japanese did not like being told what to do. They merely kept him under surveillance and reported back to Berlin that he had been "rendered harmless", which, when this exact Japanese phrase was translated back into German implied that he had been liquidated.

Sometimes the *Kempei Tai* employed female agents as well as informers. Occasionally a Japanese woman would actually be recruited into the service. One such was a Madame Nogami, an attractive woman aged about thirty-five, who was nicknamed the "Queen Cobra" in the European settlements of Shanghai on account of her dreaded reputation as the chief colleague of the commandant of the secret police. According to Walter Stennes, she held "the rank of captain in the *Kempei Tai*, which was very rare for a woman."

Commander Charles Drage, the British naval intelligence officer in the Far East, said that Madame Nogami suspected that Stennes was hiding goods belonging to Madame Chiang Kia-shek somewhere in Shanghai, so she refused to give him a permit to move any furniture. Eventually she interrogated Stennes in great detail, but without apparently learning too much. For Stennes reported that when he went back to his house at the end of the war everything was "in the same condition and the same place as it was on that day in the summer of 1937 when Madame Chiang Kai-shek paid her last visit to her house."[9]

Nevertheless Madame Nogami was a highly astute operator

and the probability is that she knew full well exactly where Madame Chiang's goods and furniture were, but that at some later date they might well be used as a bargaining counter to do a deal with Chiang—something which, as the war went on, became increasingly important. Madame Nogami was reported to have commited suicide in Peking at the end of the war.

During World War II the *Kempei Tai* were overloaded with tasks towards the end. On the surface the nation was still united behind its Emperor and government, but there were furtive defeatist activities here and there and even some instances of labour unrest which called for intervention. In 1943 the secret military police were given accommodation for their officers in the Sanno Hotel in Tokyo, where a number of prisoners-of-war and internees were also housed. There was a sound reason for this: some of the latter were being used for writing propaganda scripts for the Overseas Bureau and broadcasting. These internees helped to produce the "Zero Hour" music session, this name being taken from the Japanese fighter plane Zero. The *Kempei Tai* residents at the Sanno Hotel cooperated with the Special Security Police (*Tokko Keitsatsu*) in controlling this propaganda, utilising it for intelligence purposes and in interrogating the internees. Some *Kempei Tai* were used as spies inside the Overseas Bureau.

But some of the secret police also made suggestions for using "Zero Hour" as a means of hitting at American morale in the subtlest possible way. Indeed, so effective were they that the *New York Times*, almost doing the Japanese job for them, reported from Guadalcanal on 29 June, 1943: "Between the Tokyo Radio and Japanese bombers the nights are not always dull here. Tokyo has been beaming a programme called 'The Zero Hour' direct to the Russell Islands and Guadalcanal. The fellows like it very much because it cries over them and feels sorry for them. It talks about the food that they miss by not being at home and tells how the war workers are stealing their jobs and their girls."

The *Kempei Tai* in Shanghai and elsewhere may have disliked the Nazis, but after Japan entered the war with Germany, there were demands from Berlin that there should be a liaison between the S.S. and the secret police. The first Nazi overlord of the German colony in Japan was Herr Hillman, an aggressive business man, but he was later replaced by an even more unpleasant character, one Otto Spahn, a young Storm Trooper sent out to purge the local Nazi Party. Joseph Meisinger, the notorious "Butcher of Warsaw", went to Japan by submarine to work closely with the *Kempei Tai* and eventually he became overall manager of Nazi affairs in the whole of the Far East, undoubtedly being one of those who extended his influence to Shanghai.

F. D. Morris, an American correspondent who arrived in Japan shortly after the end of the war, discovered hidden away in the mountains at Karuizawa, about a hundred miles from Tokyo, a lost colony of some 2,000 people of all nations who had been held as spies, but including many Germans. From inquiries at Karuizawa Morris came to the conclusion that "under Colonel Meisinger's guidance the *Kempei Tai* hit a new low in ruthlessness and brutality. All Japanese house servants were enrolled by the *Kempei Tai* to report conversations and activities of their employers. One of them once said 'Please give me a piece of paper with something—anything—written on it. I have to make a report to the *Kempei Tai* today.'"[10]

16

Naval Espionage in U.S.A.

> "About 1936 the counter-intelligence activities increased. Between 1936 and 1940 there were twelve convictions for espionage in the United States. Four of these were uncovered by Naval Intelligence and the Navy played a part in two more"
> *The First Sixty Years of the Office of Naval Intelligence,*
> J. R. Green

THE EBERSTADT REPORT in 1945, dealing with the problems of national security and intelligence, came to the conclusion that between the two world wars both Army and Navy intelligence in the U.S.A. had been mediocre. It stated that "available funds were grossly inadequate, and there was considerable duplication of effort.... Few Intelligence agents were employed.... Evaluation was largely in the hands of officers untrained in Intelligence techniques."[1]

Nevertheless, despite these criticisms, some excellent counter-intelligence work was eventually done through the initiative of the Office of Naval Intelligence and a number of Japanese agents were detected. This was achieved even though as late as 1934, when the infiltration of agents from Japan had long begun, the O.N.I. was reduced to a force of eighteen officers, with only two officers and one clerk responsible for the whole of Latin America.

The Japanese, while concentrating mainly on the Californian coast and the Gulf of Mexico, took the view that espionage in the U.S.A. needed to be backed up by having agents in Central and South America. A glimpse at a map of California will show their sound reasons, especially from a naval viewpoint, for making this area their primary target. Here were key naval bases on the Pacific coast of U.S.A., while the Gulf of California extended for 800 miles and was on average a hundred miles wide. It provided a deep channel free from rocks and reefs. In the event of war with America this area would be of vital importance to Japan. While California could not easily be threatened directly from the Pacific Ocean, by infiltration, or cajoling of the Mexican Government, or even by encouraging a pro-Japanese uprising in Mexico, the Mexican side of the Gulf could provide a haven for Japanese ships. If Japan could by some means dominate the Gulf and possibly occupy Lower California from the rear, the war could be directed from there. All this was highly theoretical and it is doubtful whether any senior naval officer in Japan took the project too seriously. But it was the kind of operation which might well have created panic in San Francisco and Los Angeles while giving the Japanese a foothold, however precarious, on the American mainland.

There was also the consideration that many Japanese immigrants had settled in California and Mexico, having been sometimes very badly treated in the former territory but receiving a much friendlier reception in Mexico. Japanese Intelligence lost no time in capitalising on this, realising there was a ready-made reservoir of potential sympathisers and agents in California and a measure of goodwill in Mexico. Thus a vast espionage drive was launched into California and the whole of Central America from Mexico to the Panama Canal in the early 1930s.

Among the most favoured covers for Japanese agents in this whole area in the late twenties and early thirties were the occupations of fishermen, dental surgeons and barbers. One of the secret projects used by the Japanese for spying was that of teaching the Mexicans to fish scientifically. A special arrangement was proposed between the Japanese and Mexican governments by which the former provided the teaching and supervision and the latter gave permits for Japanese fishermen to settle at a certain point on the Mexican coast. This plan did not materialise, despite the efforts of Dr. Yochuchi Matsui who, in the mid-thirties, was sent out to Mexico to try to clinch the deal. Nevertheless Dr. Matsui was not one easily to be thwarted and he then concentrated on directing the activities of Japanese fishermen operating from California. There had been a growing number of these since the early twenties and by the time Dr. Matsui returned to Japan there were scores of such craft, supplemented by former British coastguard vessels which had been refitted in Japan. It was noticeable that the machine-gun mountings in these craft had not been removed, so that it would be relatively easy to convert the craft into armed raiders. These former coastguard ships were equipped with radio and ship-to-shore telephones. Half the crew were American-born Japanese, the remainder native Japanese. A number of the latter included naval officers masquerading as seamen. One of their tasks, set by Japanese Naval Intelligence, was to keep a watch on the United States fleet when it was conducting manoeuvres off Southern California. The ships varied in size from eighty to two hundred tons and had cruising ranges of up to some few thousand miles.

There were two main centres linking the activities of these Japanese fishing fleets. One was on the Avenida XIV in Guaymas, on the west coast of Mexico, and the other was Terminal Island, off San Pedro Bay in California. When the Japanese fishing vessels put in at Guaymas their skippers called at an address in the Avenida XIV which comprised the offices of a bottled soda water factory run by a fast-talking, energetic businessman named Matsumiya who had arrived in the fishing port about 1930. Close to his factory were the offices of Nippon Suisan Kaisha, one of the chief companies controlling the Japanese fishing fleets. This firm was indirectly linked with a Japanese Government-controlled company which had its head office in Mexico City. Employees of the latter company frequently travelled along the South Pacific Mexican railway, using their tele-lens cameras to take pictures of all installations en route.

In the early thirties there were many privately owned islands off the Californian coast, mainly the acquisition of men who had made their money in the short-lived gold boom. When the depression came, many of these islands were sold for knock-down prices or abandoned. The Japanese had been fascinated by the story of a character who called herself Princess Der Ling who had acquired a tiny island called Golondrina off the southern tip of California, setting up her own "palace" there and filling it with ex-American Marines, dressed in ceremonial Chinese robes, and Chinese dancers. They felt sure that this

must be a cover for some highly secret U.S. Navy project. It
took them a long time to realise that this was the whim of an
eccentric woman. But they were able to make Terminal Island
a regular port of call. The locals, including American fishermen, were amused by the fact that the Japanese fishermen were
always re-checking their charts and taking soundings. It was
also noted that they sent coded messages to one another. Not
until February, 1938, did any of these actions arouse suspicion.
On that date an inquisitive American fisherman decided to find
out the purpose of a number of yellow-painted drums stowed
aboard one of the fishing vessels. He discovered that the contents of these were being used for acid corrosion tests on a
broken-down vessel: he then assumed that the motive behind
these experiments could be for the eventual use of the drums'
contents to disable warships below the waterline.

The Panama Canal Zone was another prime target for espionage. Here the Japanese sought to organise a network of
informants in all adjacent territories, including Nicaragua, Costa
Rica and in Panama itself. In Panama City there were forty-
seven Japanese barbers in the mid-thirties; these were linked
together by the Barbers' Association of Japan, which was
founded by an agent named Sonada. Under the direction of an
attractive Japanese girl named Chiyo Morasawa, who had come
to Panama to run a clothes shop in the late 1920s, the barbers
were briefed as to what tid-bits of barber's shop gossip they
should assiduously collect when U.S. naval personnel visited
their parlours. Chiyo Morasawa was married to a reserve officer
in the Japanese Navy and frequently took photographs of any
military installations along the Canal.

Meanwhile at Tijuana, just across the U.S. border in Mexico, a short distance from San Diego, a large renovated and
decorated windmill bore the sign, Molino Rojo (the Red Mill).
It was run by a Japanese known as Yasahura and comprised a
bar, dance hall and bordello. But some days, when Japanese
officers visited the place, the girls were ordered to remain in
their rooms as the dance hall was to be turned into a conference
hall. Later it was learned that the "conferences" concerned
discussions on possible hiding places along the Californian and
Mexican coastline where fuel supplies for Japanese submarines
could be located.

John L. Spival, who investigated Japanese espionage in
California and Mexico in this period, has stated that he found
"Japanese engineers masquerading as common railroad work-

ers, . . . in strategic military areas just south of the American border and Japanese masquerading as farmers in areas where they could do enormous damage."[2] This may have been an exaggeration of the facts, as there is no evidence of such wide-scale operations having been discovered by the authorities. But Spival did ascertain that the Japanese had established contact with a member of the Los Angeles police when they learned that he had been supplying confidential information to an Italian agent and putting a lot of money in his bank account. They made the excuse in approaching him that they wanted information on American communists. The letter seeking this intelligence was dated 1 September, 1936, and was signed by Toshio Sasaki, vice-consul in Los Angeles. He wanted "information . . . on communistic movements in coastal districts", together with a list of Japanese of American and Japanese parents who were suspected of taking an active part in the above."[3]

Spival was also of the opinion that the Japanese were behind the abortive rebellion of General Saburnino Cedillo to overthrow the Mexican government and that they had also plotted to overthrow the Panamanian Government because it had banned Japanese fishermen in Panamanian waters. Certainly they found themselves constantly baulked by the Panamanian authorities. In 1934 the Japanese sought permission for a refrigeration plant to be set up on Taboga, a small island near to Panama. This was turned down, as no doubt the authorities suspected it was an attempt to establish a base within their territory. But later Yoshitaro Amano, a Japanese store owner who had lived for some time in Panama, formed a company named Amano Fisheries, proudly proclaiming that its flagship would be the *Amano Maru*, the largest fishing vessel of its type in the world. But then Amano overreached himself. He had heard that the United States was planning to excavate another canal in Nicaragua and that fortifications were being built in the military zone at Managua. But from the moment he left Panama he was shadowed and finally arrested on 7 October, 1937, and charged with suspected sabotage and taking photographs in a prohibited area. Fortune, it is said, favours the brave, and it certainly smiled on Amano. Whether by bribery or luck, he managed to get himself acquitted of these charges. Later he was again arrested for similar offences in Costa Rica and Colombia, but was yet again acquitted. A formidable and indestructible agent!

An eager prowler after American naval secrets was soft-

voiced, pleasantly-mannered Toshio Miyazaki, one of the
youngest lieutenant-commanders in the Japanese Navy. He had
entered the U.S.A. in 1933 and learned English as an exchange
student at Stanford University in California. Later he was assigned to Naval Intelligence by his Tokyo director, and was
responsible for recruiting Harry Thomas Thompson, a former
yeoman in the U.S. Navy, as a spy. A number of naval officers
from Tokyo came over to America in the thirties either as
genuine language students or posing as such. Another such was
Inao Ohtani, who arrived in August, 1936, in a Japanese fishing
boat at San Francisco. He, too, was a lieutenant-commander
who declared that he was going to Stanford University to learn
English. Later it was learned that he did nothing of the sort,
but made his way to the Red Windmill bordello in Tijuana. It
is doubtful whether any attempt to investigate Ohtani would
have been made but for the F.B.I. discovering a brief-case
following the death of a reputed language student named Torii
in Los Angeles in 1932. Torii was yet another lieutenant-
commander and police suspicions were aroused when a
Dr. Furusawa, the proprietor of a nursing-home at 117½
Weller Street, called to collect the brief-case.

Investigations took a leisurely course, as the attention of
the F.B.I. was not especially concentrated on the Japanese in
this period. The only grounds for suspicion were that Dr.
Furusawa seemed rather agitated when he called for the brief-
case, as though there might have been important documents
inside it. The police had only perfunctorily examined the brief-
case and not read any of the documents. They found that the
doctor had graduated at Stanford and lived for many years in
the U.S.A. President of the South Californian Japanese Phy-
sicians' Society and the South Californian Fishing Club, his
medical centre and nursing home in Weller Street were visited
almost exclusively by Japanese. Mrs. Furusawa was a founder
of the Los Angeles branch of the Women's Patriotic Society
of Japan.

Outwardly all seemed highly respectable and gave no cause
for further suspicions. Then in 1933 two items of information
were added to the Furusawa dossier and gave the F.B.I. cause
to extend their inquiries. The first item was that Toshio Miyazaki
had contact with Furusawa and that he was not at Stanford
University as he claimed. The second was a tip-off from the
F.B.I. in New York that a German named Count Hermann von
Keitel had ordered visiting cards with "117½ Weller Street"

as his address. This latter intriguing snippet of information gave the Furusawa dossier top priority as at that time the F.B.I. were rather more interested in potential German spies than those working for the Japanese.

It was Miyazaki, however, who was the first Japanese intelligence agent to be tracked down by the F.B.I. in collaboration with the O.N.I. Harry Thomas Thompson, a twenty-eight-year-old Maryland farmhand, who had been a yeoman in the U.S. Navy, was unemployed and wandering aimlessly round the San Pedro waterfront when he met Miyazaki. The Japanese officer offered him a retainer of 500 dollars a month, plus expenses and bonuses, to spy on the U.S. Navy. Thompson bought himself a Navy yeoman's uniform and, proceeding to pose as a visitor from another crew, boarded U.S. warships at San Pedro and San Diego bases. He would ask questions about gunnery data, technical innovations and even manoeuvres. Occasionally on such trips he managed to filch code-books, signal books, plans, maps and models. All this was passed on to Miyazaki who sent regular payments to Thompson from his large account in San Francisco's Yokohama Specie Bank.

This relatively easily obtained data might have continued to flow into Japanese hands, but for the fact that Thompson foolishly confided part of his story to his room-mate, a Texas youth named Willard James Turntine. Thompson told Turntine that he was friendly with a Japanese named Tanni and the Texan was worried not so much by this friendship as by the fact that Thompson was always going aboard U.S. ships even though he had left the Navy. At the end of January, 1935, Thompson told Turntine he was going away for a few days, ostensibly to meet some old shipmates aboard the U.S.S. *Pennsylvania* at San Diego. Turntine became so worried about the possible implications of Thompson's friendship with the Japanese that he decided to approach the O.N.I. They took his story seriously and immediately tracked down the mysterious "Tanni", identifying him as Toshio Miyazaki. From then onwards Miyazaki was shadowed by O.N.I. agents. It did not take them long to have Miyazaki's bank account scrutinised, confirming that he was paying Thompson 200 dollars a month.

The upshot of this was that the O.N.I. asked the civil authorities to authorise Miyazaki's arrest. This, they declined to do, saying that the naval authorities should simply warn sailors not to talk to Thompson. Thus the O.N.I. agents could not legally enter Thompson's apartment, but they arranged for his waste-paper baskets to be checked. In one of these they found all the evidence they required. It was the rough outline of a letter that Thompson was planning to send to Miyazaki, whom he addressed as "Dear Mr. Tanni". It stated: "I respectfully request that this letter be treated as my resignation from the service of your country . . . and hope that all information that has come to you through me has amply repaid for the salary paid me. This resignation is to take effect from the date of our last meeting. . . ."

That this letter was received by Miyazaki seems certain as almost immediately afterwards the naval officer was ordered back to Japan, presumably in case Thompson had reported him to the O.N.I. Thompson was then arrested and charged with masquerading in naval uniform and with selling U.S. Fleet secrets to a foreign power. He was sentenced to fifteen years' imprisonment.

Hardly had the furore caused by the Thompson case died down than a rather more serious instance of espionage was revealed. This time the culprit was a U.S. naval officer, Lieutenant-Commander John Semer Farnsworth, known to his friends and colleagues as "Dodo." He had served in destroyers in the first world war, but, after marrying a society girl, he had become a high spender and got heavily into debt. Farnsworth eventually borrowed money from a naval rating and when asked to repay, refused. He was court-martialled and dismissed from the service.

Offering his services as an aviation expert, he was turned down by several countries before the Japanese showed some interest. Gradually he was drawn into their network and asked to provide classified material. The Navy Department first became suspicious of Farnsworth when he kept pestering them for information for "magazine articles". Then a high-ranking officer's wife reported that he had urged her to show him certain naval documents. F.B.I. men joined in the hunt with the O.N.I. In May, 1935, it was learned he had borrowed a U.S. Navy handbook entitled *The Service of Information and Security*, had it photocopied and sold the copy to a member of the Japanese Embassy in Washington. It was said at the time that divulgence of its contents might necessitate a complete replanning of U.S. Fleet strategy. Eventually there was enough evidence to justify an arrest, but by that time the Japanese had wisely ceased to have anything more to do with him. It was not until February, 1937, that the U.S. attorney had been able to complete the case, as Farnsworth had persisted in denying the allegations against him. He even claimed that he had merely pretended to spy for the Japanese in order to find out about their espionage. Eventually he was sentenced to the Federal Penitentiary.

The third instance of espionage in this period was of a totally different character and directly concerned the Soviet Union and not Japan. On the other hand, as there was an unusual Japanese angle to the case, it is worth recording. Salich, an American citizen of Russian extraction, had worked for a number of years for the Los Angeles Police Department and finally obtained a position with the O.N.I. office in San Pedro. He and Mihail Gorin, the Soviet Intourist agent in Los Angeles, were charged with espionage and convicted. But the case went all the way up to the Supreme Court before the conviction was finally upheld. The defence argued that the information passed by Salich and Gorin to the U.S.S.R. was not U.S. military secret material which came under the category of espionage. They based this argument on the fact that the intelligence in question provided evidence of Japanese espionage on the west coast of America.[4]

This spate of cases of espionage in the mid-thirties led to O.N.I. funds being increased to combat the Japanese threat and, at the same time, caused the Japanese to reorganise their own intelligence services in the U.S.A. In Mexico efforts were made to recruit Yaqui Indians through their tribal chief, Urbalejo, and a good deal of information on sea and rail traffic and cargoes was provided for Tokyo through this source. Cautiously, links were established between the German Intelligence Services and the Japanese, though these never seemed to be fully developed. Count von Keitel acted as the German liaison officer and his wife was suspected of being a courier for information. But the F.B.I. and the O.N.I. found that they were so outnumbered that they could only shadow a very small percentage of suspected Japanese agents at a time. They were further frustrated by the obstructiveness of the U.S. State Department whenever they wanted some backing, or support for making an arrest.

17

The Case of Charlie Chaplin's Valet

> "The F.B.I. arrested two Japanese and Al
> Blake, a U.S. citizen, in Los Angeles last
> week. Al turned out to be no spy, but a
> hero. He had pulled off an amateur job of
> counter-espionage"
>
> *Time*, 23 June, 1941

THE REMAINING KEY figures in the direction of Japanese espionage on the West Coast of America were Inao Ohtani, Dr. Furusawa and the proprietor of a string of nightclubs in California who went under the name of Yamamoto, but whose real identity was that of Commander Itaru Tachibana.

Ohtani was resident chief of intelligence for his country in Southern California. He had teamed up with a girl named Chieko Nagai, who was also known in the Japanese colony as "Dorothy". Occasionally Ohtani would visit the Japanese intelligence chief in New York and he was also a frequent visitor at the Miyako Hotel in Los Angeles where he passed on blueprints to a Japanese photographer, K. Yamakashi, and gave assignments to a woman who answered to the name of Betsy O'Hara, but who was unmistakably Japanese. Her espionage cover was that of a beauty culture expert.

Dr. Furusawa's wife was head of the Japanese Navy Assistance League which provided her with an excuse for entertaining Japanese naval officers and sailors on leave. By this means they passed instructions through her to her husband and she gave them information to take back to Tokyo. Both Furusawa and Tachibana had organised extensive spy networks

by the late thirties and the latter helped to finance these by
opium-peddling. The F.B.I. had a tip-off from a Korean named
Kilsoo Haan that Tachibana was planning a coastal survey of
key military and naval installations, power stations and water
supply systems with a view to listing sabotage targets in the
event of war. Perhaps the evidence of this was highly coloured
and possibly Tachibana's plan was largely a matter of routine
intelligence-gathering, but the F.B.I. made little headway in
obtaining details of this probe. It did not take Tachibana's
agents long to realise that they were being shadowed and they
reported this to their boss. He set up a second team of agents
and told them to start operations in Portland and Seattle before
working their way back to San Francisco and Los Angeles. He
felt certain that the F.B.I. wouldn't pick up the trail in Oregon.
Meanwhile he ordered the team who were being shadowed to
lure the unsuspecting F.B.I. men from one nightclub to another
and then on to the bordellos to ensure that they were constantly
occupied and far away from the active team of agents. It was
a ploy which succeeded only too well, even though the whole
affair sounds like the script for a farcical comedy.

It was not until the World's Fair was held at San Francisco
in 1940 that the first chance of success in trapping the Tachibana
network occurred. A sideshow at this fair was called the Can-
did Camera Artist's Model Studio, run by a fifty-year-old ex-
yeoman in the U.S. Navy named Al Blake. He called
himself "Keeno, King of the Robots", a title he proudly displayed over the store he normally operated in Los Angeles.
His sideshow at the World's Fair consisted of providing attractive nude models for any amateur photographers who cared
to pay a small fee for this service. To an astute observer this
must not have seemed to be a particularly lucrative business—
at least not for the modest charge listed.

So, apparently, thought a middle-aged Japanese, Toraichi
Kono, who paid a visit to the sideshow and took some pho-
tographs. He put away his camera, turned to Al Blake and said:
"We have met before. Do you remember?"

Blake looked at his client blankly: "No, I'm sorry, buddy,
but I just don't recognise you."

"It was a long time ago. More than twenty years. Do you
remember you once appeared in one of Charlie Chaplin's films,
Shoulder Arms?"

"Why yes, of course . . . Must be way back in 1917."

"That's right. That's when we met. I was Charlie's valet."

This was the first of a number of meetings between Blake and Kono. Chaplin's former valet had by this time capitalised considerably on having been employed by the film star and through this having overheard many of Chaplin's conversations with politicians and other notabilities. Ostensibly, as far as America was concerned, he was a quiet, sober, hard-working Japanese running a small business. In fact he'd become a wealthy man, frequently consulted by Dr. Furusawa, whose clinic he often visited. His friendships included a few German diplomats. Each year he was in the habit of returning to Japan where he had a large estate outside Tokyo.

Blake was first put on his guard when Kono said casually that it was "a pity you aren't still in the Navy. You could make quite a lot of money."

At another meeting in Hollywood in March, 1941, Blake tested Kono by suggesting that he was thinking seriously of rejoining the Navy. Kono immediately showed interest and asked him out to dinner at the Japanese Club. Cleverly, using his talents as an ex-actor, Blake played along with Kono and at the end of the meal Kono proposed a meeting for the following day "at the corner of Sunset Boulevard and Wilton Street" and hinted that he would have an important personage with him.

Blake kept the rendezvous and was met by Kono and another Japanese in a car. They beckoned to him to get in and drove off towards the country. Kono's companion was none other than Lieutenant-Commander Tachibana, alias Yamamoto. By the end of that motoring trip Blake was convinced that an attempt was being made to recruit him as a spy. He had no intention of rejoining the Navy, as he had hinted, but, to keep the Japanese interest alive, he had invented a friend who was handling classified material in the U.S. Navy. Soon he was informed that he would be provided with funds if he procured information for them.

This was the period in which Japanese Naval Intelligence was concentrating on Hawaii and it was hinted that Blake could achieve a great deal if he went to Honolulu and Pearl Harbor on their behalf. As an inducement he was offered 2,500 dollars right away if he agreed to this mission and an additional 5,000 dollars when he returned with the information.

Blake's first reaction was to go to O.N.I. headquarters either locally or even in Washington and tell them what had happened. But he realised that this could give the game away if the Jap-

anese were shadowing him. Very soon he discovered that they
had agents watching his every move and that it would not even
be safe to use his telephone to inform the O.N.I. as that, too,
had been bugged. Blake never did learn how they managed to
tap his telephone.

But though Blake was not versed in the techniques of counter-
espionage, as an amateur he displayed coolness and resource-
fulness. Choosing a cinema which was close to the local O.N.I.
offices, he went inside and, under cover of darkness, managed
to slip away from his watchers into the manager's office. He
asked to be allowed to leave the building through a back door.
Then he paid the O.N.I. a quick visit, explained the situation
and returned to the cinema without his shadowers being aware
that he had ever left it. The O.N.I. arranged to tap Blake's
telephone and record any conversations he had with the Japanese.

Soon U.S. Naval Intelligence were hot on the trail of Tachibana. They found out that he had entered the United States in
1930 and enrolled as a language student at the University of
Pennsylvania, but that later he had switched over to the University of Southern California. The fact that he had changed
his identity convinced them that he must be one of Tokyo's
chief naval spies in the U.S.A. When the O.N.I. consulted the
F.B.I. and learned of their attempts to investigate "Mr. Yamamoto" and his nightclubs, they had little doubt that he must
be the head of a major spy network. So they urged Blake to
carry on pretending to aid the Japanese and to agree to the
mission to Honolulu.

Tachibana provided a ticket for a sea passage to Hawaii for
Blake who, once aboard his ship, was well aware that he was
still being closely watched. This time there were two agents
taking it in turn to spy on him. Later he suspected that the
Japanese were employing German agents to watch him, presumably so as not to arouse suspicion. Somewhat nervously
he awaited a furtive contact from an O.N.I. agent which, he
had been promised, would be made during his voyage. He was
uneasy because he feared that any such attempt to get in touch
with him would be spotted by the men shadowing him.

The contact was made with a skilful piece of play-acting
which the ex-actor himself could not fail to admire. Aboard
ship was one of those ubiquitous characters—the pestering
drinker. Clumsily, loudly and irritatingly, this person swayed
across the deck and in the saloons, pestering first one, then

another. Eventually even the agents shadowing Blake not only ignored him, but kept well out of his way. They were afraid that he would hinder their operations, or detract their attention from Blake. As a result it was not too difficult for the seemingly drunken passenger to get into casual conversation with Blake while the agents watched from a distance.

Blake was beginning to wonder how he could escape from this alcoholic pest when suddenly in a quick whisper the man said:

"Here are your orders. At Honolulu phone the U.S.S. *Pennsylvania* from your hotel. Ask for Campbell. Got it? Campbell. Ask him to come and see you in your room. You will identify him by a slight tear in the left-hand top pocket of his uniform. Watch out for dictaphones. That's all, but make your talk with Campbell sound convincing to the Japs. They will be listening in."

Blake hastily swallowed his drink and made an excuse to get away. The O.N.I. contact man reverted to his role of a drunk and loudly called him back to "have another with me."

"Campbell" was duly contacted when Blake arrived at his Honolulu hotel where, in his room, he found that bugging devices had been planted just as the O.N.I. man had indicated. He had to admit that the Japanese were being extremely thorough in testing him out. The meeting with "Campbell" went off smoothly and Blake took care to ensure that they sat down close to where the bugging devices had been fixed. There then ensued a further display of acting pyrotechnics for the benefit of the Japanese. Blake asked "Campbell" to provide certain information for him and the latter, after a suitable show of being both shocked and frightened, promised to provide this.

Eventually some bogus information of no real value was handed over to Blake and he passed it on to the Japanese who duly paid him. He was then told to return to the U.S.A. The O.N.I. handled this affair brilliantly, but their efforts were almost ruined by the incompetence of the F.B.I. The latter were naturally more interested in finding out full details of the sabotage programme which, they believed, Tachibana was planning all along the west coast of the U.S.A. in the event of war. They learned that some of Tachibana's agents were being given instructions in the technique of blowing up bridges and power stations. But Tachibana was, of course, fully aware that he was being shadowed by the F.B.I., though he had no inkling that the O.N.I. were on his trail. So eager were the F.B.I. to

arrest Tachibana of their own accord that they never kept the
O.N.I. properly informed.

From the naval point of view it would probably have been
useful if Blake had been allowed to carry on as an "agent" of
the Japanese right up to the moment of the Pearl Harbor attack.
Instead, as *Time Magazine* tersely reported at the time, the
F.B.I. arrested "two Japanese and Al Blake, a U.S. citizen in
Los Angeles... Al turned out to be no spy, but a hero."[1]

The two Japanese arrested were Tachibana and Kono. They
were both charged with conspiracy against the United States
on behalf of a foreign state. Bail of 50,000 dollars was demanded before either man could be released. The Japanese
Consul in Los Angeles immediately produced this sum to get
Tachibana free and he was speedily "sprung" from captivity.
Kono could not raise the bail money and nobody came to his
rescue.

Notwithstanding the O.N.I.'s coup in the Blake-Kono affair,
Japanese Naval Intelligence were able to claim substantial successes throughout this period. As in the case of Al Blake, their
attention was increasingly directed to American bases in Hawaii. In the beginning the director of naval intelligence in
Tokyo was worried about using too many native-born spies in
Hawaii. He was afraid they would be easily recognised and
suspected. So he suggested that the department might recruit
some agents of German origin. In November, 1936, the anti-
Comintern Pact had been signed by Germany, Italy and Japan,
which in itself provided one good reason for seeking aid from
Germany on the intelligence front. Professor Karl Haushofer,
a close friend of Rudolf Hess, Hitler's deputy, had spent some
time in Japan prior to World War I as a military instructor.
However, it would appear that Haushofer interested the Japanese in rather more than purely military matters. Certainly his
writings on geopolitics and his theses on astrology were highly
popular in Tokyo. In 1933–4 his son, Albrecht, was appointed
as an unofficial adviser to the *Dienststelle Ribbentrop*, a bureau
under the immediate control of the man who eventually became
Ambassador to Britain and then Foreign Minister of the Third
Reich, though Hess was its actual supervisor. Then, shortly
after the Anti-Comintern Pact was signed, Albrecht Haushofer
was sent to Japan at Hess's suggestion.

It was to young Haushofer that the Japanese turned for help
in recruiting agents in the Pacific area. In return they seem to
have given him some insight into the workings of their own

intelligence services, though this was of a very general nature. Haushofer made two interesting comments in his report to Hess on the subject of Japanese espionage: "It is typical of the conscientiousness of the more senior of Japanese intelligence officers that they study not only the languages of the countries in which they are going to operate, but their literature and culture as well. This may not seem to be worth all the effort, yet one can see how sometimes it can be turned to advantage . . . Each Japanese when overseas acts as a spy almost instinctively and similarly in his own country he sees himself as something of a spy-catcher."[2]

Three agents were recommended by Haushofer to the Japanese, though it seems probable that their names were originally provided for him by Hess. They were ostensibly a German family of father, mother and "daughter" named Keuhn, but in reality the "daughter" was Ruth Kaethe Suse, bearing no relationship to the Keuhns. Dr. Bernard Keuhn had learned to speak English fluently when he was made a prisoner-of-war in World War I, during which he served in the Navy as a wireless operator. All three were German Secret Service operators. They had settled in Honolulu and were therefore ideally placed for the kind of intelligence-gathering which the Japanese required. Dr. Keuhn's cover for such activities was his purported interest in the Japanese language and culture and the search for Hawaii's prehistoric remains. This provided him with the excuse to make frequent boat trips to the outlying islands of Hawaii. His wife acted as courier for information which she gave to Naval Intelligence in Tokyo on periodical visits. As for Ruth Keuhn, a gregarious and attractive girl, she fully played her part by making friends with American naval officers at parties and on the tennis court. Not surprisingly she married an American.

The Keuhns did well by spying for both Germany and Japan at the same time, and it has been estimated that they made something like £25,000 in six years in payments received from each country. They arrived in Hawaii in 1935 and it was not until 1937 that Dr. Keuhn was ordered to go to Tokyo through his German masters. In 1939 th Keuhns moved to Pearl Harbor where Ruth started a beauty parlour and learned a great deal by listening to the gossip of her clients, mainly U.S. officers' wives.

The Japanese Naval Intelligence Bureau had no intention of relying on foreigners for their service from Hawaii. Admiral Koroku Yamamoto insisted on having a full-time, naval-trained spy in Hawaii, one who could not only gather intelligence himself, but direct the gathering of intelligence through others in the islands. The man he personally chose was a twenty-eight-year-old ensign of the Japanese Navy, the son of a police officer. Takeo Yoshikawa was a highly dedicated naval officer who had been forced to retire from the Navy because of ill health. He had been assigned to the American desk of Japanese Naval Intelligence and had for four years studied English. Yamamoto was a brilliant naval strategist who wanted to ensure that he had all the requisite intelligence in the event of a war with the U.S.A. His view was that if Japan went to war with America, there was no chance of winning it unless the U.S. Pacific Fleet could be destroyed at the outset.

Takeo Yoshikawa was transferred temporarily from the Japanese Navy to the Foreign Office. Throughout this period of his service he was not only given intensive courses in colloquial English, but a detailed briefing for spying in Hawaii. In August, 1941, he was sent to Honolulu under the cover name of vice-consul Ito Morimura. He was ordered to report in coded messages to the consul. In many respects Yoshikawa was an unwilling spy in that he desperately wanted to return to active service. Yet though not a professional spy, he was adaptable, versatile, imaginative and he obtained results.

What he lacked in experience he compensated for in sheer determination to excel. He had been thoroughly briefed in ciphers, and espionage techniques, but he developed these in his own way. He even went swimming to get information on beach gradients and the height of tides, memorising every detail. He spent his evenings in bars around the waterfront, talking to American sailors and trying to obtain information from Nisei girls (born of Japanese parents in American territory). One of his favourite haunts was the Shuncho-ro Restaurant which had an excellent view of the harbor.

Yoshikawa's messages to Tokyo (at least those he did not regard as top secret) were sent in the diplomatic Purple Code, which was read by the Americans. Even when he included a few pithy comments in such routine cables of naval intelligence the U.S. authorities still did not seem to realise their importance. In due course Yoshikawa contacted Dr. Keuhn and almost instantly the Japanese mistrusted the German agent. He determined to use his own carefully built-up intelligence network to check the reliability of the non-Japanese agent. Yoshikawa reported back to Tokyo that Keuhn was first and foremost a German agent and that he would not hesitate to betray the Japanese cause if the one conflicted with the other.

Yet cautious as he was in many respects Yoshikawa also took the view that sometimes ostentation is the best cover. He was a *bon viveur* and this he exploited to the full, his drinking and promiscuity being little short of exhibitionist. True, he was watched by U.S. Intelligence and they learned all about his extremely busy love life by tapping his telephones. But they never realised that he was the prime Japanese naval agent in Hawaii or that he was keeping Tokyo informed of every American warship's movements in Hawaiian waters. A likeable and amusing character, he is said to have made the sage remark that "a spy without a love life is a spy doomed", according to one naval colleague. What he meant, of course, was that any man who was as occupied with the pursuit of Venus as himself would be less likely to be suspected of espionage. He also claimed that U.S. Naval Intelligence officers were voyeurs first and spies a bad second. Obviously he believed that an ardent and persistent love life was an admirable cover: he would prolong his telephone calls to girl friends in order to keep the U.S. phone-tappers unduly busy. He also avidly studied U.S. naval and technical reports which were freely available as well as a mass of technical journals. Having an eye for detail and a mass observation technique for gathering the names, numbers and technical idiosyncrasies of ships, he worked closely with the Keuhns while never involving himself too deeply in their affairs.

His views on the importance of mass observation of trivialities ranged from studying the food and drink preferences of high level U.S. naval officers to repeated censuses of the garbage bins at Pearl Harbor. He reckoned to know approximately how many U.S. ships were in at a given time simply from statistics on garbage bins, and a prolonged study of these provided a pattern of movements. His talents were surprisingly versatile and, in the best Japanese tradition, he never hesitated to adopt a menial role as a disguise. Sometimes this took the form of posing as a barefooted Filipino labourer, while at others he flamboyantly played the role of a Japanese night club "Champagne Charlie". He was a skilled photographer, taking pictures of U.S. ships from the hills and even hiring a small plane to obtain aerial photographs of the hangars at Wheeler and Hickam airfields.

If Yoshikawa had not sent a fair amount of his communications by the Purple Code, he would have been suspected. Some of these messages contained information which should have worried the Americans, but they seem never to have realised the implications. The Americans believed that the Japanese were not specially interested in naval movements around Hawaii any more than anywhere else in the world for the simple reason that all their other embassies and consulates supplied Tokyo with just as much naval intelligence as from Pearl Harbor and Honolulu. The truth is that this was part of the Japanese cover plan: provide as much general naval intelligence from Stockholm and Cape Town, Naples and Tangier as was sent from Hawaii.

Yoshikawa also relied on the fact that the Americans were often slow to decipher his messages because of a shortage of Japanese translators. For this reason he speeded up transmission and asked Tokyo if he could report three times a week instead of once. Often the Americans were three weeks in arrears in deciphering such messages.

But on really vital matters Yoshikawa had other means of communication, because he expected that sooner or later he might be interned, especially if war occurred. He also organised secret communications in Hawaii itself. For example, he received messages from Dr. Keuhn and others of his spy network by a system of bonfires and house lights; the figure 7 (representing, say, the number of ships of a certain class) would be symbolised by two lights shown in the window of a house on Lanikai Beach at a certain period of the night, or by two sheets during a similar period in daytime. Bonfires were sometimes lit on distant hills, and Yoshikawa also showed ingenuity in having a code system disguised in advertisements for "wanted" items broadcast over K.G.M.B. Radio Station. By this means he managed to reduce personal contacts with his agents to a minimum.

All Yoshikawa's messages to Tokyo in the Purple system were signed in the name of his Consul-General, Nagai Kita. From 27 March, 1941, right up to the time of the attack on Pearl Harbor the Japanese secret agent poured out a steady stream of intelligence. It is fascinating to study how Japanese Naval Intelligence, under the direction of Admiral Yamamoto, planned that first devastating attack. A key question which Tokyo put to Yoshikawa was "on which day of the week are there the most ships in Pearl Harbor?" He replied: "Sunday.

Kimmel invariably brings his fleet into Pearl Harbor each week-end."

They were also interested in how the warships were moored and Yoshikawa informed them that the U.S. battleships were usually moored in pairs. Yamamoto had called for urgent reports from his naval attachés in London and Rome as to what lessons could be learned from the British Fleet Air Arm's torpedo attack on Italian warships in Taranto Harbor. The reports showed that the depth of water in Taranto Harbor was forty-two feet or less. This had always been considered too shallow for aerial torpedoes, so Yamamoto wanted to know how these weapons had been fired. Intelligence from his agents in both Rome and London confirmed that wooden fins had been attached to the torpedoes so that they would run on an even course through shallow waters. So Yamamoto was determined to find out whether this tactic could be applied against the Americans in Hawaii, but this meant finding out whether they had adopted anti-torpedo nets in the harbor at Pearl Harbor.

Now while these inquiries were specifically sent to Yoshikawa, they were also made in Berlin and Rome. Possibly, too, Yamamoto may have thought there was a better chance of obtaining some of the information he wanted from the Keuhns. He need not have worried. Yoshikawa eventually came up with the news that Admiral Husband E. Kimmel, C-in-C, U.S. Fleet, Hawaii, had rejected plans for torpedo nets in the harbor "on the grounds that they 'would restrict boat traffic by narrowing the channel'." By this decision he doomed many ships.[3]

But through their double-agent, Dusko Popov, the Yugoslav who operated for Britain's Double-Cross System, British Intelligence learned that the Japanese were inquiring via the Germans for detailed information about ammunition dumps, mines, airfields, naval installations, submarine depots, torpedo protection nets at Pearl Harbour. The questionnaire on these subjects was so detailed that Popov was convinced that this could only mean that the Japanese were planning a surprise attack on the U.S.A. But the British, having obtained this item of intelligence, blundered by failing to pass it on to the President of the United States direct and to the O.N.I. Instead, incredibly, it was sent to Edgar Hoover, head of the F.B.I. This was to prove disastrous. Not only did Hoover mistrust Popov and suspect he was simply a Nazi agent who had fooled the British (something which the latter could and ought to have shown was totally untrue), but he made no effort to follow up the evidence provided by the Pearl Harbor questionnaire. Hoover denounced Popov as "an immoral decadent" to one British intelligence officer. When asked why he made this false assertion, he replied: "Look at the man's goddam code-name, 'Tricycle'! It means he likes to go to bed with two girls at once."[4]

And so the one vital warning was ignored and the massacre of Pearl Harbor occurred exactly as the Japanese had planned. In the meantime they obtained all the answers to the questionnaire so carefully prepared. Yoshikawa not only filed information, but even compiled his own highly specialised maps of Hawaii, specially designed so that on the strength of his coded messages the positions of the U.S. Fleet could be noted in Tokyo with exactitude. Colonel Allison Ind has told how once, disguised as a Filipino labourer, Yoshikawa had swum "to a point inside the guarded zone. But the sentry had been alert. He had been an uncomfortably good shot."[5]

On 5 December, 1941, Yoshikawa was still passing messages to Tokyo, indicating that three battleships had arrived in Pearl Harbor, making a total of eight anchored therein. These last minute messages were speedily relayed by the Foreign Ministry in Tokyo to the Naval Ministry. The following day he reported that on the previous evening "the battleship *Wyoming* and one sweeper entered port. Ships at anchor today are 9 battleships, 3 minesweepers, 3 light cruisers, 17 destroyers. Ships in dock are 4 light cruisers, 2 destroyers. Heavy cruisers and carriers have all left. It appears that no air reconnaissance is being conducted by the Fleet Air Arm."

No doubt he was in too much of a hurry to get the information passed to check every detail. In fact he made one mistake, naming the *Wyoming* when it should have been the *Utah*, and missing the presence of two heavy cruisers."[6]

On the fatal night before the attack on Pearl Harbor twenty-seven Japanese submarines had surrounded the area. Before he was interned by the Americans, as he knew he must be, Yoshikawa burnt his code book and all compromising material in his possession. It was not until long afterwards that it was realised he had been the ace Japanese spy in Hawaii. Under the arrangements for an exchange of diplomats between two warring nations he was duly released from internment and returned to Japan. There he worked on in Naval Intelligence throughout the war.

The Keuhns were not so fortunate. Bernard Keuhn was still sending out signals even during the attack on Pearl Harbor. From the attic window of his home overlooking the bay he sent light signals to the Japanese Consul, Otojiro Okudo, who was watching for them. These messages were then relayed to the Japanese naval commander. But an American intelligence officer saw the lights flashing from the Keuhn household and promptly informed the F.B.I.

Dr. Keuhn and Ruth were arrested together and later Mrs. Keuhn was rounded up. Bernard Keuhn was sentenced to death, but this was later commuted to 50 years' imprisonment. But in 1946, largely because of information he gave to the U.S. authorities, he was released. His wife and "daughter" were deported after the war.

18

The Intelligence Probe in S.E. Asia

"Every advantage lay with the enemy. There had been minute pre-war study of the ground and conditions. Careful large-scale plans and secret infiltration of agents, including even hidden reserves of bicycles for Japanese cyclists, had been made"
Sir Winston Churchill,
The Second World War

THIS WAS HOW Churchill succinctly summed up the background to the fall of Singapore in World War II. Yet not even he could have known how the Japanese intelligence probe into not only Singapore, but the whole of South East Asia had commenced three decades earlier. Japanese espionage in Singapore had begun in World War I when their officers were able to go all over the colony quite freely. This is not to suggest that any attack on Singapore was being planned at that time, but those officers observed every detail and reported what they saw.

A great deal of this intelligence-gathering in S.E. Asia was devoted to commercial espionage in the late twenties. There was a positive link between this and the tremendous trade drive launched a few years later. From about 1930 onwards the Japanese, as a result of clever assessment of market trends, consistently undersold the Western powers enabling their trade to rise by more than 30 per cent. But as far as intelligence-collecting was concerned, no subject was left unexamined. For example in the 1930s a team of Japanese medical officers was sent out to the Dutch East Indies to study sanitation conditions

and disease statistics in the territory. Their detailed and conscientious reports enabled the Japanese authorities to plan how
to avoid outbreaks of disease among their troops when the
invasion came.

One of these doctors made another discovery: discussions
with Dutch officers and a census-taking in some of the local
brothels revealed that a large number of the upper-class Javanese working in the Dutch administration were homosexuals.
This information was used to launch a number of male brothels
in Java in order first to lure and then recruit Javanese admin-
istrators as spies. Japanese agents were active in the Dutch East
Indies throughout this period, their resident director being a
prominent merchant named Tomegoro Yoshizumi who was
eventually ordered to return to Japan when the Dutch authorities
became suspicious of him. Japanese fishing vessels operated
as the ever-watchful third arm of naval intelligence around the
Dutch East Indies and this probe by the fishing fleets was even
extended to Singapore.

One report received by the Dutch was that two Japanese
reserve officers had operated in the disguise of laundrymen in
the hope of finding documents carelessly left in tropical uniforms of Dutch officers. Certainly when the Japanese secured
a timber concession near Balikpapan in Borneo in 1938, they
took the opportunity to clear tracts of forest land which were
scheduled as secret landing grounds for aircraft. Apart from
this they obtained details of nearly all the Dutch air strips. John
Gunther, who travelled all over S.E. Asia at this time, told the
story that "when a Japanese cruiser visited Cheribon, Java,
they cleverly invited the native population aboard and secretly
recruited agents."[1]

British security in Singapore was sound enough in a straightforward, unimaginative way, prior to World War II, but it left
much to be desired. Indeed it was so unimaginative that it was
quite easy for the Japanese to exploit it. Precautions were taken
to keep people out of defense areas and all dockyard workers
were fingerprinted. But the authorities failed absolutely to note
the fact that the Japanese restaurant, the Tamagawa, had a
perfect view of the Johore beach, and that close to the Singapore
air base at Pongan there were Japanese beer gardens and fish
ponds.

Complacent British intelligence officers, chortling over their
gin-slings, would laugh at the Japanese fishing crews who took
soundings in waters which, they claimed, had been already

accurately charted by the Admiralty and such charts were freely obtainable. I asked a Japanese naval officer about this and his reply was: "Well, I am afraid they laughed too easily. In the first place what they said about the charts was perfectly true—up to a point. They were easily available, but, as you as an ex-naval officer will know, charts are always being amended and the navigating officer is always kept busy making these corrections on his own set of charts. So, lesson number one, all charts must be checked at intervals with personal observation. Of course, we need not have taken soundings quite as ostentatiously as we did. We need not have taken soundings at all as a general rule. But your people were convinced that soundings were all that we took and so didn't take us seriously. The soundings were a cover for other observations."

During some Far East Fleet manoeuvres in 1938 a Japanese freighter, *Borneo Maru*, dropped anchor off Blakang Mati, one of the islands defences some distance from the Singapore docks. Because of this the British decided to alter the whole operational programme.

Extraordinarily enough, Churchill, who in the pre-war days kept his own mini-intelligence service on events in the outside world, seems to have been singularly ill-informed on Singapore. Colonel Masanobu Tsuji, who was chief of Operations and Planning Staff of the 25th Japanese Army in Malaya, has stated that "Singapore had no rear defence—a fact unknown to Churchill at the time". One can only assume that he was disgracefully misled, because he was anxious to learn all he could about Japanese activities in other parts of the world. On 17 February, 1941, for instance, Churchill was inquiring of General Ismay, his military adviser: "What are the arrangements in British Columbia for dealing with the Japanese colony there should Japan attack? The matter is of course for the Canadian Government, but it would be interesting to know whether adequate forces are available in that part of the dominion. About thirty years ago when there were anti-Japanese riots, the Japanese showed themselves so strong and so well organised as to be able to take complete control."[2]

Even in 1941 when pre-war tension was at its height in Singapore security was abysmally slack. At an officers' club in the naval base was an Asian steward named Shawan, who had been there for years, was regarded as markedly pro-British and had an excellent record. He was responsible for selecting and employing the other club servants. It was generally assumed that he was Chinese, but the counter-intelligence people had never bothered to check up on him.

One day a visitor to the club commented on the careless talk that was carried on in the presence of this steward. He suggested, despite protests from his brother officers, that he should invent some top secret information and mention it in fairly loud conversation when Shawan was in attendance. "We shall then see what he does," said the visitor who had himself been appalled by the poor quality of security measures in the colony as a whole.

Sure enough Shawan was seen to make a quick note on a winelist, after which he tore off the corner of the page on which he had made this note: "PW end November", a fairly obvious reference to the projected visit of H.M.S. *Prince of Wales*, which the visitor had conjured up. Yet it was only the insistence of this man which caused the club members to get hold of the scrap of paper and question the steward. It then transpired that his identity was that of Colonel Tsugunori Kadomatsu, of the Japanese Army, who had been working for military intelligence ever since 1930 when he had been sent to West Point to study American training methods. It was after this, and on the strength of his fluent English, that the Japanese sent him to Singapore from which post he had kept Tokyo informed with a weekly stream of intelligence.

Colonel Tsuji was one of the most dynamic of the younger Army officers and, for a time at least, had been a member of the Society of the Cherry and a supporter of the East Asia League theories of that secret organisation. However, he was never one of the extreme nationalists and it is understood that when there was a pre-war conspiracy to assassinate the Prime Minister, Captain Tsuji, as he then was, reported the plot to the War Ministry.

It was Tsuji who commanded the group of officers who planned Japan's seventy-day campaign for the conquest of Malaya and the invasion of Singapore. On 1 January, 1941, he set up the Taiwan Army No. 82 (Research Section) Unit, under the direct command of General Itagaki. It comprised only thirty people. Previously he and his team had experienced life in the sub-arctic regions of Manchuria. Now they had to live and work in tropical jungles under the most primitive conditions. "For the first time in history," he stated, "an army carried out a blitzkrieg on bicycles."[3]

Using all manner of disguises, this team infiltrated British colonial territory and made some of the most thorough topographical and military reports of all time. They decided that whereas Singapore was well defended on the sea side, it was defenceless in the rear facing Johore province. Once again it was the courage and discipline of officers in undertaking espionage in conditions of great discomfort which helped to pave the way for victory. There was a spy such as Major Asaeda, who, disguised as a coolie, going without food and sleep, infiltrated into Singapore, Thailand and crossed the Malayan frontier, "bringing back a valuable report on conditions".[4]

Sergeant "Fukui" (this seems to have been his code-name) was made the leader of a special espionage squad to keep Johore Strait under constant surveillance during the ten days before the attack on Singapore. His duties were to obtain details of enemy positions and to study the ebb and flow of tides, a factor which was always given a high priority by Japanese Intelligence.

Later Colonel Tsuji was promoted to the Operations Division of the Imperial General Staff. When war ended he was listed by the British as a war criminal, though there was little hard evidence to suggest he should have been dubbed as such. He avoided arrest by disguising himself as a Buddhist monk and in this pose travelled around South East Asia and China for three years after the surrender. He only returned to Japan after the war crimes trials had ended, publishing a book, *Underground Escape*, in which he described his experiences while on the run.

In 1951 he was arrested for violating the purge ordinance by making a political speech in which he expounded neutralist theories. Following this he was elected to the Diet with a large majority as an Independent and later he joined the Government Party. He was associated with right-wing politicians and associations advocating rearmament. His conception of neutralism, however, seems to have been quite different from the definition of that creed in the West. In 1955 he visited China and Russia; on his return he spoke favourably of the former and extremely critically of the U.S.S.R. He organised a Self Defence League in 1953, insisting that Japan should hold aloof from both the U.S.A. and Russia. According to a Japanese Intelligence report, he gave a secret address in the early fifties in which he stated that the U.S.A. was likely to lose World War III and that Japan must not be involved in such a holocaust.

While the Japanese had convinced themselves that S.E. Asia

was theirs for the taking and presented few problems, as early as 1938 intelligence officers inside China had indicated that there was a very real danger that the war in China could drag on indefinitely and become a drain on Japan both financially, economically and militarily. It was about this time that Chinese and Japanese agents met secretly on the neutral territory of Portuguese-held Macao to seek a way out of this prolonged and totally unsatisfactory war. The truth was that many spokesmen at the League of Nations, hypocritically not anxious to do anything to stop the war beyond making speeches, only aggravated the situation. The countries who made fiery anti-Japanese speeches at Geneva only strengthened the hands of the extreme nationalists in Tokyo. General Sir Ian Hamilton summed it up when he declared that "all the trouble in the Far East is the fault of those who forced us to break our alliance with Japan. The League has done much, doubtless unwittingly, to blow fire into the blaze first by irritating the Japanese, then encouraging the Chinese, and now it wants us to pull their chestnuts out of the fire." This speech was warmly received in Tokyo. Yet it is significant of the strength of moderate opinion in Japan even then that the government declined to be hustled into leaving the League of Nations. They reiterated that they had no intention of repudiating the Kellogg Pact or the Nine-Power Treaty. It was not until December, 1935, that the Washington Naval Treaty was abrogated by Japan.

Yoshio Kodama was one of those agents in the field who felt that a settlement could and should be made with the Chinese. Born in 1911, he was an active member of the Patriotic Youth Corps before being sent to China as what was euphemistically described as an "irregular official". In China he founded the Kodama Agency and is said to have made a fortune by import-export deals. When he went to China he had hardly any money at all, but when the war ended his assets in Japan were worth more than £250,000. One of his outstanding achievements was in providing an uninterrupted flow of supplies to the Japanese Navy. He started life as a factory worker and at one time was a fervent radical. When he was eighteen he volunteered to approach the Emperor to ask him to provide work for a million unemployed. Later he was arrested on various occasions for his ultranationalist activities and some say he was dispatched to China as a secret agent in the hope that this would keep him occupied and curb his political ardour.

The situation in the Sino-Japanese War was always puzzling

to an outsider. While the armies battled against one another, the secret agents were frequently making undercover deals, sometimes exchanging prisoners, more often helping one another with trade bargains, probing all the time for a solution which would enable both sides to reduce fighting to a minimum. With hindsight the Japanese would probably agree that they ought to have achieved a peace settlement without loss of face before 1936. The Western powers were as much to blame as anyone for this not actually being achieved.

Morris "Two-Gun" Cohen, Chiang Kai-shek's Secret Service officer, sums up the atmosphere of this unreal wheeling-dealing in his stories of the Japanese Army deciding to put an end to arms trafficking by occupying the Hong Kong frontier. Cohen was watched by one of a team of Japanese spies. One of them called on Cohen in his office. "He was the most anonymous bloke I'd ever seen. I've always prided myself on being able to tell a lot from a man's appearance. With this chap you couldn't tell a thing, neither his race, his class, nor even his age within twenty years. I guessed he was a Levantine of some sort, but he might have come from anywhere between Gibraltar and Manila." The Japanese agent wanted to make a deal—for Cohen to obtain a permit for the export to Shanghai of one million dollarsworth of raw sugar, while he would arrange the delivery to Chiang's China of one million dollarsworth of gasoline. Cohen commented that this was "one of the best bargains I ever made".[5]

Much has been said about the Japanese use of drugs both in the financing of espionage teams and in undermining the morale of the Chinese. Richard Hughes, a former correspondent of British and Australian newspapers in Tokyo, Hong Kong and other parts of the Far East in this period, has asserted that "the Japanese military used drugs deliberately and systematically to debase the Chinese people during the pre-Pearl Harbour days."[6] But then so did the British in the mid-nineteenth century, though for sordid commercial reasons only. What drug trafficking there was was usually aimed at winning over informants among the Chinese and bribing them with a regular supply of drugs. Cigarettes known as Gold Bat were sold in China and were said to contain doses of opium and heroin: these were to be seen in many of the brothels where prostitutes were engaged as spies for the Japanese. The opium cigarettes were manufactured by the Japanese in Formosa and smuggled into so-called "Free" China.

Hong Kong was no different from Singapore when it came to the crunch. The Japanese took over the New Territories and Kowloon in four days and the whole island in two weeks. Judging from the highly efficient round-up of suspected Chinese saboteurs and undercover agents, intelligence had been planned just as effectively here as in Singapore. But in Hong Kong female agents on the Japanese side were more in evidence than in Singapore. Emily Hahn has told how she met a mysterious character named "Bubbles" just after the surrender of Hong Kong. "She sent word to me through a Russian girl I knew pretty well that she would like me to come to tea at the Gloucester Hotel," wrote Emily Hahn. By this time the hotel had been taken over by the Japanese and named the Matsubara. At the party were three Chinese boys who, along with Bubbles plied her with questions: "Bubbles was certainly that mythical creature, a beautiful female spy, and for the Japanese. She was investigating me! . . . Had I heard from any of my friends in the concentration camp? Did I know any method of getting word in to them?" Later Bubbles came to call on her and "every time I turned my back she hastily took a photograph of me with a small camera she had concealed in her handbag. . . . I lost patience after a while and opened the cupboard where I kept my photograph albums. 'Here,' I said, tossing her a portrait of myself . . . Bubbles calmly thanked me and . . . said 'will you autograph this, honey?' "[7]

Emily Hahn managed to pick up scraps of information about Bubbles. She had a safe-conduct pass bearing Japanese seals, her protector was the Japanese manager of Hong Kong Food Control Office. Apparently she had been a Japanese agent long before the war, specialising in making friends with American seamen and British soldiers who talked freely to her in the belief that she was one of Chiang's supporters. Later in the war Bubbles became a hostess at the Parisian Grill in Hong Kong, which was owned by a Turk and his Russian wife. One day the Japanese police walked into the restaurant and informed the owner that he had a requisitioning order.

And the new Manager? Bubbles, of course. Who else?

19

Soviet Network in Japan

"It was brilliant detective work by the
Kempei Tai which finally broke the Sorge
Ring in Japan"

Allen Dulles

SO MUCH HAS been written about that notorious double agent, Richard Sorge, that the author must be pardoned if the name inevitably occurs yet again in this book. Sorge was but one man, albeit the all-important one, in various Soviet spy networks which the Japanese managed to track down in the 1940s.

It was arduous work calling for enormous patience, skilled interrogation of numerous informants and suspects and, above all, intelligence from Japanese spy centres all around the globe. In keeping an eye on the Russians the major Japanese listening posts were Vienna, Sofia, Istanbul and Ankara, Geneva and Zurich and, of course, Shanghai and Manchuria. It was a prolonged battlé, but a measure of the extent to which Japan maintained the upper hand can be gauged by the fact that as late as April, 1941, she was able to sign a five-year Pact of Neutrality with the Soviet Union. This solved the Russian problem as far as Japan was concerned.

Russia was much more worried about the possibility of a Japanese attack from Manchuria or elsewhere between 1940 and early 1941 than about a threat from Germany. One of the reasons for this concern was that the Soviet Union's intelligence from Japan had been beset by failures until the arrival of Sorge and even then Sorge was regarded with suspicion on account of his being a double-agent and a close friend of European agents of the U.S.S.R. recently liquidated on Stalin's orders. The *Kempei Tai* had kept a tight watch on any potential Soviet spies, especially those attached to the Tass News Agency. Captain Malcolm Kennedy, the Reuter correspondent in Tokyo, states that he knew all three successive Tass correspondents in that capital: "I came to know Romm and his successor, Nagi, quite well during their respective periods as Tass correspondent in Tokyo. I liked both of them. But I was struck by the curious reasoning of these two extremely intelligent journalists: when Soviet hopes and wishes conflicted with reality, they always tended to give priority to the former in their assessment of any particular situation."[1]

Perhaps this was why both Romm and Nagi were liquidated on trumped-up charges during the late 1930s. They were not the only Soviet intelligence officers in Japan to suffer; both Colonel Rink, the military attaché, and Golkovitch, the G.P.U. man, were also purged in November, 1937, along with one other agent in Japan, Constantin Yurenev. Obviously something had gone seriously amiss with Russian intelligence in the Far East for all these to be liquidated on orders from the Politburo. From then on Russia depended almost entirely on the network set up by Richard Sorge, who was a G.R.U. agent (that is, Soviet Military Intelligence) as distinct from the N.K.V.D., as the predecessor to the K.G.B. was known. Richard Sorge, born in 1895 at Baku on the Caspian Sea, was the son of a German father and a Russian mother. He had served in the German Army in World War I, then joined the Communist Party and was recruited into Russia's spy network in 1924–5. He was sent out to the Far East to organise the "China Unit" and became Resident Director of Military Intelligence for the Far East. It was Sorge who impressed on Moscow the absolute importance of obtaining detailed intelligence from Japan. It was also his suggestion that he should return to Germany, establish contacts with the leading Nazis and then go to Japan as a Soviet spy, but ostensibly seeming to be in the German camp.

That the paranoically suspicious Stalin should agree to such a risky undertaking was perhaps an indication of how desperate the Russians were to improve their knowledge of what was going on in Japan. Stalin was fully aware that Sorge had been one of the best friends of Ignace Reiss, another secret service operator who had been liquidated on Stalin's personal orders.

At the same time the Soviet Union was perturbed at various attempts by the Japanese to penetrate their own secrets. They were well aware that a mere handful of Japanese in Afghanistan had cycled into that territory and were selling their bicycles for nominal sums in order to win friends and hire spies. A fairly minor and harmless venture in spying, but one which alarmed the Russians out of all proportion to the actual incidents. There had also been rather more serious leakages of Soviet secrets to Tokyo via Switzerland and a number of cases of Russians defecting to Japan via Manchuria.

There is no doubt that there was cooperation between the Germans and the Japanese on such matters as intelligence on Pearl Harbor, as has been seen from the mission to the U.S.A. of Dusko Popov. The questionnaire which he took over to America was so vital to Japanese naval interests that it is incredible that its importance was ignored by Hoover just as it is equally incomprehensible that the British did not pass it on to the O.N.I. The Germans also used the Japanese as intermediaries with their own agents in Britain prior to Pearl Harbor. The agent, Wulf Schmidt, parachuted by the Germans into the English countryside in 1940 and known by the code-name of "Tate", was captured and "turned" into a double-agent who, throughout the rest of the war, transmitted false information back to Germany. His *Abwehr* masters continued to send him funds, all of which fell into British hands. Once, having received a radio message from Hamburg, "Tate" went to London to receive funds from an intermediary. The money was passed to him in notes hidden inside a copy of a newspaper while "Tate" was a passenger on a bus sitting alongside a Japanese attaché from the London Embassy. British intelligence officers picked up the trail, identifying the Japanese as Lieutenant-Commander Mitinory Yosii.[2]

What worried Moscow far more than anything else was the constant fear that they were being fed false information on Japan. By early 1941 they knew all about Britain's "Double Cross" game (the "turning" of German agents to work for the British) through their own sleeper agents inside the British Security Services. Their greatest fear was that somewhere along the line bogus intelligence might be supplied to them on the same lines. Then, in the latter part of 1941, with the Germans launching an attack on Moscow itself, another and far greater fear manifested itself. This was that highly accurate intelligence on their own dispositions, troop movements and military problems was being relayed to the *Abwehr* from Japanese sources.

A great deal of intelligence was somehow escaping from anti-Stalinist senior officers in the Red Army. It was known that there was a leakage from them to a Russian general who had escaped to Vienna. But in September, 1941, the Japanese had obtained photocopies of Soviet files which had been captured by the Germans, the kind of material which they had asked the Germans for in vain a year previously. The material came in a variety of ways, via a senior Red Army officer who had defected to Japan in 1939, from unofficial German sources and from agents in the Balkans. In many respects it was one of Japan's most successful intelligence coups of the era. Yet the full truth of this is still difficult to ascertain. Was there a two-way agreement between the Japanese and Admiral Canaris, chief of the *Abwehr*, for an exchange of intelligence on Russia, something totally unknown to the Nazi hierarchy? Or did the Japanese share their secret intelligence on the Soviet Union with the Germans through their man in Sofia, Isono Kiyosho, a journalist operating in Bulgaria and the Balkan states?

How good was Kiyosho and what were his sources? Not even the intelligence section of *Fremde Heere Ost* (Germany's Eastern Armies) knew about the Japanese journalist. But it was apparent that suddenly the most astonishingly detailed intelligence on the Red Armies was getting through to the Russian department of the *Abwehr* from an agent whose code-name was "Max". At first German generals felt the news was too detailed and extensive to be true and they suspected fake material was being planted on them. "Max" insisted on protecting his source. At this stage of the war Japan needed more than anything else to be able to manipulate both the Soviet Union and Germany and there is some indication that, by mid-1942 at any rate, there were signs of such string-pulling in both Berlin and Moscow. A report of the *Forschungsamt* (Research Agency) of 11 May, 1942, stated that "the Japanese Embassy in Moscow is undertaking attempts designed to bring about a separate peace between Germany and the Soviet Union. We have learned this from telegrams we have intercepted and decoded. . . . We will not have peace with the Soviet Union until she is beaten."[3]

In the meantime, of course, the Sorge Ring in Tokyo had scored many successes in the Japanese capital. Though the *Kempei Tai* relentlessly hunted down all possessors of radio transmitting sets, somehow by using couriers in and out of the country and ordering the Ring's radio set to be moved after each transmission, Sorge kept one jump ahead of his hunters. The Fourth Bureau arranged the courier traffic, a very slow business usually through Hong Kong or Shanghai. But by the summer of 1941 Inspector Osashi of the secret police had become convinced that a major foreign spy ring was operating in Tokyo. Japanese radio-detectors reported that they suspected the presence of an illegal radio transmitter somewhere in the Tokyo area. But at that time they were not certain whether the spy network operating this set was American, British or Soviet.

Allen Dulles, the master-mind behind the U.S.A.'s intelligence organisation in Switzerland in World War I, was full of admiration for what he called "the brilliant detective work" of the Japanese secret police in tracking down the Sorge Ring. It was the result of painstaking inquiries and clever interrogation in hunting down native communists, who had been suspected of espionage. One such man who was questioned was Ito Ritsu, who had nothing whatsoever to do with spying. Though in this sense he had nothing to fear, he thought it would be wise to pretend to cooperate with the police. He did this, while being interrogated, by naming a number of people as suspects, choosing those who had deserted from the underground Communist Party, or anyone he personally disliked.

One such person he named was a Madame Kitabayashi, who had once been a Communist Party member, but after going to live in the United States had ceased all contact with Communists and had joined the Seventh Day Adventists. In 1936 she came back to Japan and was clandestinely approached by Miyagi Yotoku, a communist who had lived for some time in the U.S.A. and Okinawa. The latter was a member of the Sorge Ring for whom he operated under the pose of an artist. Mayevsky, Sorge's Russian biographer, has stated that the Japanese secret police only discovered the existence of the Sorge Ring because of "a traitor who called himself a communist".

This was not quite accurate. Ito Ritsu did not deliberately betray anyone. He named Madame Kitabayashi only because she had *ceased* to be a communist, and he knew nothing about her having been seen by Miyagi. It was the incisive and prolonged cross-examination by the *Kempei Tai* which caused her to mention Miyagi. From Miyagi the trail led the secret police on to other names, first to Hozumi Ozaki, Sorge's top agent and a counsellor to the Japanese Government, and then to the rest of the Ring. Possibly Hozumi Ozaki survived as long as he did because he had never joined the Communist Party and he was trusted by Prince Konoye as an unofficial adviser on China to the Japanese Cabinet.

However, it is by no means certain that the *Kempei Tai*, or possibly some other branch of Japanese Intelligence, did not discover the existence of the Sorge Ring long before they admitted doing so. There is the fact that Klausen, Sorge's German communist radio operator, noticed that a radio detector van was parked near his apartment and he had to report to Sorge about casual visits from an "electrician" and a man who said he must have been given the wrong address. If the secret police, or others, had narrowed the quest for a transmitting set down to the immediate vicinity of Klausen, it is hard to believe they did not establish the location of the apparatus beyond all doubt. It was long after this that Klausen was arrested. There is also considerable evidence to show that it was by not arresting Klausen there and then and simply tapping his transmissions that the *Kempei Tai* were able ultimately to round up the whole of the Sorge Ring.

Now, while it was imperative for Moscow, threatened by direct German attacks, to know whether or not Japan would invade Siberia, there was no special urgency for Tokyo to stop Sorge from radioing his information to the Russians. Sorge was telling Moscow that Japan posed no military threat to the U.S.S.R.: only when he made reference to a possible attack on Hawaii did it become imperative for him to be silenced. By listening to all the messages Sorge was sending to Moscow Japan could learn all the techniques and individual characteristics of Klausen's transmission, as well as learning more about the Ring. It is not beyond the bounds of possibility that they were able to operate with bogus messages *after Sorge's arrest*— at least for a brief period. This is a theory that is held by some Japanese today, but there is no positive proof of it other than circumstantial evidence. However, I will cite what a former Japanese intelligence officer has to say on the matter: "You must remember that by this time some Soviet ciphers were in our possession. More than that, the code being used by the Sorge Ring was a numerical one based on a standard reference book. This would not be too difficult to break when one considers the volume of traffic put over by the Ring—some 200,000 word groups. Then there is also the strange case of Kinkazu Saionji.

"Saionji, who was arrested by the *Kempei Tai* about this time, was one of those young men who were sometimes cynically referred to as Prince Konoye's Breakfast Club. He was an adviser to the Foreign Ministry and as such was charged with being a member of the Sorge Ring on account of his having given information to Ozaki. The actual charge was that of 'having violated the Military Secrets Protection Law'. He was found guilty, but escaped with a suspended sentence. At the time it was suggested that he was let off because he was a grandson of Prince Kimmochi Saionji, the former elder states-man of Japan. But there was more to it than that. I believe that the clue to all this lies in the fact that in the end the Sorge Ring was unmasked long before Sorge was arrested."[4]

Saionji remains an enigmatic and fascinating figure to this day. Born in 1906, he was educated at Oxford University where he took a degree in P.P.E. In 1934 he joined the Japanese Foreign Ministry. A member of the inner circle of the Emperor Hirohito's court, he scandalised his family and pre-war Japa-nese society by marrying a geisha and embracing proletarian causes. In 1936 he went to the United States to attend confer-ences of the Pacific Problems Research Association and a year later he became President of the Japan International Problem Research Association and a part-time employee of the Cabinet. During his service with the Foreign Office he visited Russia with Foreign Minister Yosuke Matsuoka and was said to have been introduced to Stalin as "a Japanese Bolshevik". He also visited Germany and Italy.

When he was at Oxford this brilliant young man's great ambition was to be a successful playwright. It was only when he failed in this that he decided on a career in the Foreign Office. The image that has been created of him (and it is one to which I myself at first subscribed when researching my history of Chinese Secret Service) is that of an oriental Vicar of Bray, who worked for the Russians while in the Japanese Foreign Service and then later backed the Chinese Communists against the Russians. I should now revise this judgement. That Saionji had Marxist sympathies is not questioned, but I think these always lay more with the Chinese Communists and that he was never wholly taken in by the Russians. If he joined the Communist Party, it was not to spy for the Russians, but to ally himself with those in Japan who wanted to make peace with China. As for his membership of the Foreign Service that, too, was to use his influence for a *rapprochement* with China. It is significant that in 1937 he carried out an undercover mis-sion to Shanghai in a fruitless bid to head off Japan's invasion of China. Incidentally, he claims that it was an Oxford don who introduced him to Marxism.

Saionji was elected a member of the House of Councillors in 1947 and he also re-established the Pacific Problems Research Association and became its director. His friendship for China was unabated even at a time when any mention of that country was anathema in Tokyo. In 1958 he took his family to Peking with the unofficial blessing of the Japanese Government. There he made a Maoist-style recantation of "former errors" and worked first with the Chinese Communists against the Russians (this was before the Sino-Soviet rift became official) and later with Peking against his Japanese Communist comrades.

Then in 1970, after being given a farewell banquet by Chou En-Lai, the Chinese Foreign Minister, Saionji returned to Japan, stopping off at Hong Kong where he was the guest of one of that colony's leading Communist bosses, Dr. K. C. Wang. For more than twelve years he had been Tokyo's unofficial ambassador in Peking and he even called his residence "the little Embassy". While in China he had been allowed more freedom than any other foreigner. He passed the time writing essays on Chinese food, wines and music, but in 1963 he had set up the Sino-Japanese memorandum under which a Japanese delegation travelled to Peking each year.

On 18 October, 1941, Inspector Osashi, accompanied by the Japanese Procurator, Mitsusada Yoshikawa, arrived at Sorge's home. The Soviet agent was promptly arrested and soon after the rest of the network were rounded up. By the end of October the Soviet spy ring in Japan was virtually destroyed. Altogether some thirty-five people were arrested. Ozaki and Sorge were executed on the same day, but, surprisingly, this was not until 7 November, 1944. This delay in executing Sorge raised queries in some quarters as to whether or not he was still alive, or used in an exchange deal, while another man was sent to the gallows in his place. The probability is that it was neither in the Germans', nor the Russians' interests that this spy scandal should be publicised. For the Germans it could have been acutely embarrassing, as Sorge was a confidant of the German Ambassador, Major-General Ott. The Japanese obviously wanted to get the maximum information out of him which eventually they did in the form of a detailed confession. Possibly right up to the last moment they regarded Sorge as too valuable a prisoner to be executed.

But there can be no doubt that he paid the penalty as his Japanese mistress traced his grave in a cemetery at Zoshigaya after the war and, when this and the coffin were opened, she claimed to recognise the gold fillings in the teeth of the skeleton as well as other identifications.

20

Pearl Harbor and Thereafter

> "Japanese Naval Intelligence became a
> highly efficient and dangerous presence in
> the world of intelligence"
>
> Allen Dulles

IN AN OBLIQUE kind of way the Japanese did try to comply
with the Hague Convention prior to their attack on Pearl Harbor.
They sent an ultimatum to Washington at 1300 hours Washington time, while launching their attack at 0730 hours Hawaiian time (1330 hours Washington time), thus giving the
U.S.A. a mere half hour's notice of possible attack. The actual
text of the message was that "the Japanese Government regrets,
in view of the attitude of the American Government, it considers
it impossible to reach an agreement through further negotiations."

It was a fairly definite indication of a declaration of war,
but the U.S. Navy even then failed to realise the urgency of
the situation. This is perhaps best illustrated by the complacent
comment of a member of the Naval Operations Staff that "we
wondered why the Japanese had insisted on the message being
delivered at 1300 hours." In fact, the O.N.I. had picked up
the message some hours before this deadline. Yet, quite apart
from this warning, U.S. Naval Intelligence should have realised
weeks before that war was imminent. The Joint Congressional
Committee investigating the attack on Pearl Harbor afterwards
found that "the fact the Japanese codes had been broken was
regarded as of more importance than the information obtained

from decoded traffic. The result of this rather specious premise was to leave large numbers of policy-making and enforcement officials in Washington completely oblivious of the most important information concerning Japan."

In September, 1941, for example, the O.N.I. was given a deciphered message to the Japanese Consulate in Honolulu asking for full details of the location of ships in Pearl Harbor. Astonishingly, this message was not even relayed to Pearl Harbor for information, despite the fact that the request was repeated twice weekly.

The Pearl Harbor bombardment was a brilliant success for Japanese Naval Intelligence. It was not dependent solely on men like Yoshikawa, though he was the supreme example. The Japanese had hundreds of agents in the whole Pacific area, though not thousands as has sometimes been suggested. Secret agents had bought their way into controlling several brothels patronised by U.S. personnel. The Japanese knew that on a Sunday the largest number of vessels would be found at anchor in Pearl Harbor and they knew exactly where each ship would be positioned. The result was that, apart from the damage done to the U.S. base, the Americans lost 18 ships, 300 aeroplanes and 2,500 men.

The British were beginning to read some Japanese diplomatic ciphers pre-war and, when the U.S. entered the war after Pearl Harbor, they greatly aided the Americans on the subject of deciphering. From then onwards rapid progress was made by the United States until in the long run they actually won the cryptographical war. The Japanese had been lured into believing that their ciphers were safe by General Tojo's chief of signals, Kazuji Kameyana.

David Kahn has suggested that "the Japanese trusted too much to the reconditeness of their language for communication security, clinging to the myth that no foreigner could ever learn its multiple meanings well enough to understand it properly."[1] In the early days this was no doubt true and may have been one reason for the rash assurance given to General Tojo who, by this time, had become Prime Minister.

After Pearl Harbor there was a tremendous increase in personnel attached to the various deciphering units. Foreign language schools were drawn into the cryptographical organisations. *Tokumu Han* had developed into a unit employing thousands of people, female as well as male. This Special (Cryptanalysis) Section had Rear-Admiral Nimura as its head and comprised three branches—General Affairs, Code-breaking Research and the Owada Communications Unit—under Captains Amano, Endo and the extremely able Morikawa.

Just as it is now admitted that the Americans were guilty of grave errors of judgement in failing to realise what was going on through inability to analyse Japanese messages efficiently, so a picture has emerged of a Japanese cryptographical organisation which failed abysmally after Pearl Harbor. But this picture seems to owe more to Japanese modesty than an accurate reading of the situation, and possibly to a certain amount of disinformation. That the Americans rapidly improved and that the Japanese became careless is unquestioned. Certainly the Japanese do not seem to have realised how easily their cipher systems were eventually broken. But one should not take too seriously the comment of Lieutenant-General Seizo Arisue, chief of Army Intelligence, who declared after the war that the Army could not break the Allies' codes. The Japanese Army may not have been as good at deciphering as their Navy, but it must be remembered that their track record in earlier years, especially in obtaining some Soviet ciphers, was quite impressive.[2]

Where the Japanese were undoubtedly cleverer than the Allies was in their cryptanalysis. When they broke a message, their interpretation of its meaning and, more important, its implications, was quite astonishingly brilliant. They were also adept at deception and baffling the enemy with bogus messages, something which the U.S. Admiral Nimitz himself ruefully admitted.

Some naval intelligence from the United States was acquired in a remarkably bizarre way even in secret service history. On 22 June, 1942, a badly typed and misspelt letter, originally addressed to Senora Inez Lopez de Molinali in Buenos Aires, was returned to Mrs. Mary Wallace of 1808 East High Street, Springfield, Ohio. Her address was on the envelope. The letter read:

"The only new dolls I have are THREE LOVELY IRISH DOLLS . . . You wrote me that you had sent a letter to Mr. Shaw, well I went to see Mr. Shaw he destroyed YOUR letter . . . His car damaged but is being repaired now . . . Mary Wallace."[3]

What astonished Mary Wallace was that, though her name was on the back of the envelope, she had not written that letter. The longer she examined the letter and envelope the more suspicious she became. Something very odd was going on. She queried the matter with the postal authorities who in turn referred the matter to the F.B.I.

Nothing very much might have been done about this mysterious letter but for the fact that yet another letter marked "unknown at this address" was returned from Buenos Aires to another woman at Portland, Oregon. She, too, had not sent the letter and passed it direct to the F.B.I. This other note read:

"I just secured a lovely Siamese temple dancer. It had been damaged, that is tore in the middle. But it is now repaired and I like it very much. I could not get a mate for this Siam dancer, so I am redressing just a small ordinary doll into a second Siam doll . . ."

In due course, by the F.B.I. prodding censorship into taking notice of such things, a curious correspondence was revealed, all concerning dolls. Other letters told much the same story: "I have a splendid Andalusian dancer doll in perfect condition and ready for immediate dispatch". The censors noted that in most of these letters there were misspellings and erratic typing. "A broken doll in a hula grass skirt will have all damages repaired by the first week of February," states another letter writer. "The broken English dolls will be in a doll hospital for a few months before repairs can be completed. The doll hospital is working day and night."

The whole puzzle was eventually too much for the F.B.I. and was handed over to the cryptologists and cryptanalysts. As each letter was detected and examined so a pattern emerged: "You asked me to tell you about my collection a month ago. I had to give a talk to an art club so I talked about my dolls and figurines. The only new dolls I have are three lovely Irish dolls. One of these three dolls is an old Irish fisherman with a net over his back, another is an old woman with wood on her back and the third is a little boy."[4]

From all this detail the cryptanalysts decided that the dolls represented a jargon code for naval intelligence. After a few trials at deciphering this oddball code they decided that one message indicated that a light cruiser of the U.S. Navy would be ready for action at a certain date and that some severely damaged British warships would be laid up for some months before repairs could be carried out. "Three lovely Irish dolls" was decoded to mean "three new American warships", while "Irish fisherman" meant an aircraft carrier and an old woman with wood on her back was a ship with a wooden superstructure.

But for a long time there was no indication of the writer's whereabout or her name. Then at last came a letter which gave as an address a place where the writer had once briefly had accommodation. The F.B.I. man who called at this address inquired whether anyone might have stayed there briefly who could have given such an address. One name of a temporary visitor was that of Mrs. Velavee Dickinson, who owned a rather exclusive shop specialising in dolls in Madison Avenue, New York. She was a frail, tiny fifty-year-old widow who seemed to be the most unlikely of spies. Nonetheless further inquiries were made and these revealed that before moving to New York she had managed brokerage accounts for Japanese living in the Imperial Valley of California. Many of her friends there included not only many Japanese and Japanese-Americans, but some Japanese naval officers.

At this stage the F.B.I were not certain that there really was a code in these mysterious letters. But what convinced them was when an astute cryptologist pointed out that "Mr. Shaw" almost certainly referred to the U.S.S. destroyer *Shaw* which was damaged at Pearl Harbor, but undergoing repairs. U.S. secret agents visited Mrs. Dickinson's shop in the guise of customers and kept a careful watch on the premises. They learned that the shopkeeper was passionately fond of all things Japanese and that she had been desperately in debt through heavy expenses of medical and hospital bills for her late husband's illnesses.

Mrs. Dickinson was quick to suspect that she was being watched and that some of her "customers" were not genuine. She had been put on her guard as a result of not having had a reply to the letter she had sent to Buenos Aires. So one day she determined to try to give the F.B.I. the slip. She shut up her shop and travelled to Portland, Oregon. What she had not bargained for was that the F.B.I. had telephoned through to Portland to get one of their agents in that city to meet her train and take over the surveillance. In an oriental restaurant in Portland she met a former Japanese naval officer.

She was arrested on 21 January, 1943, when she returned to New York and visited a bank where she kept a safe deposit box. In this box was a sum of 18,000 dollars, part of an estimated 40,000 dollars which the Japanese had paid her for services rendered. She was charged with spying for the Japanese Government and violating censorship laws by sending coded letters outside the United States. The only connection

Mrs. Wallace had with the case was that she had innocently purchased the three dolls during a trip to New York and the writer of the letter had obtained her address as a result.

Mrs. Dickinson pleaded guilty to the lesser of the two charges against her—violation of the censorship laws. Government attorneys agreed to this plea because they had been advised that Mrs. Dickinson's defence would place the blame on her husband, Lee, who had died recently. She was sentenced to ten years' imprisonment.

The reference to South America in this coded correspondence was noted by the F.B.I. as further evidence of growing suspicions that the Japanese had a network of spies not only in Argentina, but in Central America and Brazil as well. In April 1942, reports had come through of Japanese "turning up [in Brazil], equipped with everything from illegal radio transmitters to detailed charts of Brazil's shoreline. One raid unearthed 400,000 rifle cartridges and a quantity of automatic riot rifles . . . a raid at Sao Paulo deprived the Japanese of forty-two high-powered speed-boats."[5]

There was some unofficial cooperation between the Americans and the Brazilian police and this resulted in the discovery of Japanese agents developing a small port near Jaquia, about ninety miles south-west of Santos, and fitting it out with fuel stores and a special dock for submarines. Though no Axis power submarines had appeared in Brazilian waters, the Brazilian Government was sure that what was going on at Jaquia meant that such visits were being planned.

On the Ilha das Flores, Brazil's equivalent of the U.S.A.'s Ellis Island, in the bay of Rio de Janeiro, the Brazilian Government had interned 200 enemy agents, including some Japanese. One farm labourer who was arrested was eventually identified as General Yusci Tonogawa and yet another Japanese agent turned up in the uniform of a Brazilian officer of the Reserve. But it was in the kitchen of a Brazilian industrialist that the strangest agent of all was detected. Brushing back the coarse black hair of the family's cook, Brazilian police found not a native female, but a captain of the Japanese Imperial Army. For five years he had been posing as a woman and was regarded by the household as a splendid cook—the best they had ever had![6]

All of which exemplifies the extraordinary talents and genius for disguises possessed by Japanese agents.

Once and once only during the war was the dolls deception code adopted by the Americans to be used against the Japanese. It was perhaps a dangerous ploy to repeat, as repetition in espionage is always risky. Allen Dulles, operating in the American O.S.S. office in Berne, had a very important spy, who took the code name of "George Wood", working inside the Berlin Foreign Office. Wood was in the habit of keeping Dulles supplied with a regular flow of German documents and cables. Late in the war Dulles urgently needed to contact Wood directly in Berlin to ask him to provide more intelligence on the Japanese. Dulles and Wood had arranged for any such messages to be sent to Wood in the name of a fictitious Swiss girl. One day Wood received a postcard from Zurich telling him that a girl friend who ran a toy shop wondered whether any worthwhile Japanese dolls could be bought in Germany. Sure enough Wood got the message correctly and sent Dulles a detailed series of reports on the situation in Japan. Prior to this a great deal of inaccurate information had been coming out of Tokyo through diplomatic channels. The American diplomatic staffs in Tokyo and Yokohama, for example, had been fooled into believing that the major part of the Japanese Imperial Fleet was in home waters on the eve of Pearl Harbor. This was due to the fact that large numbers of Japanese agents in both cities had been dressed in sailors' uniforms and paraded in the streets.

The almost instinctive impulse to neglect no opportunity of obtaining intelligence among even high-ranking Japanese officers was in evidence on some of the military missions to Berlin during the war. Even as early as 1940, when Reichminister Hermann Goering gave a banquet in honour of such a mission, an undercover American agent working inside Goering's headquarters at Karin Hall reported: "General Ernst Udet, surrounded by several Japanese colonels, explained to them the organisation and tactics of our airborne troops [i.e. the German troops]. He drew numerous sketches that he explained and then carelessly tossed them on a nearby table. I noticed how one of the Japanese collected them and put them in an inner pocket of his tunic."[7]

Another story, which I have been unable to verify, though it was solemnly recorded by the same agent (a female) inside Karin Hall, was that Lieutenant-General Tomoyuki Yamashita managed to persuade Goering to take him up in a Junkers 97 bomber over London while the city was being bombed by the

Luftwaffe. This was first-hand intelligence of the most remarkable kind. How many high-ranking officers of other nations would take such a risk?

A great deal of the intelligence on Japan which the United
States acquired before entering the war was obtained from
sources in Germany. But, with the O.S.S. not yet launched
and the U.S. Secret Service mounting only negligible operations, there was a lack of skilled analysers of such information.
Too often it was mistrusted because it came from inside Germany. The Americans had warnings of possible Japanese landings in Malaya as well as a report in early 1941 that "Japan is
also busily engaged in organising fifth columns in the territories
she expects to invade. Special attention is given to sending into
these countries large numbers of pangees—Buddhist monks
who are either Japanese or have been educated in Japan. They
are expected to be especially useful in influencing the native
populations and in gathering military information. . . .
According to Stahmer, the Japanese General Staff dispatched
a Colonel Yakematu to Singapore a year ago. There he hired
himself out as a coolie on a small rubber plantation and worked
at menial jobs on Singapore Island until he had learned the lay
of the land. Then he obtained a job as a longshoreman in Keppel
Harbor, receiving point for all supplies for Fort Canning headquarters, fortress of Singapore, nearby. Next he hired out as a
construction worker at the principal naval base on Johore Strait.
Eventually he became foreman on a Japanese-owned rubber
plantation near Tampin, in the Malay state of Negri Sembilan,
where he established a secret headquarters. Colonel Yakematu's actual job was collecting and mapping all information of
military and economic interest to the Tokyo General Staff."[8]

Colonel Yakematu was the head of a secret mission comprising some 180 Japanese army and navy officers who recruited numerous agents in the local populations. Between them
they charted the channels along the Straits of Malacca and
studied the beaches for landing operations. Some were disguised as coolies, others worked as tugboat captains and fishermen. A few officers actually undertook labourers' work in
the rubber plantations; a few others became truck drivers around
the tin mines and even on two new airfields which the British
were building. Using a wide variety of occupations, they were
able to find the maximum amount of intelligence, covering
naval bases, roads, depots, which places were well guarded
and those sites where there was negligence. Some of the agents

became watchmen on waterworks and on the causeway connecting Singapore Island with Johore Bahru on the Malayan mainland. All this intelligence was coordinated by Colonel Yakematu and a full report sent by him to Tokyo. It was shared equally between army and navy staff officers. The boast in Tokyo—and there is much still to support it—was that the Japanese had a more detailed picture of conditions, defences and security in Singapore and Malaya than the British themselves.

Apparently the Germans were so impressed that one senior *Abwehr* officer told Goering that "when the time comes to invade, the Japanese will know even more accurately where to go and what to do than we Germans did in the Norwegian campaign."

In April, 1941, news came to America, and was broadcast on 17 April, 1941, that "six Japanese divisions are on the island of Hainan, training in the complexities of jungle warfare. Since the terrain of Hainan is very similar to that of Malaya, the conclusion is obvious."

The fact that the United States was confronted by so efficient an enemy and forces so courageous and patriotic that they would die rather than be taken prisoner and commit suicide if that was the only way they could die, caused much rethinking in Washington. Ladislas Farago, a Hungarian who worked in intelligence under Secretary of the Navy James Forrestal during the war, told the author: "The war unhinged Forrestal. He had been at Iwo Jima and seen the appalling slaughter there. He wanted to avoid any further slaughter of U.S. troops on this scale. So I was asked to work on psychological propaganda, the aim being to persuade the Japanese to surrender.

"It meant a lot of research and some strange facts emerged. We found that the Dowager Empress of Japan was a great admirer of Douglas Fairbanks senior. At one time we thought we could use this as a ploy. We found that the Japanese people, contrary to popular belief, are a peace-loving people. We had to do enormous research because Japan had only been involved in foreign wars twice in its history. But they were often involved in clan conflicts. We actually found some eighteenth century surrender leaflets of theirs. Yet we did not have a single agent in Japan to help us. In fact we worked from a suite of rooms in the Library of Congress. We finally established direct contact with the Imperial Household."[9]

But it was a long uphill battle for the U.S.A. and Britain,

not least in the game of propaganda and espionage. British
Force 136 dropped thousands of matchboxes in Siam where
there was a grave shortage of matches. At first this was a great
success and people picked them up and sold them. It was known
as Operation Lucifer and intended as one way of winning friends.
But the Japanese retaliated by forcing Siamese Radio to broadcast warnings that the "wicked British" were dropping matchboxes containing explosives.

21

A Decisive Defeat in the Ciphers Game

> "U.S. awareness of the Midway operation was the result of brilliant intelligence work and the amazing success of American experts in breaking Japanese communications codes"
>
> Masanori Ito

JUST AS IT was a brilliantly planned and well organized communications operation which made the attack on Pearl Harbour a success almost beyond the dreams of the Japanese Naval Staff, so it was an equally well planned counter-intelligence project which eventually enabled the United States to win the cryptological war.

This is now admitted on the Japanese side, for as Masanori Ito, an historian of the Japanese Imperial Navy, states: "The American High Command were almost as well informed of plans for Midway as was the Japanese Imperial General Staff. This was due to Japan's relaxed security measures. They broke silence despite orders in fog. The Japanese Navy was hampered by inferior radio communications, radar and intelligence from Midway onwards."[1]

The Japanese faced cryptological problems on two fronts. In Europe a good deal of their communications contacts with the Germans was being intercepted. At Bletchley the British were reading all German signals which included some intelligence on Japan, while Allen Dulles' agent inside the German Foreign Office was also providing the Allies with some information on the Far East. But the impact of the Pearl Harbour

disaster had been a tremendous spur to the American cryptological teams in the U.S.A. and Hawaii deciphering Japanese
signals. Gradually analysis and interpretation of such intelligence improved considerably so that when the Midway operation was being planned by the Japanese the U.S. Naval
Intelligence was well aware of it, having at last broken more
of the Japanese codes.

Why suddenly had the Japanese become more complacent
and careless on communications? Certainly such complacency
was untypical. They had begun to worry about their cipher
security, and wondered whether the Purple Machine was not
perhaps infallible. But the Germans assured them that their
own Enigma Machine was unbreakable and offered to send a
shipload of Enigma machines to Japan. This offer was taken
up with alacrity. The machines were put on a ship and the
Germans signalled full details of its route and time of arrival.
When this message was intercepted by the Bletchley decipherers there was great glee. The ship sailed to Japan and no
effort was made to interfere with it, as the Allies then knew
full well that once Japan had these Enigma Machines, it would
be easier still to read their ciphers.

Thus it was that the Americans anticipated the Japanese plan
to invade Midway. The first clue they had was that certain
signals suggested a major Japanese attack on a target coded as
"AF". This could refer to the Aleutians, Hawaii or Midway.
Admiral Chester Nimitz made an intelligent guess that Midway
was the target. To lure the Japanese into confirming this for
him, he ordered the garrison commander in Midway to send a
signal in plain language saying there was a desperate shortage
of water there.

This deception ploy worked perfectly. The U.S. cryptographers awaited some indication that Tokyo had picked up this
easy-to-read signal. Sure enough a few days later a Japanese
message reporting a shortage of water at "AF" was intercepted.
This meant that "AF" was Midway. So when the Japanese
arrived the Americans were ready for them and won a victory
which marked the turning point of the war in the Pacific.

Yet carelessness had played a part in all this. There was a
serious breach of security rules when, in a dense fog, Admiral
Nagumo's First Carrier Force broke radio silence. As Masanori
Ito has written, "It is hard to believe that the same men who
had done the careful intelligence work for the Pearl Harbor
attack could have done the haphazard job of the Midway op-

eration. Every estimate was bad, every guess was wrong."[2]

The setting up of the Allied Intelligence Bureau in mid-1942, under General MacArthur, also made things harder for Japan. The American section of this Bureau managed to infiltrate the Japanese-occupied Philippines, while a branch of Britain's S.O.E. (Special Operations Executive) launched its own deception tricks in S.E. Asia. There is not much evidence, however, to suggest the S.O.E.'s Force 136 was much more than marginally successful in a very limited manner. It was after all being controlled from places as far from the scene of fighting as Meerut, New Delhi and finally Kandy. The Japanese managed more than once to capture British S.O.E. codebooks. They must have been thoroughly amused to read these somewhat turgid instructions:

"Suppose you wish to inform the field commander that the date of the next drop has been changed to 18th. April and that you will drop twelve containers and three Chinese bodies. This would be your text:

"'We change date for next dropping stop date April eighteen repeat eighteen stop will drop containers twelve (designatory particle large objects) and Chinese three (designatory particle for humans).' To indicate past tense insert 'already'."

A great deal of money, manpower and valuable time was wasted almost criminally by both Americans and British in some of the crazy projects launched against the Japanese by agents in such organisations as Force 136, Burma Detachment 101 and Morale Operations HQ in New Delhi. One such project was the printing of several million Japanese railway tickets from Tokyo, Osaka and other Japanese cities to various other cities and places all over Japan. The idea was for American bombers to drop these tickets over Japan in the misguided belief that they would paralyse the railway system. Oliver Caldwell, who worked in the American Office of Strategic Services in World War II, stated: "I received conflicting accounts regarding the success of this plan. I still think it was as sensible as an O.S.S. idea someone else dreamed up which led to the release of thousands of bats from American aeroplanes over Japan, each bat carrying a small firebomb set to go off hopefully after the bat found a new home under the eaves of a Japanese house. The bats were expected to start great fires in Japanese cities. For reasons I never learned, the bats were not successful arsonists."[3]

A rather better ploy was that adopted by the Japanese in the

Dutch East Indies. On 23 September, 1942, they announced on Tokyo Radio the foundation of the Virgins' Association, indicating that it was intended to "rally all Indonesian girls to cooperate with the Japanese Army".

Japanese radio propaganda, including some deception tactics, was skillfully directed by intelligence officers during the war. The head of the War Office Information Bureau was Lieutenant-Colonel Akiyama, whose most frequently quoted spokesman was Major Kametaro Tominaga, who was connected with the Army Intelligence Sector and also worked at Imperial H.Q. The *Kempei Tai* also kept a close watch on any operations master-minded by the propaganda team and scrutinised and shadowed any Japanese-Americans (*nisei*) they employed. The screening of such people was undertaken jointly by the *Kempei Tai* and the Special Security Police (*Tokko Keitsatsu*).

Perhaps the best tribute that can be paid to these Japanese-Americans from the viewpoint of Tokyo is that their instinctive patriotism to their homeland remained constant. The vast majority of them were interned in case they attempted to form an underground resistance. The government need not have worried: there was, as far as can be seen, not a single instance of espionage or disloyalty to the Japanese Government among any of them.

The principal figure in organising the Overseas Bureau of the Japanese Broadcasting Association (American Division) was a Major Shigetsugu Tsuneishi, who joined the Eighth Section (Psychological Warfare) in November, 1941. He coordinated all interested bodies including the Foreign Office, Home Ministry, Army, Navy, Great East Asia Ministry and the news agencies and radio companies. One special project of his was the monitoring of all news of local disasters in the United States emanating from medium wave domestic radio stations in America. Tsuneishi then relayed news of these disasters to American front-line troops. This had a double impact: first, the news was true, and not propaganda; secondly, it was news these troops in the Pacific would not otherwise hear. It made listening in to Tokyo a "must" for many G.I.s and sailors.

Much has been made of the mysterious "Tokyo Rose" (as G.I.s called her) who broadcast to American troops during these years. It was assumed at the time that there was one girl who conducted this work. But Edwin O. Reischauer, the American historian, has written: "There was certainly no single 'Tokyo

Rose', nor was any person ever discovered who had traitorously engaged in propaganda activities against us in that fashion attributed by some to 'Tokyo Rose.' Most American listeners had actually developed a whimsical affection for the American-sounding feminine voices offering them programmes of music they enjoyed hearing."

The story goes that the *Kempei Tai* interrogated a Japanese-American girl named Iva Toguria who came from California, but was living in Japan at the outbreak of war. They told her to register as a Japanese citizen, but she refused to do so. Reluctantly she agreed to broadcast for them. It was perhaps ironic that the sole Japanese-American who showed some resistance to even the mildest form of collaboration should be the victim of a witch-hunt after the war. She was jailed for being "Tokyo Rose", though it is now admitted that this actual role was filled by several girls. Eventually she received a pardon from President Ford.

There were other subtler broadcasters who deserve some mention if only because their contributions probably did more damage to American morale than half a dozen spies. One such was "Orphan Annie" who was extremely adroit and astute in publicising news of disasters in the U.S.A. to front-line troops. A typical quotation from "Orphan Annie's" repertoire is the following:

"Hello, you fighting orphans of the Pacific. How's tricks? This is Annie back again on the air, after her weekend, strictly under union hours. Reception O.K.? Well, it had better be, as this is All Request Night and I've got a pretty nice programme for my favourite little family—the Wandering Boneheads of the Pacific Islands. The first request is made by none other than the Boss. And guess what? He wants Bonnie Barker and 'My Resistance is Low.' My, what taste you have, sir, she said.

"Now let's have more close harmony from the New Guinea Nightingales and other chapters of the Pacific Orphan Choir. It's dangerous enemy propaganda, so beware."

Another time she would harangue the British: "Greetings, all. How are my victims this evening? Are you all ready for another vicious assault on your morale. Too bad, I hear that your film stars and actors and actresses who visit your troops at home won't risk the journey out to the jungles of Burma. Too far, too damp, too hot, too much risk of disease. But too bad for you poor blokes who are suffering all these things."

This radio propaganda was for a very long time much more effective than anything the Germans did, most of which produced mirth rather than any decline in morale. The reason for this initial success by the Japanese in this field was undoubtedly the role played by their intelligence officers in controlling it.

Inside China the Japanese Secret Service in all its multifarious guises was probably much more effective than elsewhere. Indeed these successes were so pronounced that it is difficult to understand how Japan failed to make peace with Chiang Kai-shek, especially after his own secret service had been infiltrated. The Japanese Army may have been too intransigent, but a major factor against some kind of peace was the fact that the Chinese Communists were carrying on a guerrilla war of their own. Two young Chinese girls, refugees from Malaya, were recruited to play the part of double-agents in China. They were taken out of Malaya and trained in a secret Japanese agents' camp, being fully briefed on how they were to establish contact with the military intelligence organisation of Tai Li, Chiang Kai-shek's spymaster. They were to join that team and, on account of their mastery of English, persuade their Chinese masters to send them to India. There they would infiltrate the American Intelligence set-up.

The training must have been extremely thorough, for this very complicated project was carried out to perfection. The two girls joined Tai Li's outfit and duly arrived in Calcutta with the story that they had managed to escape from Singapore. They were desperately anxious to carry on the war against Japan, they said, and volunteered to undergo any task set them. To their mortification, however, while the Americans were more sympathetic than the British, the only work offered to them was in a mission school. On the other hand they realised that this could be a cover that nobody would suspect.

Nor would it have been, but for the fact that American Intelligence in New Delhi discovered that some of the information which they shared with the Chinese was being leaked to the Japanese. This could only mean that somewhere along the line Chiang Kai-shek's secret service had been infiltrated. So a close watch was kept on any contacts between their own people and Chiang's and also any strangers who might have contacts with American O.S.S. officers.

For a few years both girls were able to obtain enough intelligence to keep Tokyo interested in them. This they achieved without arousing any suspicion in either New Delhi or Calcutta, the two cities in India where the O.S.S. kept a constant watch. Then, by sheer luck, the O.S.S. discovered that one of the girls had been buying components for the building of a small radio set, while the other was in the habit of being taken out by American officers. After this a close watch was kept on both girls, yet no proof of espionage was obtained.

At last one of the girls became engaged to an American major and plans were made for an engagement party. The O.S.S. were convinced that among the guests at this party they would be able to detect the suspected Japanese agent's intermediary. Constant shadowing of the sister who had bought the radio parts had not revealed any evidence of her transmitting information from her home. Therefore, they argued, the probability was that she went to the Chinese consulate and radioed a secret Japanese station in Burma from there.

The engagement party duly took place and Oliver Caldwell tells what happened: "A Chinese major from the embassy, a Tai Li man, was one of our suspects. He led the girl to a sofa in front of a fireplace and they sat there talking. I sidled over and sat on the other end of the sofa and leaned back, pretending that I was taking a nap. All I heard was a long lecture from the elderly general on the evils of sexual frustration and finally a proposition to the girl. Thereupon she started to laugh and leaned over and kissed me on the cheek, then left both the general and me on the sofa. I assumed that she was telling me she knew I was a plant, an American intelligence officer."[4]

Before any action could be taken the attractive Japanese agent vanished without trace. But from that time onwards the Americans became convinced that there was treachery somewhere in the Chiang Kai-shek secret service. It has not been easy to trace this vanishing spy because her real name had long since been abandoned. But a Japanese intelligence officer who helped to direct some operations in South East Asia during the war had this to say: "This sounds to me to be very like one of about four girls we infiltrated into Tai Li's organisation. Two of them survived until after the war, the other two were murdered. The one you have in mind moved between New Delhi and Calcutta and we had to pull her out on one occasion when she was suspected by the Americans. Eventually we got her to Chittagong where she reported on the British landing-craft arrivals. When the war ended she went to ground in Burma for two years. She is alive today, but I don't want to say where."

This same intelligence officer told me that in South East

Asia the Japanese Army studied the tactics of Sun Tzu, the Chinese strategist: "The same was done prior to Pearl Harbor. And Sun Tzu is compulsory reading even today. We Japanese were the first to translate Sun Tzu as the greatest expert on the arts of espionage. You might like to note that the first English translation of his works by Captain E. F. Calthrop in 1905 depended very much on Japanese help in interpretation of certain passages. He called his book *Sonshi*, which is the Japanese translation of Sun Tzu's name."

I asked this Japanese intelligence officer whether he had studied Sun Tzu with a view to understanding Tai Li, as it seemed to me quite extraordinary that somehow two nations at war with one another could have this exchange of intelligence in the field of espionage.

"To understand Tai Li one had to know one's Sun Tzu," he laughed. "We needed to build up a considerable dossier on Tai Li so that we knew his strengths and weakness, how he could be manipulated. He was not a man of any distinctive background. He had joined Chiang Kai-shek's military police back in 1925. But we discovered something very interesting: between 1923 and 1927 he was secretly working with the Communists. We knew he did this not for ideological reasons but simply to safeguard his own position if Chiang failed to consolidate his position. But we found much else about his early life of which he wished to keep Chiang in ignorance. Do you know that he burned all records of his early life and actually ordered the murder of people who knew him in his teens. He was a ruthless butcher. But he was a great believer in employing female agents and it was never very difficult to bait him with one of these."

As the war drew to a close so Japan's vast army of agents dwindled. In 1941 there had been 20,000 Japanese in Peru, many of whom were deported. In November, 1944, it was reported that the bodies of seven Japanese—two entire families, the Shimizus and the Tomayasus—were found in Lima. Looking for clues, police found a large wooden chest in which were German and Japanese propaganda, maps and photographs of vital installations and bridges, many of them in the U.S.A. There was also a Japanese flag and some secret society insignia.[5]

Japan had managed to maintain an effective espionage network in Turkey for longer than almost anywhere else in Europe. They had been helped to some extent by contacts made many years previously by the Grey Wolf, White Wolf and other societies. There was a team of twenty-four Japanese and Turkish members, attached to the Ministry of Home Affairs in Tokyo, with links to Istanbul and Ankara. In Turkey itself the Japanese Foreign Office sponsored two newspapers, printed in French, German and Turkish—*Ayin tarihi* and *La Turquie Ré-maliste*, as well as a number of publications printed only in French. One confidential Japanese Foreign Office paper names four Turks employed part time as intelligence agents—Vedat Nedim Tor, Barhan Belge, Sabri Ehhem and Neehet Halil Atay. Their duties were not only to gather information required by Tokyo, but "to organise a centre for foreign publications . . . to give guidance on the press and meet the demands from the various movements [presumably the secret societies] . . . and to influence the media."

In January, 1945, the Japanese Embassy in Ankara feverishly burned all their papers when taken by surprise at the news that Turkey had broken off relations with Japan. The Japanese had inherited all the Nazi contacts when the Turks had broken with Germany some five months earlier. In the interim the Japanese had themselves relayed intelligence to the Germans in an exchange deal. A key member of the network which was taken over by the Japanese was an ex-midwife, Fraulein Paula Koch, who had run a news agency in Adana. It was rumoured that she ruled some 2,000 secret agents who roamed the Middle East, providing her with intelligence of Allied shipping and troop movements.[6]

By this time Japan's links with Admiral Canaris's *Abwehr* were totally severed and Canaris himself had been executed by the Gestapo. Major-General Hiroshi Oshima, who had seen service in Berlin first as military attaché and later as ambassador, had struck up a close friendship with Canaris in the early thirties. He and Canaris both favoured an Anti-Comintern Pact which was solely an alliance against the Soviet Union and no other nation, though Oshima himself was personally anxious for Japan to have a free hand in South East Asia. For a while relations between Japanese Intelligence and the *Abwehr* were cordial and close and they extended even to joint operations in Britain, France and French North Africa. But as the rival secret services of Himmler and Schellenberg took precedence, so the links with the *Abwehr* became of less importance.

22

Starting From Scratch

> "Bullets they took from us, they took our rifles;
> Minerals they took and comrades too:
> But while our mouths have spittle in them
> The whole country is still armed"
>
> Marina Tsvetayeva

PROBABLY NO NATION in modern times has lost a war in quite such a dignified and disciplined manner as Japan in 1945. Captain Walter Stennes, the German officer who had worked for the Chinese against the Japanese, commented that after the atomic bombs were dropped at Hiroshima and Nagasaki, "the Japanese still policed Shanghai admirably until the Americans arrived, and Japanese troops, despite the end of the war, behaved with strict discipline and efficiency. In defeat the Japanese showed at their best and their behaviour at this time was exemplary. . . . In defeat they were dignified and often showed to great advantage. For a while after the surrender in the summer of 1945, they still performed some military duties, mounted guards and so on. . . . I have seen a line of Japanese soldiers standing to attention with their rifles in their hands and their bayonets fixed, remaining absolutely motionless while Chinese children came up and insulted them and actually spat all over them."[1]

It was a case of the whole nation starting all over again their race for world power status. But this time it was from scratch, while others were given a handicap advantage. But in the words of Marina Tsvetayeva in her *Poems to the Czech Lands*, while there was spittle in the people's mouths, "the whole country is still armed." Armed this time not to dominate militarily, but certainly to become an equal with any other world power.

On 4 October, 1945, a comprehensive order was issued by the Allied Occupation authorities for the removal of certain officials from the Ministry of Home Affairs downwards, including the *Kempei Tai* and the entire network of "Thought Police". All secret police and departments which had been concerned with the control of free speech were abolished. All political prisoners, including many communists, were immediately released. This situation regarding the communists was to some extent reversed when the Korean War started. Then while the Japanese Communist Pary was not outlawed, certain measures against it were brought in. Just before the Korean War General MacArthur, as Supreme Allied Commander-in-Chief, recommended that there should be a purge of the twenty-four members of the Central Committee of the party. The result of this was that they immediately carried on their activities clandestinely. Thus was the purge of extreme nationalists and the right-wing followed by a purge of the far left. This latter move, however, in no way reversed the action taken against the extreme right. As late as April 1952, when the Peace Treaty came into effect, there were still 8,711 people who had not been released from purge restrictions. Among these were 3,039 *Kempei Tai.*

The Black Dragon Society was dissolved during the Occupation and, in addition, the financial and business interests which had been linked to the society were also purged. By December, 1951, some 233 right-wing organisations had been dissolved under the terms of Occupation decrees. At the end of World War II Yoshio Kodama, founder of the notorious Kodama Agency, was appointed as an adviser to the Higashi-kuni Cabinet. This former undercover agent had, of course, much to offer in business experience quite apart from his wide knowledge of China and South East Asia. But the Occupation authorities intervened and he was tried and sentenced as a war criminal, being released in 1948 after a short sentence. From then onwards Kodama once again became an influential figure in the land, though this time he reappeared as a cautious and moderate right-winger who condemned terrorism. He also strongly criticised militarism in his book, *I Was Defeated*, claiming that he had been offended by brutality he had witnessed during the war. A strong anti-communist, he urged Japanese youths to "use your physical strength only when we are in danger of a leftist revolution in Japan."

Gradually Japan earned the respect and trust of the Occupation regime and was treated more as an ally than an ex-enemy. General MacArthur, whose role in all this has been underestimated by many historians, visualised the nation as being ready for a Peace Treaty as early as 1947. But the Russians stubbornly opposed these early moves towards ending the occupation. By this time the Cominform was set up, replacing the pre-war Comintern, and there was considerable evidence that the Soviet Union had embarked upon a policy of indoctrination of Japanese prisoners-of-war, of whom they had a huge number, many of them being used as slave labour. Through the Soviet radio stations propaganda was pumped out not merely to some of the prisoners-of-war, but to Japan itself. Other propaganda, mainly directed against the Americans, was launched through such organisations as the Japanese-Soviet Cultural Relations Association, the Soviet Study Association and the Japanese Communist Party.

The four-power Allied Council for Japan comprising the U.S.A., U.S.S.R., China and Britain, established in Tokyo was more of a hindrance than an asset. Its principal task was to monitor directives issued by the Far Eastern Commission in Washington and to lend what often proved to be conflicting advice. In practical terms probably both bodies could have been easily dispensed with, as it was General MacArthur who really formulated and carried out the policy of the Occupation. In most respects he was the outstanding pro-Consul of the century. In comparison with him Earl Mountbatten of Burma, who made a most unfortunate impression in Japan, was a disastrous last Viceroy of India. As one liberal elder statesman commented after India was granted independence, "at least MacArthur did not cause Japanese to kill Japanese as Mountbatten's divisory tactics caused internal bloodshed in India."

The Soviet Union's representative on the Allied Council, General Kuzma Derevyanko, deliberately tried to divide the Japanese nation and to undermine its recovery. His comments ranged from blatant propaganda to open attacks on MacArthur, while demanding that there should be "continuous surveillance of the activities of all former Japanese officers." The last demand was denounced by MacArthur as an attempt by the Russians to turn Japan into a left-inclined police state.

Article Nine of Japan's new constitution stated that the Japanese would "... forever renounce war as the sovereign right of the nation and the threat or use of force as a means of settling international disputes." At the same time, and as a necessary response to the possible hazards which the Korean War could produce, it was conceded that "Self Defence Forces" should be permitted. Not unnaturally, this was vehemently attacked by the Russians, who set about organising various "united front" organisations to supplement the work of the Japanese Communist Party and, as Allen Dulles pointed out, they used the trade unions especially in Japan in "skilfully exploiting local issues".

Russia's aggressive attitude in the Far East, the risks that the Korean War could escalate into a larger conflict, made a certain amount of rearmament of Japan inevitable. MacArthur acted speedily in instructing that a 75,000-strong Police Reserve Force should be established within a few weeks of the outbreak of war in Korea. On 15 October, 1952, the new Security Agency (*Hoancho*) was set up and given jurisdiction over ground and maritime forces as well as the maintenance of internal order. Two years later the Diet passed bills which introduced a new and revised security agency called the Defence Agency (*Boeucho*) and the ground, sea and air Self Defence Forces were formally legalised on 1 July, 1954.

A secret service in the old sense of the word was tacitly forbidden under the original Occupation terms, but naturally and logically any Self Defence Force must have an intelligence-gathering agency. Thus in July, 1952, the Public Security Investigation Agency (*Koan Chosa Cho*) was launched as the successor to the Special Investigation Bureau (*Tokushin Kyoku*). Two years later the police Guard Division (*Keibu Bu*) of the Police Agency (*Keisatsu Cho*) was established largely to keep a watch on subversive groups whether of the right or the left. In many respects the Police Guard Division, working in concert with the P.S.I.A., was an intelligence-gathering body aimed at snuffing out any subversive movements whenever they should appear. This was not, however, a repressive move and far greater tolerance was shown than had been the case pre-war in any similar bodies. Though possessed of powers of arrest and raiding, these agencies were rather in the nature of serious students of the causes of subversion and unrest. Proof of this came with the publication by the Police Agency Research Association (*Keibi Keisatsu Kenyyukai*) in 1952 of a study of right-wing movements, *Uyoku Undo*.

Naturally the setting up of these bodies did not please everybody. Mr. Omori, chief of the National Salvation People's General Federation, criticised the Japanese Government in 1954 for some of their security measures: "Recent changes in the direction of the Second Section of the Public Security Investigation Agency suggest that the authorities are tightening their control over the activities of right-wing groups. In particular they are trying to introduce the demon of mutual suspicion among right-wing comrades, to instigate disruptive tendencies to prevent our union, and to weaken or even block the concentration of power that we are achieving. Inasmuch as they are exerting their evil influence in this way and confronting us with malignant schemes reminiscent of the former special secret police, we must all exert the greatest care not to fall victim to their plots."

Opposition of genuine nationalists, however, was not so much the concern of the internal intelligence community as the disturbing knowledge that many ex-communists were appearing in right-wing organisations. Some—probably most—of these were genuine converts, but as the members were so large there was a real fear that "sleeper" communists might be infiltrating right-wing movements merely to create trouble and confusion. So there was a very special watch on new nationalist bodies, as well as the anti-communist associations. Sometimes the latter were given the most esoteric names as, for example, that of the Peerless Poetry Association (*Fuji Kado Kai*) whose declared aims were "to foster the great virtues of devotion to the gods and respect for the Emperor." But here there was no need to worry: the society was more cultural and religious than political and aimed to keep alive the ancient culture and traditions.

Slowly, almost imperceptibly, yet democratically and unambiguously, Japan once again developed an intelligence service. It was, of course, not to be compared with the pre-war buccaneering John Buchanish Secret Service. But, as will be seen in later chapters, it has emerged as highly efficient not only in preserving Japan's defences internally and externally, but as a new, radical and highly fascinating concept of Intelligence.

From the late forties to the early sixties the major targets for Soviet espionage were the U.S.A., the N.A.T.O. powers, West Germany, the British Commonwealth, France and Japan—in that order. The K.G.B. did its utmost to foment strife, strikes and riots in Japan itself, using its disinformation tactics as well as agitators to bring this about. Mainly they encouraged every possible manifestation of anti-Americanism. Richard Pipes, director of the Russian Research Centre at Harvard University, stated when in the early seventies plans were discussed for the U.S.-occupied Okinawa to be ceded to Japan, "in Tokyo the masses roam the streets to protest the terms on which Okinawa is to be transferred to Japan, but there is no news of demonstrations against Soviet refusal even to discuss the transfer of the Kurile Islands." This situation has drastically changed in recent years when the intransigence of the U.S.S.R. over the Kurile Islands has at last been realised throughout the nation. These islands had been seized by the Russians after the war, despite the fact that Japan had honoured her neutrality pact with the Soviet Union.

Soviet espionage against Japan in the early post-war years was directed from Harbin in Manchuria. In being able to cope with this, while not yet having a fully effective intelligence agency, Japan was greatly helped by the Americans. When Juri Rastorov, a high-ranking Soviet intelligence officer, defected to Tokyo, the Americans gained a fairly detailed picture of Moscow's designs for Japanese infiltration and subversion. It was a serious setback for the Russian Secret Service and, as a result, by the early sixties only Ceylon and India were areas where the influence of Moscow was still dominant in the Far East. In the rest of Asia and the Pacific theatre generally the K.G.B. had been forced on the defensive partly because counter-intelligence operations were effective but also through being bogged down by having to watch the disillusioned Chinese.

Nonetheless in this period the Soviet Union was not without some successes. Professional burglars employed by the K.G.B. stole secrets from a number of embassies in Moscow and managed to obtain Japanese diplomatic ciphers. The Seventh Department of the K.G.B. was responsible for espionage targets in Japan, India, Indonesia and the Philippines.

Japan's first chance to show some cautious initiatives in the sphere of intelligence came at the end of the Korean War. For the first time since the war they entered into negotiations with South Korea, but found that lack of information about policy-making in Seoul was hampering them. It was some years before this was largely corrected by the cryptanalysts in Tokyo's Cabinet Investigation Board (*Naikaku Chosashitsu*). They deciphered the South Korean codes and so gave Japan a chance to be better prepared for negotiations. South Korea eventually discovered what had happened and immediately decided to send all messages by diplomatic courier instead of by cabled messages.

It was after the Korean War that Red China decided the time had come to set up a spy network in Tokyo where that nation had not yet been able to establish diplomatic relations. To achieve this the Japanese dispatched a Red Cross team ostensibly to handle the repatriation of Chinese in Japan. The titular head of the mission was a charming and disarming female, but the Intelligence chief who used the cover of the Red Cross to start up his network was one Liao Cheng-chih, later to become ambassador to Burma.

Very soon the Japanese discovered the nature of this operation. There was a strange paradox in Japan at this time. While there was no law against the gathering of secret information from Japanese sources by outsiders, the collecting of secrets concerning U.S. troops in Japan and about American weapons provided for the Self Defence Forces was punishable. It was a ridiculous situation and one realistic Japanese political commentator, Kazuo Kuroda, wrote in the *Japan Times* in 1965: "Japan has renounced war in its constitution, but whether it is necessary to go so far as to open the country for espionage cannot readily be affirmed."[2] He recommended incorporating anti-espionage legislation into the Criminal Code.

North Korean intelligence agents, who appeared to abound in Japan and some of whom almost certainly worked for Moscow, when caught, were generally charged with subsidiary offences—illegal entry, transmitting without a licence, but the penalties were light and Tazuo Furuya, writing in March, 1969, described Japan as "a principal base for international spies".[3]

This may have been an exaggeration, but the point was taken and the situation gradually rectified. There were well over half a million Koreans in Japan and the new Japanese Intelligence made an assessment that about half this figure supported North Korea, with the remainder being either neutral or supporters of South Korea. North Korea had a great initial advantage in having a ready-made intelligence-gathering set-up in its General Association of Korean Residents in Japan (*Chosoren*). Eventually it was found that North Korea had been clandestinely pouring in millions of pounds in various currencies into Japan since the late 1950s. Instructions to agents were passed by a numerical code from Radio Pyongyang.

Commenting in 1967 on the North Korean espionage drive in Japan, David Wise and Thomas B. Ross wrote: "Information flows back by way of repatriated Koreans. Since December, 1959, the Japanese have permitted more than 85,000 Koreans to return to their homeland. Often they hide intelligence messages among their personal possessions ... Japanese intelligence is convinced that in this manner North Korea pulls in a wealth of information about Japanese technology and the United States military establishments in Japan."[4]

Chinese espionage in Japan largely concentrated on collecting theses and data on missiles, space development, electronics and especially on the production techniques of Japanese computers. All such material in the late fifties and early sixties found its way from Tokyo University to certain libraries in Peking. It was believed that these theses and data were sent to China by bookshop agents handling left-wing publications in premises in Kanda, near Tokyo University. Students at the Engineering Department and the Research Institute of the University were then said to cooperate in the microfilming of documents. The students were not public servants and thus could not be prosecuted under the National Public Service Law. But this loophole has since been closed.

Russia has paid very close attention to Japan's fishing fleets ever since 1945. Even in 1946, when there was no conceivable threat from this direction, the Russian representative on the Allied Council was asking: "What was the composition of the Japanese fishing fleet at the beginning of the war, at the moment of surrender, and at present: the total tonnage of the fleet and separate tonnage according to the types of vessel?"[5]

Japan claims that 10,987 of their fishermen have been charged by the Russians with "illegal entry into their waters" and some 1,300 fishing vessels have been seized up to May, 1971. No doubt the Russians were aware of the Japanese fishing vessels which indulged in espionage off the Californian and Mexican coasts before World War II, but their attitude towards these Japanese fishermen has been openly aggressive rather than defensive. This was positively exemplified in 1975 when Tokyo uncovered a plot by the Russians to subvert Japanese fishermen into supplying them with information. This case brought to light the plight of those fishermen operating around the Soviet-held southern Kurile Islands, who went in constant fear of being arrested for poaching. Under pressure, some of these fishermen had traded minor and relatively harmless information to the Soviet officials in exchange for what they called "poaching rights." No classified documents were handed over.

All this was discovered when the skipper of a fishing boat was arrested by the Hokkaido police on his return from an expedition to the waters of Kunashiri Island. It had been noted that there was rather too swift a release by the Russians following the Japanese being "captured" by them. The skipper was charged with violation of the Ships' Officers Law and then discharged. According to the police, Masanori Sawada had on several occasions supplied military and other information on Japan to Soviet officials in return for a guarantee of his safety while fishing near Russian-held islands. In this instance no particular harm was done and indeed the possibility is that the actual information was outdated.

The existence of spy vessels similar to that of Sawada had apparently been an open secret for some years in Hokkaido. These vessels controlled by the U.S.S.R. under duress were known as *Repo Sen*, an espionage network, but the Japanese authorities were well aware of such machinations and knew that Sawada's vessel had made contact with the Russians eleven times in two and a half years. Some twelve fishermen were believed to be on the Soviet pay-roll.[6]

It was President Roosevelt, acting somewhat furtively, though abetted by Winston Churchill, who allowed himself to be tricked into agreeing that the Kurile Islands should be handed over to Russia as part of the bargain that the U.S.S.R. would enter the war against Japan. Roosevelt was actually led to believe that these islands had been illegally annexed from Russia by the Japanese. In fact, they were legally ceded by Russia to Japan in 1875. It was a foolish bargain to make, based only on the Allies' expectations that the war against Japan would last until 1947, an indication of how poor was their intelligence on what was happening in that country in 1944–5. In 1978 the Soviet Union reinforced its garrisons in the Kurile Islands and, by the following year, there were some 5,000 Russian troops there. Aggressive action against Japanese fishing vessels was stepped up in the seventies: in 1975 alone some forty-three boats were seized along with 291 crewmen. No agreement on this vexed question has ever been reached.

Moscow and Tokyo were involved in a territorial dispute in 1977 after the Japanese Government's refusal to recognise the Russians' decision to impose a 200-mile fishing zone around the four Kurile islands of Habomai, Shikotan, Kunashiri and Etorofu. Eventually there was an interim agreement which gave Japanese vessels limited rights inside this zone. The Japanese

Maritime Safety Agency is responsible for maritime security, but this presents many problems with a 200-mile offshore fishing zone.

Chinese sympathy is on the side of Japan on the question of the continued occupation of the Kurile Islands. Even as long ago as 1968 Mao Tse-tung took Japan's part on this subject. Soviet ships are constantly probing around the whole area. In 1976 it was reported that Japanese defence officials were studying reports that some of their fishermen had claimed to have caught a Russian submarine in their nets. A newspaper account stated that "fishermen said they were trawling in the Okhotsk Sea when their boat was suddenly turned two hundred degrees and dragged backwards at high speed. They found themselves confronted with a Russian conning-tower, and the Russians used a chisel to cut the nets".[7]

23

Post-War Intelligence

"It is extremely important for Japan with
its exclusively defence-orientated policy to
constantly conduct surveillance on such
military trends as ship and aircraft movements in peripheral waters and air space
of Japan . . . it is equally important to collect information on world trends"
                Japanese Defence White Paper,
                                    1978–9

THIS DEFENCE WHITE PAPER statement summed up the basic
requirements for Japanese military and naval intelligence in the
coming decade. It went on to reaffirm that the Japan-U.S.A.
security arrangements were "indispensable to Japan" and that,
to implement the surveillance policy, anti-submarine patrols
both by ships and aircraft were imperative.

The rebirth of Japanese Intelligence Services has been parallel with the development of her Self Defence Forces. Under
the Defence Agency come various sections comprising the Defence Division, Operations Division, First Research and Intelligence Division and the Second Research and Intelligence
Division. All these are linked to the National Defence Council
and the National Security Council. Arrangements for consul-
tation, supervision and coordination are meticulously worked
out. Equally important, however, is the Security Bureau which
is composed of the First, Second and Third Public Safety Divisions, the Foreign Affairs Division and the Security Research
Division.

The Public Security Investigation Agency, which copes with subversion, comes under the Ministry of Justice and is in turn linked to the Public Security Commission which makes decisions regarding subversive bodies and controversial problems. It is perhaps worth noting that today there is a Civil Liberties Bureau. The Security Bureau comprises three Public Safety Divisions, a Foreign Affairs Divisions and a Security Research Division. This is quite separate from the Foreign Affairs Ministry's own intelligence and research organisation which includes separate bureaux for Asia, America, Europe and Oceania, the Middle East and Africa as well as an Economic Affairs Bureau.

If there might seem to be a preponderance of divisions and sections, it should be stressed that this is not reproductive bureaucracy multiplying, but that each link fits admirably into all the others and that, by and large, this conglomerate provides a balanced overall picture to the government of the day.

Much of the intelligence gathered—especially in the early days of the new set-up—came from enthusiastic amateurs operating quite legally and in a practical commonsense manner. For example, in March, 1958, the Japanese magazine, *Air Review*, published photographs of U-2s landing in Japan at a time when little was known about them in the outside world. These photographs were taken by a sixteen-year-old student of aeronautics who happened to be on the runway of the airfield and had managed to remain unnoticed. A year later members of a Japanese glider club were photographing landings at Fugisawa airfield forty miles south of Tokyo, when an unmarked black turbo-jet made an emergency landing close to them. The glider club members were quick to note that there was something highly secret about this aircraft as the pilot had no uniform but carried a pistol at his waist. Next day Eiichiro Sekigawa, editor of *Air Review*, was supplied with details of the whole incident.

During the years 1963 to 1965 the Japanese Communist Party swung towards Peking. At last they realised just what the U.S.S.R. had done to repress the peoples living under the Warsaw Pact and how high-handed they had tried to be with their Chinese comrades. But it had also dawned on them how Soviet operators were trying to steal Japanese secrets. In 1969 Japanese police had arrested an Indonesian exchange student, Mabe Odantara, for stealing industrial secrets. It was discovered that the Indonesian had previously studied at a Soviet university and had been recruited by the K.G.B. On another occasion Japanese Intelligence, in collaboration with the American C.I.A., unearthed communist forgeries, one of which was a fake agreement between the U.S. Secretary of State and the then Japanese Premier, Nobusuke Kishi, permitting the use of Japanese troops anywhere in Asia.

Cooperation with the intelligence services of other countries was, of course, inevitable and essential in post-war years. Naturally there was a close relationship with the C.I.A. of both the United States and South Korea. During the mid-sixties Japanese investors were used by the U.S. C.I.A. in an attempt to boost the South Vietnamese economy. It was thought that the Japanese could play a useful role, but after prolonged talks nothing came of this project. In this instance Japanese caution prevailed, probably due to their much more highly attuned commercial intelligence.

It was, however, in naval intelligence that Japan progressed most rapidly in the sixties and seventies. What can be called instant naval intelligence is of paramount importance to any world power today. For while the round-the-clock "nuclear watch" for land-launched weapons can be coped with in a fairly straightforward manner, the lurking, ever-moving submarine-borne underwater missile is what presents the real problem. There is as yet no hundred per cent certainty that nuclear-weapon-carrying submarines can be tracked around the globe. In 1968 Japan's Maritime Self Defence Force dispatched a survey mission to the United States, Canada, Britain and France to gather data on developments in anti-submarine warfare. Priority in the S.D.F. was given to the island of Hokkaido because this had Soviet territory on three sides with only narrow strips of water between. One problem has been that the seas around Japan provide some complicated sonar features. The thermal layer depth is generally shallow, becoming deeper in the summer. It is difficult to detect by sonar any submarine lying below this thermoline, so that this feature favours the submarine and is unfavourable to the submarine-detector. But, as sound channels favourable for conveying sound waves also lie at relatively shallow depths, this feature is advantageous to those who can set up a fixed detection system along the seashore. Except near the Yamato Seamount, at the centre of the Sea of Japan, the bottom of the sea is generally flat and therefore favourable to the successful operation of long-range passive sonars from fixed stations.

It is highly probable that Japan's round-the-clock underwater watch is as highly sophisticated as that of any other power today. The nation has all the technical knowledge required to perfect such a system, both under the water and above it, not least in her capacity to produce space research vehicles. One practical way of building a big merchant navy and a small but effective defensive navy at the same time is to spend more money on oceanological research. Japan's Federation of the Economic Organisation (*Keidanren*) has been encouraging such research since the late 1960s, especially in the Malacca Straits.

This is in no manner a reversion to expansionist policies, but dictated by the Soviet menace. In 1978 Makoto Momoi, a staff member of Japan's Defence Research Institute and a specialist on Soviet naval affairs and security problems in N.E. Asia, summed up the strategic imbalance in the Far East as follows: "Japan is ten years behind recognising the Soviet threat because we accepted the American theory that the Soviet Navy wasn't to be taken seriously." But Japan had already learned the lesson, for in her fourth post-war White Paper on Defence there was this statement: "The activities of the Soviet Fleet around and beyond Japan are intensifying and these appear to be aimed at increasing political and psychological influence over this area, and not merely for training and intelligence purposes."

But Japan has matched this threat with a far-seeing vigilance. Radar scopes scan the seas around Japan and the northern regions and also probe inside Siberia, while all Soviet ships in these waters and the Tartar Strait, which is Russian territory, are tracked by electronic intelligence. The Japanese Defence Agency stated in 1971 that it was going to establish two dozen sets of submarine-detection devices on the sea bottom at the entrance to Soya, Tsugaro and Tsushima.

It was in some degree due to her own naval intelligence that Japan has drawn closer to China in recent years. She has been forced to keep an anti-submarine watch around her coasts. The American Seventh Fleet takes care of this problem outside Japanese territorial waters, while Japan's own Intelligence Services, in close collaboration with the U.S.A., maintains an inshore watch. Following this day and night check, Mr. Michita Sakata, Director-General of the Japanese Defence Agency, reported that, at the end of 1975, the Soviet Navy had about 750 ships, totalling 1,200,000 tons, in the sea of Japan, based on the ice-free port of Vladivostock. This Russian force comprised ten cruisers, eighty destroyers and 120 submarines. But what concerned the Japanese even more were the facts that, firstly, more than forty of these submarines were nuclear-powered and equally divided between strategic (long-range) missile carriers and the "hunter-killer" type. The Russians had the additional advantage that the average age of their vessels was ten years or so younger, while the Americans' Fleet confronting them was much older. The Soviet Fleet had been under the command of one highly experienced, intelligence-minded commanding officer, Admiral Sergei Gorshkov, for all of twenty years. There was the added warning for Japan that the Russians had no intention of relying only on Vladivostock for a base, but that they were developing bases at Korsakov in Sakhalin Island and the submarine base of Sovetskai on the mainland. There was also evidence of the creation of a summer base for the Soviet Navy at Petropavlovsk Kamchatsky on the Kamchatka Peninsula.

Russian probes into Japanese waters continue remorselessly. On 15 May, 1976, Japanese police announced that Alexandre Matchekhine, a correspondent of the Novosti news agency, had been arrested on charges of espionage. It was alleged that he had tried to obtain codes of the U.S. Seventh Fleet and naval radar secrets by trying to bribe a Japanese chief petty officer. He was released later that month as there was a decision to drop the prosecution on the grounds that the U.S. Navy believed that no vital secrets were revealed. That was the official version: the probability is that Matchekhine gave the Japanese sufficient information to justify leniency. Yet at the same time the Russians were carrying out a probe into the efficiency of the scrambling system of the Japanese Home Defence Forces.

A year later a North Korean spy, Sin Yong Man, was arrested for gathering military information in Tokyo with the aid of five accomplices. The tracking down of spies on Japanese soil had been considerably improved by the seventies. A new menace was that of the self-styled Japanese Red Army which had linked itself to various terrorist groups ranging from the Red Brigade in Italy to the Baader Meinhof organisation and the various Palestinian Freedom guerrilla forces. The Red Army was a breakaway group from the Japanese Communist Party. Its leader, Fusako Shigenbo, was a friend of Leila Khaled, the Palestinian guerrilla. Together, Shigenbo and Khaled set up a training centre for revolutionaries in the Lebanon. There they formed the Kamikaze Group, the members of which dedicated themselves to suicidal missions. The Japanese Red Army's principal projects were directed by Fusako Shigenbo, who lost her husband in the 1972 massacre at Lod airport. Later, in conspiracy with the Black September group, the Japanese Red Army attempted the blowing up of an oil refinery at Singapore, but were foiled by the Singapore police. They occupied the Japanese Embassy at Kuwait, when the Tokyo government agreed under duress to supply an aircraft to fly the terrorists to Kuwait. At the time of writing Shingenbo, now in her forties, is still at large. Another member of the Red Army is Mariko Yamamoto, a graduate of Tokyo Women's Christian College, who at one time ran a gift shop in Paris as a cover for her terrorist activities.

For a while Japanese Intelligence was kept busy coping with the low-profile activities of Chinese intelligence-gatherers. "You can hardly call them spies," a Japanese informant told me. "They just operate through such agencies as *Seinenkai*, the Young People's Group, or the Yokohama Chinese League. Then they sometimes enrol sympathetic Japanese as agents. It is the latter we need to watch, for quite often they do not realise what they are doing. I was watching a Japanese in his early fifties—let us call him S. He had served for a period in the Intelligence Department of the American Occupation forces after the war. He had made several journeys to China and appeared to be engaged in selling Chinese products to department stores in Yokohama. He was a member of the Friendship Association through which channel he had received invitations to visit Peking.

"S also maintained close contact with local Chinese friendly to the Taiwan Government and in fact I would not altogether rule out that he is a double-agent, though you can be pretty sure that his real allegiance is to the Communists. The chief reason why the Public Security Force is interested in S is that he still keeps good relations with his former employers, the U.S. Army, and often visits bases in the Yokohama area."

By the early seventies Japan was embarking on a substantial measure of limited rearmament and the Self Defence Forces announced in 1971 plans to expand its intelligence organisation with the establishment of a Central Intelligence Office, to be manned initially with a hundred military analysts. It was however stressed that on the intelligence side they would continue to work closely with the U.S.A.

Such a policy was increasingly dictated by Soviet expansion

in its naval build-up in the Pacific and Indian Oceans, yet at this time Japan's military budget was still only about one per cent of the country's gross national product compared with the U.S.S.R. (12 per cent) and the U.S.A. (7 per cent). Public relations activities for the Self Defence Forces have been extremely good. On the practical side the Forces have been effectively used in the event of such catastrophes as severe typhoons and in encouraging the youth of the country to participate in their physical education schools. But a close watch is kept on public opinion to ensure that if there are any grounds for criticism, they will be noted. The Prime Minister's Office regularly conducts a poll of the nation on problems concerning the S.D.F. and national defence every three years. The result of the poll for 1978 was recorded in the Defence White Paper for 1978–9, in a report entitled "Opinion Survey on the S.D.F. and Defence Issues". This showed that 86 per cent of the population thought the S.D.F. should be maintained, 76 per cent considered it was "good", while only 13 per cent and 5 per cent respectively thought it should be discontinued and was "bad". Questioned as to its future role 38 per cent thought the S.D.F. should be used for the preservation of national security and 33 per cent considered it should be for "disaster-relief operations."

The nation's Police White Paper for 1978–9 stated that "espionage and other underground activities by agents of foreign countries have intensified with the improvement of Japan's international status." However, the only case they cited was that of the employee of the Nippon Telegraphic and Telephone Public Corporation who had stolen restricted research materials and sent them to China. A few years before this Japanese public opinion had been outraged when the South Korean Central Intelligence Agency kidnapped a Korean Opposition leader from a Tokyo hotel room and took him back to Seoul. When this man, Kim Dae Jung, was sentenced to death in 1980 the Japanese threatened South Korea with cuts in economic aid and train drivers all over Japan sounded off a one-minute hooter protest.

On 6 September, 1976, a Russian pilot, Lieutenant Viktor Belenko, defected together with his MiG 25, landing at Hakodate airfield. In advance of his arrival he had written out a message in English: "Immediately contact a representative of the American Intelligence Service. Conceal and guard the aircraft at once. Do not allow anyone near it."

Japanese and Americans jointly investigated this plane, which clearly was one of the very latest models. Explosive charges had been planted in those parts of the plane which the Russians evidently were anxious that no foreigner should see: the Japanese most skilfully located these and removed them. Fearful that the Russians might send in planes to destroy the aircraft (Soviet fighters were hovering high overhead), the Japanese arranged for the MiG 25 to be transported to Hyakuri Air Base some sixty miles north of Tokyo. There it was thoroughly investigated with that precision and detailed analysis for which the Japanese are noted. Meanwhile the Russians made repeated demands for the return of the plane. Eventually it was delivered to them in sections packed into huge crates which were loaded on to a Soviet ship at Hitachi. The Japanese sent the Russians a bill for "transportation charges and damage to ground facilities", while the Russians asked for damages for "unfriendly handling". Neither side paid anything.

Japanese Intelligence experts probably obtained full value for their highly efficient investigation of the MiG 25; "the experts who gave the plane a preliminary once-over were astonished to find the body and wings covered with spots of brownish rust. Clearly, the MiG wasn't made of the strong light-weight titanium used in U.S. interceptors. But what was it made of? The Japanese pulled out a magnet and a loud 'thunk' confirmed their suspicions: the Foxbat was plated with old-fashioned steel. Yet some experts were awed at what they found. One said it was 'brilliantly engineered'. Another said 'the MiG 25 does the job well, at less than it would cost us to build an equivalent plane.' Another said: 'It is apparent that the Soviet designers are efficient cost managers who only use as much quality as is needed to solve a problem.'"[1]

This shows how in collecting intelligence the Japanese pay attention not merely to matters of design, construction and performance, but to materials used, costs and cost-effectiveness. In matters of defence they are fully conscious that wasted money in this direction means a lower standard of living for their people, that the cheaper one can produce ships and aircraft and weapons, the more that can be spent on boosting the economy.

Worsening relations between Russia and China and the initiatives introduced by Saionji and others in Peking led in 1977 to a surprising about-turn in Sino-Japanese affairs. Then there was a move by the Chinese People's Liberation Army to draw closer to officials of the Japanese S.D.F. Director Iwashima of the National Defence College visited Peking in April of that year, and this was followed by a five-man mission in May of the Ocean International Problems Research Institute (*Kaiyo Kokusai Mondai Kenkyusho*).

Japan, unlike the rest of the Asiatic world, has maintained relations with South Africa in trade and diplomacy. A Japanese naval flotilla has even been sent to South Africa on a goodwill visit. Most probably the Japanese are better informed on South Africa than many Western nations. Scandals involving relations with other nations have been relatively few. In February, 1977, there were disclosures in Washington alleging huge pay-offs by the Korean C.I.A. to members of Japan's Liberal Democratic Party and wholesale bribes to Japanese firms dealing in Korea.[2] Later impressions were that the whole business was largely exaggerated out of all proportion by enemies of the Korean C.I.A. in Washington.

In the same year a former Australian diplomat claimed in Tokyo that Western Powers had been monitoring and decoding Japan's secret and diplomatic cables for years. He was Gregory Clark, a close aide to the former Australian Premier, Gough Whitlam, and whose book, *Japanese Tribe: Origins of Uniqueness*, suggested that the Australian Security Intelligence Organisation (A.S.I.O.) intercepted and decoded such messages. Gregory resigned from the Australian Foreign Affairs Department in 1965 because he was bitterly opposed to policy on the Vietnam War. Great play was made of the fact that A.S.I.O. had decoded messages between Canberra and Tokyo, setting out Japanese proposals later discussed at the Australian-Japanese ministerial talks in 1973. Both the Australian Embassy and the Japanese Foreign Office denied Clark's claims.

Espionage directed against Japan has certainly been stepped up in recent years, as the Police White Paper indicated, but counter-espionage measures have been improved in consequence and have resulted in some spectacular successes. In August, 1978, Tokyo police broke up a Chinese spy ring which had specialised in stealing secret and valuable electronics research papers connected with the national defence system. A former senior official of Japan's public telephone and telegraph corporation and two owners of Tokyo bookshops dealing in Chinese publications were arrested. Most of the documents were taken from the Ministry of Trade and Industry and the Ministry of Transport, but some were taken from private companies engaged on defence work. Police stated that the book-shops used the post to send the stolen papers to China: "a search of the two stores and the homes of their owners turned up hundreds of papers concerning Japan's defence and electronics equipment. Apparently most of the documents and research papers had been supplied to Japan by foreign governments and private-level corporations under agreements preventing them from being transferred to other countries, especially the com-munist states."[3]

Studies on the subject of improved security measures were carried out by the Intelligence Services in the mid-seventies. There are now two security-related research institutes set up and supported by both government and business. One was the Institute for Peace and Security Research, launched in 1976 and backed by the S.D.F.; the other is the Japan Security Research Centre. The Institute is headed by Masamichi Inoki, former superintendent of Japan's military academy, and it is patterned on the London-based International Institute for Stra-tegic Studies. In its first report, published in 1979, it opined that "the presence of U.S. military bases in Japan is essential to the U.S. security commitment to South Korea and for mil-itary stability in North East Asia."[4]

Japan is, of course, fully cognisant of the fact that, as Gen-eral Goro Takeda has made clear, she "cannot defend herself alone".[5] Criticisms have also been made of some of her defence policies. There was concern that, according to intelligence reports received in Tokyo, three Soviet air bases with a total of five runways were being built in the Kuriles in 1979. That same year the U.S.S.R. moved some 3,000 troops on to the islands of Etorofu and Kunashir, along with tanks, heavy ar-tillery and surface-to-air missile batteries. By March, 1980, it was reported that Russian nuclear weapons were deployed in the Kuriles.

Relentlessly the Soviet Union and her allies have stepped up their aggressive operations in the Far East. For this reason the United States has recently increased pressure on Tokyo to assume greater responsibility for its own defences. Under the terms of their constitution, of course, the Japanese may still not deploy elements of their Self Defence Forces outside their own territorial waters or air space. Further, they may not engage in any "offensive" action, which in effect means that they may not open fire until they have been fired upon. In the current world situation this is still something of a frustrating anachronism. But it is not only the United States who would like to see Japan strengthen her defences: the governments of other Far Eastern nations, Thailand, Malaysia, Singapore, and the Philippines and Indonesia among them, take much the same view.

Threats come from many quarters and the Intelligence Services have not been slow to assess them realistically. It was a Japanese agent who first reported the fact that North Korea was providing Russia with a training ground for guerrillas from El Salvador, Costa Rica and other parts of Latin America. This same agent also provided information on a drug smuggling network organised by the North Korean Diplomatic Service to help finance communist propaganda and subversive operations. This came from a tip-off in Warsaw where the smugglers had established the European headquarters of their network.

Much more disturbing were the disclosures following the breaking up of a Soviet spy network in Japan in 1980. On 29 January, 1980, Japan's Defence Agency Director, Enji Kubota, accepted the resignation of General Shigeto Nagano as Chief of Staff of the Ground Self Defence Force (Army) because of the discovery of suspected spies in the force. General Toshimichi Suzuki was appointed in his place.

Tokyo police questioned the three suspects for eleven days to determine what types of intelligence had been delivered to the Russians and for how long. The exposure of a Soviet spy ring actually inside Japanese Military Intelligence stunned the military establishment, as treachery within their own ranks was practically unheard of. The ensuing arrest of a retired Major-General, Yukhisa Miyanaga, aged fifty-eight, one-time intelligence chief, and two serving intelligence officers, First-Lieutenant Eiichi Kashii and Warrant Officer Tsunetoshi Oshima, came as a devastating blow. It was the first time in history that any serving Japanese Army officers had been arrested for alleged espionage.

The ridiculous paradox of this situation was that if the men accused had leaked secrets on radar and weapons supplied by the U.S.A., they could face a sentence of up to ten years' imprisonment under the terms of the Japan-U.S. Security Treaty. On the other hand under the Self Defence Laws, under which passing Japan's own secrets would come, the maximum sentence would only be one year.

Japanese press reports speculated that the men might have passed information on Japan's own intelligence activities, on

the deployment of forces on Hokkaido, and possibly with information on Chinese troop deployments. It was alleged that
documents had been passed to the Russians for sums of money
of up to £1,000 each. Clearly, the organiser of this spy ring
was Major-General Miyanaga himself. Two Soviet agents believed by the police to be involved in receiving the documents
had served as Service attachés in the Soviet Embassy in Tokyo.
One of these was Colonel Yuri Kozlov, who had left Tokyo
with his wife only hours after the arrests became known. In
the pre-dawn raid the Tokyo police seized papers and copies
of classified documents in the desks of the two serving officers.
The original tip leading to the detection of this spy ring came
from a Soviet defector, Stanislav Levtchenko. Miyanaga had
foolishly kept a diary of the instructions he received from the
Russians, giving the actual dates on which he had coded radio
messages. Apparently the Japanese police began intercepting
enciphered short-wave messages beamed to Tokyo from Vladivostock several months earlier. The investigators said that a
table of random numbers discovered at the retired general's
home permitted them to decode the messages, proving that they
were specific instructions for future espionage operations. Thus
patient work and effective counter-espionage measures enabled
the Japanese to acquire considerable intelligence themselves
before the men were brought to trial.

Major-General Miyanaga not only confessed to receiving
the Russian instructions, but showed the investigating officers
how he had connected his complex radio apparatus to a tape
recorder to avoid losing any part of the messages. The trial of
the three men revealed that altogether the Russians handed over
some £6,200 in bribes to the defendants. Major-General Miyanaga was sentenced to a year's imprisonment—the maximum sentence allowed—and the other two officers were jailed
for eight months each.

Immediately there was a demand in the Diet for new legislation to prevent espionage more effectively. For too long
Soviet agents and their local sympathisers had been able to
operate with relative impunity, and even when caught the situation had frequently been that they could only be charged with
violating customs laws, while civilians could not even be prosecuted under military law.

24

Espionage For Prosperity

> "At the time of Emperor Meiji the Japanese were already used to thinking twenty to thirty years ahead, and they are still the same this day"
>
> Hakan Hedberg

THE TITLE TO this chapter may well be critised on the grounds that it is both ambiguous and ambivalent. So it is, but, on reflection it will be seen to be recognisably intelligible.

How many of the world's intelligence services have set out with the prime aim of making their nations more prosperous and improving the standard of living of their peoples? With the sole exception of Japan, the answer must be none. Of course this statement must be qualified and clarified. Naturally some of the work associated with Japan's intelligence services is concerned with defence: it would be a rash nation which acted otherwise. But one can estimate that something like eighty-five per cent—possibly even ninety per cent—of Japan's intelligence-gathering is directed towards making Japanese more prosperous.

Given Japan's traditional tendency to seek useful information abroad and apply it in the homeland, this was not so much a new policy as a rational method of finding new work for intelligence-gatherers. As that astute observer, Hakan Hedberg, has indicated, since the restoration of the emperor in the last century, the Japanese have made a habit of thinking thirty years ahead of their time.[1] Wisely, sensibly and without fuss, they set out to turn what at first seemed a disadvantage into a positive

251

advantage. The disadvantage was that after World War II Japan
was only allowed very limited forces barely sufficient for her
own defence, which also meant that she must have no secret
service in the old sense. The days of buccaneering espionage,
of cloak-and-dagger activities around the world and secret societies plotting new empires were ended in Japan's new constitution.

As Japan could clearly not be allowed to spend very much
on defence forces for many years to come, it also restricted
orthodox intelligence-gathering requirements to a minimum.
There was some money to spare as a result of all this and the
Japanese decided to spend it by organising a global intelligence-
gathering system which was not espionage as it is known in
the West, but provided the nation with a steady stream of information on trade, commerce, markets, technological developments, economic research and almost everything which would
produce ideas for improving their living standards. In fact the
actual targets for such intelligence collection were much broader
than this, for to a Japanese "knowledge" is comprehensive and
indivisible; it includes management and organisational as well
as technological knowledge and anything that may be pertinent
to production such as how other nations handle the trade unions,
what the consumers in other areas of the world most require,
and even such subjects as ecology.

The results of this global probe, which started a few years
after the war, have been truly phenomenal. Somewhere in all
this there are lessons for both the affluent Western powers, the
Soviet bloc and the Third World. Indeed if the Third World
copied Japan instead of perpetually taking a begging bowl to
Washington, London, Bonn and Paris, they might more easily
escape from their self-made poverty. As to the Western World,
they, too, might look eastwards with profit to themselves and
haul in the lesson that, if you want to be prosperous, you need
to plan for it.

National characteristics have, of course, greatly helped Japan in implementing this project of what can best be called
total intelligence. The Japanese are by nature anxious to learn
from others, eager to adapt that knowledge and improve upon
it; their labour force is far less resistant to labour-saving ideas
than is the case in Europe; they make first-class analysts of
intelligence. They have also been helped by the very small
percentage of their gross national product devoted to defence.
Dr. Hisao Kanamori, who in 1967, was appointed chief econ-

omist of the Japan Economic Research Centre, laid it down as almost an axiom that "never more than one per cent of the G.N.P. should be devoted to defence". It is unlikely that this axiom will be maintained over the next twenty years, but up to date it has worked well.

Dr. Kanamori is a splendid example of the new type of coordinator of intelligence. Born in 1924, he was a law student at Todai University, after which he spent five years at the Ministry for International Trade and Industry (M.I.T.I.) before going to the Economic Planning Agency. He was at Oxford University for two years and has acquired something of an international mind which perhaps more than any other of his qualities has enabled him to make the Japan Economic Research Centre (J.E.R.C.) the world's best forecasting institute, a reputation which has been enhanced by the work of Professor Miyohei Shinohara. However, Dr. Kanamori himself has directed some of J.E.R.C.'s future-gazing assignments.

While most of the intelligence-gathering and analysing organisations are new, Japan had a number of valuable non-governmental bodies of this type to build on. There was the Kikagaku Research Institute, which was founded in 1917. This had proved a valuable asset to various business firms as well as the government. Something of the philosophy and approach to the work of these researchers can be gauged by this comment of a shrewd European businessman: "The Japanese conception of a first-class boss is first of all one who can find the right men for the right jobs and then let them have a fairly free hand, while still encouraging team work. His role is not so much that of a decision-maker and boss in the Western sense of the word as of an educator and manager. And secondly he must be the type of man who is devoted to what one can only call perpetual knowledge-seeking. He coaxes his team on the right lines, but he does not dictate. He welcomes ideas from wherever they come. The result is the kind of admirable consensus of executive opinion such as you don't often find in the West."

This is reflected in the real success of this whole intelligence-gathering operation which has become a superbly coordinated enterprise linked to private industry and the universities, which are the prime developers, and spearheaded by government. Private trade schools are almost as numerous in Japan as in the U.S.A. University courses have been geared to providing the type of personnel required for intelligence-gathering overseas. The men sent out may be classified as salesmen (and, of course, selling is a vital part of their job), but all the time they are urged to collect information and assess it. They do not take a narrow view of this latter task: nothing is so small that it can be ignored. Two examples of this may suffice. In the mid-fifties the Japanese compiled statistics of the numbers of amateur photographers they observed in various parts of the world. From this they built up a picture of prospective markets; from casual conversation with some of these photographers they built up a picture of the kind of cameras they most wanted. The result was that Japan anticipated the world-wide camera boom and were geared to meet its demand long before many other nations. Then there was the story I was told first-hand by a Japanese who happened to be driving across southern England and came to the National Trust-owned village of Lacock. He broke his journey to make a spontaneous report. "You see," he explained, "we have nothing quite like this in Japan. So I thought that the administration of a village like Lacock in Wiltshire might provide some ideas for those rural cities which some of our future-looking town-planners have in mind."

It was in 1956 that a systematic pattern of economic diplomacy began to develop. From about this date Japanese management sent no less than 10,000 personnel abroad—principally to the U.S.A.—to bring back new techniques and technology. Commenting on this, William H. Forbis, who spent six months researching every corner of Japan, says: "For a grand total of 2.5 billion dollars, which is only a tenth of what the United States spends every year on research and development, these emissaries bought virtually all the technology of the Western World."[2]

How can Japan manage to do all this so much better for so much less? There are several answers. One undoubtedly is that this kind of intelligence work is regarded as just as patriotic and just as vital as military intelligence gleaned in time of war. But the sheer range of the Japanese conception of total intelligence is that much greater, so the volume of information collected is greater. The Japanese are tireless, perpetual-motion observers, quite capable of duplicating the jobs of salesmen or technicians, engineers or academics with those of information-gatherers. So the cost is minimal. Then there is this talent for thinking twenty or thirty years ahead. It was this which enabled the Japanese to foresee the markets for electronics, the high-speed train and the boom in cameras. "The most efficient economic intelligence in the world," is how Hakan Hedberg has described the set-up, adding that "flocks of technological missions are seen queuing up every day at the Haneda airport departure gates" to be sent on "permanent watching assignments."[3]

Even more important perhaps is the close link-up between business and government. As E. T. Hamilton, president of the U.S. Chamber of Commerce, declared in 1970, business in Japan is "government-guided and the two act as a group. They have a planned arrangement which gives them great strength."

At the pinnacle of this intelligence network is the Ministry of International Trade and Industry (M.I.T.I.). It is M.I.T.I. which forges the partnership of government and industry. It could almost be called the arbiter of planned capitalism, for M.I.T.I., which was founded shortly after the war ended, directs Japan's growth and keeps the economy moving. Through M.I.T.I. Japan has managed to a remarkable degree to marry the seeming incompatibles of capitalism and state direction. A shrewd observer of the Japanese scene has detected that while there was a great deal of Marxist economic theory taught in the Japanese universities after the war, both teachers and students picked out what was relevant and discarded the ideology. It is M.I.T.I. which has thrust Japan into the forefront of world powers, providing its own research teams around the world, setting up its own technological laboratories and aiming at the all-embracing know-how required for world-wide operations, for investment and planning for the future. While Japan's Foreign Ministry has a staff of 2,517, M.I.T.I.'s amounts to 15,449 at the time of writing.

Linked to M.I.T.I. is the *Keidanren*, the Federation of Economic Organisations. Its aims are roughly threefold: (1) to adjust the fluctuating interests and requirements of various businesses; (2) to formulate policy recommendations for the government; and (3) to promote international exchange and collect information. One of *Keidanren*'s ablest leaders was Yoshizane Iwasa, who, in 1964, led an economic mission to the U.S.A. One of the information-gathering objectives which he set for the mission was to listen to a broader cross-section of American businessmen than the Japanese had previously met and to get their reactions on a variety of subjects, including the then vexed question of trade with China. As a result Iwasa set up wide regional contacts in the U.S.A. and was foremost in building up the Japan-California Association. He had been appointed president of the Fuji Bank in 1963. Astutely, Iwasa opined that

Japan should in future make regional approaches to the American continent and that the first of these target areas should not be the New York-Boston complex, but in California and elsewhere on the West Coast. Next on the list was the Mid-West and after that another Japanese-American Association solely for the southern states.

Naturally, Japan's appetite for intelligence on a global scale aimed at making her more competitive and more prosperous has raised cries of "industrial espionage" in some quarters. Some of these allegations may be justified, but others are sheer hypocrisy, especially when one considers that some of the most blatant industrial espionage is practised not only in the Western World, but all the time by nations of the Soviet bloc. West German estimates of the actual losses incurred through the operations of East German industrial spies and actual thieves range as high as £230 millions. When a nation is in a hurry to catch up with its competitors, as Japan was in the late fifties, some short cuts to business intelligence-gathering are inevitable.

"An estimated 10,000 commercial spies honeycomb Japanese industry," stated an American correspondent in Tokyo. "In Tokyo alone there are 380 detective agencies that specialise in stealing corporate secrets. Last week industrial espionage achieved a new pinnacle of respectability in Japan with the opening of the Institute for Industrial Protection, a school avowedly established to train spies and counter-spies for Japanese corporations."

". . . There is no law in Japan against stealing trade secrets so long as no patents are violated and products still in development are naturally not patented."⁴

A career diplomat and one-time ambassador to Turkey, Tadashi Kurihara, became president of this new school. On his nine-men staff were such seasoned intelligence operatives as Yuzuru Fukamachi, formerly a naval code specialist, and Tatsuo Furuya, an intelligence chief who had wide experience in Shanghai during World War II. Among the first fifty students at the school were some promising young executives in their late twenties. Their companies had selected them to attend the Institute and paid for their tuition. During their four-month course they were taught such techniques as how to tap a telephone from a distance by beaming a ray from an infra-red listening device into the receiver and how to coat documents with colourless dye that will penetrate even through leather gloves to blacken the fingers of anyone touching them. But these were the trivia of the course.

These young men were among the modern counterparts of the Japanese who, nearly a hundred years earlier, had gone to the Western World to learn its industrial secrets. A few of the pioneer intelligence-gatherers had taken jobs in the Lancashire cotton industry, returned home and provided the information for Japan to compete. Mr. W. F. Cartwright, formerly managing director of the once highly successful Steel of Wales company, told the British Association for the Advancement of Science as long ago as 1966, in an address at Nottingham that British industry should follow the example of the Japanese and go out and seek information overseas: "'Find out the best practice in the world and improve on that' is the motto of Japan," he said, "and British industry would be wise to adopt this policy."

There are a number of organisations which help provide the type of overall economic intelligence which Japan requires. Some operate solely as information-gathers, others as "think tanks" which provide suggestions for further research and improvements that can be made on discoveries achieved. A few fulfil the role of both. It is calculated that today there are more than a hundred private research organisations which can be called "think tanks". Outstanding among these is the Nomura Research Institute which acquired a tie-up with the Interactive Data Corporation of the U.S and was founded in 1965. The Nomura Institute employs some 550 people, of which 270 are researchers, and has offices in New York and London and subsidiary organisations in Hong Kong and Brazil. Its research covers almost everything from investment and industry to regional planning, environmental studies and all the sciences. The material gathered goes into a computer application centre which has a data bank and a documentation section. Its managing director is Ikuro Ishikawa.

Mitsubishi Research Institute is also one of the leading "think tanks", directed by Noburo Makino, and has many graduates on its staff. Like Nomura, it covers Europe, America, the Middle East, Africa and South East Asia. The Mitsui group is the oldest and one of the largest institutions in Japan, having been founded in 1616. It was also one of the first national companies to send its employees abroad to study in 1891. During the post-war period more than 700 of its staff have studied abroad. Mitsui has 185 offices in major cities around

the world extending from London to Lahore and New York to
Nairobi. Its Technical Development Division explores business
possibilities outside the country and has recently been especially active in Indonesia.

Diversity has been the secret of Mitsui's success, ranging
from the development of the petrochemical industry to real
estate, from communications to aircraft construction and the
manufacturing industry. All this could not have been achieved
with such rapidity but for the twenty-four hours a day computer
network at Mitsui which serves to process the tremendous amount
of information produced by the company's operations round
the world. The history of the computerisation of Mitsui dates
back to 1957. What it calls its "System Administrative Division" not only decides the company's computerisation policy,
but promotes the effective utilisation of computer systems
through information-gathering and research. Mitsui's main
computer systems are structured to process the various types
of information required for the efficient conduct of a wide
variety of business activities.

Planning for the future is undertaken by a number of research
units, most notably Yujiro Hayashi's Institute of Future Technology and also the Energy Research Unit which explores the
possibilities of all kinds of energy from fossil fields to nuclear
fuels, and specifically covers research into what it calls the
"behavioural sciences". These include location strategy, analysis of the feasibility of leisure businesses, studies on earthquake disasters and relief supplies systems, the development
of nuclear cities, analysis of urban congestion and the recycling
of waste. Much attention is paid to information from other parts
of the world for this analytical work. For example, a detailed
study has been made of the theory held in some earthquake
areas around the globe that animals provide a semblance of a
warning system by their behaviour prior to an earthquake. This
was monitored in China and elsewhere, it being noted that
while the theory seemed true in the case of some earthquakes,
it did not apply on every occasion. Similarly, the International
Studies Department which covered South East Asia, made a
basic survey for the possibility of building industrial estates in
Indonesia. The same was also done in the Sultanate of Oman.
Tolyo Research Division sends out researchers to New York
and London to collect on-the-spot surveys on investment, while
similar surveys have been conducted in Brazil and other parts
of Latin America.

But, it may be argued, other nations of the world carry out similar surveys. True, but frequently such surveys are haphazard and uncoordinated, or those conducting them lack the requisite technological background to make adequate assessments. And far too often there is a lack of partnership with government, or, worse still, the results of the surveys lie in pigeon-holes without any action being taken. In Japan one may be sure that few surveys are carried out which do not have both government backing and, even more important, about which the government are kept informed directly or indirectly. The Japanese were quick off the mark in sensing that with the coming of the technology of the computer a whole new age was dawning. When General Electric purchased the French computer producer, Machines Bull, they were convinced that continental Europe had shown themselves to be incapable of sustaining an independent computer industry. From that moment onwards, backed up by intelligence reports from all over Europe and the U.S.A., the *Keidanren* and M.I.T.I. gave full backing for computer research. There was something approaching a crash programme of development, supported by world-wide studies of the subject, and this was all achieved with remarkable unanimity and a consensual approach in decision-making. The Diet directed an Electronics Industry Deliberation Council to be established with M.I.T.I., in itself an excellent example of consensus between government and private industry.

The M.I.T.I. Bureau of Heavy Industries set up an Information Room with a Special Survey Group reporting on the U.S. computer industry. The result is that today Japan and the United Kingdom are the only two countries other than the giant colossi of the U.S.A. and the U.S.S.R. to sustain independent computer industries. Not unnaturally America's so-called "Silicon Valley" along the south-west edge of San Francisco Bay has been one area to which the Japanese have sent research teams. This fertile strip of land, once noted for its orchards, is now the centre of dozens of semi-conductor companies. In 1978 a report by Gene Bylinsky asserted that "Japanese agents are aggressively gathering information by both overt and covert means and they eagerly buy samples of new tools and instruments and send them back to Japan. They go for yields, production rates and future plans. What normally might take them a year to discover at home with a tremendous amount of costly research and development can often be obtained in a single conversation in Silicon Valley."[5]

Most of these agents operated from local offices set up by Japanese companies. These offices were in effect listening-posts, a main function of which was to collect intelligence on computers with the same precision one would expect from a professional military team of agents. Most of their work was perfectly straightforward and consisted of attending conferences and courses, calling on computer companies. But there was another side to it. Agents attached to these local offices set out to become friendly with executives and engineers of American companies. They not only tracked down these people after they had left their offices, but when they had left one company and were waiting to take up a job with another. Job turnover in this industry runs at anything up to twenty per cent per year, so the Japanese had quite a large pool in which to probe.

It was the personnel in the waiting pool to which most attention was paid. Often they were tempted with consultancy fees for information provided. On the other hand, as the Americans have had to confess, the Japanese try scrupulously to keep within the laws of the land in such deals.

In the mid-seventies photomasks used to make semi-conductor silicon chips for a local semi-conductor company disappeared from Silicon Valley and were later reported to have arrived in Tokyo. Extensive inquiries were made, but the case was never solved. Yet as a result the Japanese made rapid strides in breaking into the advanced semi-conductor memory components. Within two years the Japanese took advantage of the fact that American manufacturers were having production problems owing to the complexity of the circuits. A great sales drive was launched and at exactly the right moment the Japanese were selling millions of dollars' worth of silicon chips to American semi-conductor companies which could not match them in turning out components.

There is, of course, another aspect of this quest for silicon secrets. The Japanese are not only anxious to keep abreast of the Western nations in the field of electronics, but ahead of the Soviet bloc. This provides them with a distinct advantage in any trade negotiations either in the West or the East. Another factor in the drive for electronic intelligence is that counter-espionage tactics are almost equally important. Most Western nations have made it illegal to export electronic equipment without a licence, which is rarely given for any proposed sales to the Soviet bloc. So the Russians are even more ruthless than the Japanese in their own quest for silicon secrets. By all manner of devious operations the Russians have sought to steal electronic equipment from the Western world, usually by bribing unscrupulous dealers in the N.A.T.O. countries. The Japanese helped to expose one of the more flagrant of these operations when they leaked information to the Americans and the British that the Soviet Union had acquired through a middleman a small Californian bank which held in its records information on many of the engineers and electronics experts who worked in Silicon Valley.

Every move in the economic field in Japan's intelligence probe is decided not merely by technical information received, but by diplomatic and political assessments. In no other country in the world do diplomacy and trade march so well in step. Similarly, the Self Defence Forces have close links with the *Keidanren* which can almost be compared to the British Defence Ministry having an arrangement with the Confederation of British Industries. In 1970 the Defence Agency asked private industry to employ some 10,000 military men separated from the Services each year in a technological exchange system between the military and industry. At the same time the Defence Agency started regular meetings with the *Keidanren*.

The vital need for combining industrial and military intelligence was indirectly stressed in Japan's White Paper on Defence for October, 1980, when it was stated that "Japan, with its exclusively defensive posture, continues constant intelligence activities to collect information necessary for warning, surveillance and defence within Japan proper and Japan waters and airspace . . . it needs to improve satellite reconnaissance."

The reasons for this were clearly shown by the Defence Agency's statistics for the year which showed that 360 Soviet warships had passed through the Tsushima, Tsugaru and Soya Straits each year and that 157 flights by Russian planes had been made over the Japan Sea.

One of the most outstanding of the "think tank" operators is Saburo Okita, managing director of the J.E.R.C. and a member of the future-minded Club of Rome. Gregarious, amusing, quick-thinking, he was one of the master-minds behind the plan in 1960 for Japan to double its national income. On reflection he felt that perhaps the intensity of this drive created pollution problems for Japan, but he was not slow in formulating a project to reduce environmental hazards. It is true that in an overpopulated, intensely industrialised society such as Japan pollution inevitably becomes a serious problem, and that some of its largest firms tended to regard this as a necessary evil. But progress has been made in this direction and most of it has been due to monitoring the anti-pollution measures of other countries. This in its turn has enabled the government to put pressure on private enterprise which has resulted in a company such as Nippon Steel planting ten million trees around its eleven steelworks to "achieve ecologically balanced vegetation."[6]

Japanese intelligence research teams study politics as much as material resources and functions. For example, the mission sent to Malaysia in 1962 specifically reported on the stability of the new government. The drive in South East Asia has been phenomenal and as C. L. Sulzberger has aptly observed, "Japan's gross national product today is such that Japanese businessmen are rapidly taking over markets in a way the generals who preached a Greater East Asia Co-Prosperity Sphere never imagined."[7]

In China, too, the *Keidanren* is cooperating actively with the Japan-China Long-Term Trade Committee, having set up the Japan-China Ad Hoc Committee on Joint Ventures in December, 1979. The next year the Japanese sent in a group of experts to the Fujien province and Shanghai for joint-venture studies.

Any new development in any part of the world, whether a change of government, or some new discovery, is swiftly examined by teams of information-collectors. Thus it was that when huge bauxite deposits were discovered in Australia, Mitsui was not slow in promoting Mitsui Alumina in Australia to mine and process bauxite for export to Japan. Similarly, on the political front, the Japanese were quick off the mark in September, 1980, when they sent a forty-four-member delegation, representing the whole business community, to Zimbabwe, following the declaration of independence in that country only six months previously.

25

B.P.I. Rather Than G.N.P.

"We must enter the knowledge industries . . . we must switch from an era of raw
material waste to an era where we use as
few raw materials as possible"

Naohiro Amaya, M.I.T.I.
planning chief

DR. HISAO KANAMORI forecast as long ago as 1970 that Japan
should beat the United States' G.N.P. per capita by 1982. It
was about this time that M.I.T.I. set out its planning targets for
the 'eighties and that Naohiro Amaya insisted that the emphasis
should be more on acquiring new knowledge than on mere
production. This in turn gave Japan a new slogan—"B.P.I. is
better than G.N.P.", that the nation's aim should be not so
much on G.N.P. as on Brain Power Index.

It is now calculated that, as a result of carefully planned
intelligence, Japan's B.P.I. is today at 318 compared with 100
in 1955, thanks largely to the Economic Planning Agency and
the various research bureaux.

This has been achieved by the nation putting a larger share
of its G.N.P. into research than even the U.S.A. and twice as
much as West Germany. But with the emphasis on B.P.I. rather
than G.N.P., this has meant that sometimes, in a quest for
rational consensus, Japan has proceeded rather more slowly
and cautiously in certain fields. The early enthusiasm of some
Western politicians about what nuclear energy was going to do
in boosting living standards was not always shared by Japanese
scientists. They felt that in the field of nuclear research much
more needed to be learned before a positive programme could

be launched. The experiments and nuclear energy programmes of other nations, including the Soviet bloc, were monitored, while Japan's universities turned out an increasing number of nuclear scientists each year: the figure is said now to be more than 300.

The caution has paid off. In 1976 Japan was thinking in terms of backing the more advanced fast breeder nuclear reactor, and the following year she signed a private agreement with the U.S.S.R. calling for cooperation in atomic energy development, including nuclear power reactors and nuclear fusion. The two sides agreed to exchange experts on fast breeder reactors and nuclear fusion, with the Russians wanting to purchase nuclear equipment from Japan. It is ironic that whereas Britain, which had a lead in nuclear energy development at one time, has allowed much of her nuclear technology to go to the U.S.S.R. without getting anything in return, Japan has at least made a reciprocal bargain with Russia.

In 1980 Susunmu Kiyonari, acting chairman of the Atomic Energy Commission, stated that "like it or not, we shall have to use fully energy obtained from nuclear fission, if we want to maintain our present living standards for long."[1]

The present figure for nuclear power stations in the country represents about twelve per cent of the nation's power supply. But the aim is to push this percentage up to 31 per cent by 1990. "We feel we are now on the right track," said a spokesman, "but if we do make a great leap forward in the late 1980s, it will be because we did our homework in studying other nations' mistakes. All our power plants operating nuclear reactors are located in remote and depopulated coastal areas. One problem on which we required to spend a great deal of time in research and information-gathering was that of developing earthquake-proof nuclear systems. As a result an expert committee of M.I.T.I. should soon produce final proposals for improved safety measures in this direction."

Here again the fundamental differences of approach to such problems by the Japanese compared with Western nations is worth noting. The Japanese emphasis on education and attitude to life are just as important as their will to work. Perhaps they are fortunate in that there are various societies all over the country which in their different ways encourage the right kind of outlook. There is the *Jissin Rinri Koseikai* group which has more than a million members and is described as a "moral culture and educational group". To underline the importance of early rising, this society holds its meetings at five o'clock in the morning, beginning with a singing session in which members pledge that "all day long we shall work willingly without forgetting about the three blessings of society, teachers and parents. We shall not talk of other people's wickedness, or of our own goodness. We shall not get angry, or feel dissatisfied. Eliminating the three wastes—of things, time and mind—we shall live a new life."

This outlook can also be seen to some extent in the *Soka Gakkai* (Value-Creation Society), which has a membership of ten million and extends to more than thirty countries. Its leader is Daisaku Ikeda, the son of a Tokyo seaweed vendor, and is based on the teachings of a monk named Nichiren Daishunin who lived in the thirteenth century. It would be unwise to try to read too much into the building up of any of these post-war organisations, and they should certainly not be seen as successors to the pre-war nationalist-cum-espionage societies. Yet they are worthy of study as organisations which stimulate research of all kinds and are capable of being utilised in the national cause. *Soka Gakkai* has some 200,000 converts in the U.S.A. alone, operates its own university, Soka Digaku, near Tokyo, and has a daily newspaper, *Seikyo Shimbun*.

Japan's defence budget for 1980 showed that 28.8 billion yen were set aside for the Technical Research and Development Institute, which employs some 958 civilian personnel. Much progress still needs to be achieved in purely military and naval technological developments, especially as Soviet forces in the Far East include forty-three divisions in Siberia. While Japan has been able to achieve great success in economic and commercial intelligence-gathering, it has been assumed by some Western defence experts that one of her weaknesses is lack of a comparable ability to collect information on the technical characteristics of other nations' forces. This assessment may be true in some respects, but it is undoubtedly erroneous in others. The United States, of course, shares some of its intelligence with Japan, but this is largely general in character and there is probably room for improvement here. On the other hand the Japanese are in a strong position to supply information on critical undersea movements, on the airspace around her territories and adjoining land areas, especially the Soviet maritime provinces. The value of this intelligence to the United

States has probably not even yet been fully grasped by some in Washington. Yet its importance in the future is likely to be far greater.

Yet while the Self Defence Forces chiefs press for more money to be spent on defence and intelligence-gathering in the military field, there is considerable resistance to this among politicians of all parties. Some have been so outspoken as to declare that twice the amount should be spent on research into fighting environmental and pullution problems as for defence. Certainly the emphasis on being better informed on how to tackle ecological problems has been stepped up in the last few years. There has been a feeling that while many industrialists pay lip service to the need for anti-pollution measures, some of them are dragging their feet. It was partly for this reason that the research survey for the Sunshine Project was launched in 1975 with a view to establishing "clean new energy technology" in both the solar and geothermal fields. Similarly the Moonlight Project was set up to examine further energy conservation in solar homes.

When Masayoshi Ohira became Prime Minister he personally directed his Nine-Policy Research Groups to concentrate on environmental problems. A Christian who also participated in New Year Shinto rites, Mr. Ohira insisted that he neither wanted "yes men", nor theoreticians in his research teams: "we want the kind of facts which will make us a healthier society." More than 200 people were recruited into these groups which examined separately a wide range of subjects from a "Rural Nation Plan", "Life Interests of the Multiple Society" and "Pan-Pacific Solidarity" to "Family Basis Consolidation" and "plans to cope with the new age of culture."

Some of the nation's finest brains helped coordinate this research. Tadao Uchida master-minded the analysis of the results of Japan's external economic policies, while Saburo Okita himself directed the study of Japan's relations with her Pacific Ocean neighbours. Masamichi Inoki, the head of the Peace and Security Research Institute, had charge of the study of "Overall Security". What was particularly illuminating about the terms of reference of the last-named group study was that it ranged far beyond the narrow confines of security, but touched on "appropriate diplomatic approaches in such fields as economy, education and culture." Similarly, Ryuchiro Tachi undertook studies into "new type economic management", while Shichihei

Yamamoto headed a team studying new plans to cope with "the new age of culture".

Some of the most fascinating innovations and discoveries have been made from these studies, many of which may lead to astonishing developments. Perhaps the fact that Japan had had to pay dearly in terms of pollution for its rapid industrial progress tended to make research in this field more determined than in any other. One outstanding success which has come out of all this is the Kashima industrial complex, now said to be the cleanest group of petrochemical companies in the world. Yet another is the Honda motor company's development of the pollution-free engine, an achievement which surpasses anything attempted in the U.S.A. to date. Lead pollution has been studied in other countries and, by monitoring levels of lead pollution in certain areas of Japan and Australia and then compiling statistics on children's health, the Japanese research teams came across some figures which were disturbing enough to warrant further investigation. These showed that in certain urban areas where lead pollution was highest, it was found that "where anti-social or delinquent children were examined, they all had raised Pb-B (blood lead) levels." This has led to examination of the possibility that "lead intoxication" can not only cause brain damage, but be a cause of violence and hooliganism.

The nation's globe-trotting information-collectors are also encouraged to make suggestions as to how their intelligence can be utilised. Just as the "suggestion box" is a feature of Japanese businesses which is taken seriously by their staffs, so this habit is maintained when they are sent abroad. It was as a result of certain observations made by seven of their ideas spotters which produced such surprise items as the Capsule Inns, an edible music record and a cure for cirrhosis of the liver. It was reported that in some capitals of the world the high prices of rooms were leaving many hotels half empty. This tallied with a growing tendency in Japan itself for opposition to prices of £12 to £40 a night for standard hotel rooms. So the mini-room hotel idea was mooted. This has been developed through the Capsule Inns offering for less than £5 per night long rows of cubicles slightly larger than a telephone booth, containing bed, television, radio with alarm, mirror, clock and air conditioning. The experiment has been an enormous success not only with businessmen, but people who miss their last trains home and find the cubicle cheaper than a taxi home. It is not too difficult to see how the Japanese could export this idea to other countries with similar problems. Another suggestion from overseas resulted in a Japanese record-producing company developing a disc made of rice paper which, when not wanted any more, could be eaten. One of the challenges from Tokyo to the big American and European drug companies came from Nihon Nohyaku, which produced an unique liver drug NKK-105 which aims to cure cirrhosis of the liver and a hangover.

Some of these suggestions, of course, have resulted from the diligent collection and assessment of "consumer intelligence" in other countries as well as Japan. The main object of this is to ensure that the prospective overseas consumer of Japanese products will get what he wants and that exports remain competitive. Great care is taken in this research to understand the psychology of the consumer just as much as his or her known likes and dislikes. The results of foreign consumer research are also carefully compared with similar surveys at home. Dentsu's survey on consumer attitudes, conducted solely in Japan, came up with four new trends among native consumers of its goods: a greater emphasis on healthier conditions of living, a trend to plan life systematically, a growing desire to escape from urban life and a marked trend towards individualism. The conclusion was that in many ways people were less radical than they had been in 1975.

It is not always easy to assess how valuable this consumer intelligence is and how competently it is analysed. If there is a weakness in contemporary Japanese intelligence analysis, then perhaps it is a tendency towards arriving at too optimistic conclusions. The conclusions of the Dentsu system survey may be overall correct, but some might say this was an oversimplification. But as a result of their probes into what consumers in other nations think, Japan is fully conscious of the problems which lie ahead, and believes that something better will have to be put in the place of the drive for increased productivity. Research shows them that what is needed is better education to stimulate improved use of leisure, a lower-houred working week to give the time for such leisure pursuits, a more determined drive against pollution and the development of the robot worker.

The drive for increased productivity has brought with it the kind of accidents which cause pollution in one form or another.

This was almost inevitable. A recent example was the radiation leak in which fifty-six workers were exposed at a nuclear power station, when the Japan Atomic Power Company failed to report the leak of contaminated waste water from Tsuruga City power station in March, 1981. But such accidents have touched off a genuine desire to conquer the pollution problem.

Saburo Okita paved the way to what he called "knowledge-intensive electronics". Out of some of his star-gazing proposals have developed such ideas as robot technology on a big scale, electric cars, the government's Machine Technology Research Centre and pollution-control equipment. These are projects which Japanese industrialists are taking seriously. As Okita himself has put it: "We may yet be the canary that survives." What he means is that in the turmoil that is likely to embroil the whole world in the next two decades, Japan is probably as well equipped as any nation to come through them successfully.

Highly sophisticated robots which can replace two human workers are already operating in Japanese factories. It is estimated that there are now more than 42,000 of them and one new factory opened by Fujitsu Fanuk has increased its output of robots to a rate of 350 a month. At the Nissan car factory robots bend and weld pieces of metal into the shape of a two-door small car in less than a minute. They cost about £28,000 each and Japanese managements are able to install them speedily because there is no resistance from their work forces. In such firms as Nissan workers are guaranteed jobs for life and resistance to the idea of being relieved of the dirtiest and most boring part of their work would seem ridiculous.

Yet such success would not have been achieved without studying the psychological problems aroused all over the world by the prospects of employing robot labour. The intention is to expand production while freeing workers from their less pleasant tasks. By 1983 it is calculated that Toyota, the car manufacturers, will have 930 robots and many other firms are following suit. None of this would have been achieved but for research and intelligence-gathering plus M.I.T.I.'s contribution of £43 millions for development in this sphere. The truth is that Japan is heading for what their futurologists see as "the fifth generation computer revolution", with the certainty that before long all night shifts at factories will be undertaken by robots, with humans checking for errors when they come on duty in the mornings.

There are countless examples of how Japan has borrowed

the germ of an idea from elsewhere in the world and then turned it into something which has astonished other nations. She was laughed at when she persisted in producing the giant oil-tanker, yet ultimately proved to adapt this idea more effectively than anyone else. Then again, having closely examined the process of blast-furnacing intended to produce 1,500 tons a day, the Japanese adapted the process to turn out 2,500 tons. They again perfected the one-gun colour television tube, the ocean-probing bathyscaphe and petrochemical research in the laboratory.

Meanwhile the *Keidanren* keeps the closest possible watch on international developments and trends. Japanese intelligence is particularly good on Middle East affairs and Tokyo was given warning long before the coming to power of the Ayatollah Khomeini that supplies of oil from Iran could be in jeopardy. That this intelligence was acted upon is clear from oil import figures. In 1974 39 per cent of Japan's Middle East oil came from Iran. Two years later this figure was reduced to 20 per cent and supplies from Saudi Arabia, Iraq and elsewhere were pushed up. By 1979 Japan was relying on Iran for only nine per cent of her Middle East oil requirements.

As regards trade with Russia and her satellites Japan has maintained her traditional friendship with Poland and thus has done more trade with this nation than any other in the Soviet bloc. The *Keidanren*'s activities for economic exchanges with the Soviet Union are conducted mainly through the Japan-Soviet Business Cooperation Committee, which was established in 1965 for the purpose of promoting bilateral economic exchanges. Just as the *Keidanren* have taken the view that in their Indonesian projects they need to work hard because they are behind time, in Siberia, where projects have been entered into, they are working hard because they want to be prepared *ahead of time*, waiting for the day when Soviet terms will be more realistic and when Japan's economic base is ready to cope with the large-scale projects which must be required in this area. Indonesia has been given specially close attention by Japan ever since economic relations were resumed after the overthrow of President Soekarno. Japan felt that, as a result of the set-back suffered while Soekarno was in power, she was behind the times in the surging international competition in that area of the world. The *Keidanren* took the initiative and set up a standing committee on Indonesia, urging swift investment in the territory and sending out an exploratory mission.

At the moment there is joint Soviet-Japanese cooperation to a limited extent in as many as seven projects in Siberia. These include development of forest resources, prospecting for natural gas in Yakutya and exploration for oil and gas on the continental shelf off Sakhalin. There is ample scope for obtaining a detailed overall picture of economic prospects for this still largely undeveloped territory as the Japan Committee has twelve sub-committees studying all questions relating to Siberian development schemes from coal and natural gas to timber, paper and pulp.

This cautious association with Russia has not prevented Japan from keeping in line with the U.S.A. and Western Europe in applying certain economic measures in the light of the invasion of Afghanistan. Nothing is done which would in any way endanger the alliance with the U.S.A. There is certainly more enthusiasm shown by the Japan-China Long-Term Trade Committee, chaired by Mr. Yoshihiro Inayama, who became chairman of the *Keidanren* in 1980. It would probably be true to say that the research conducted overseas both by the *Keidanren* and M.I.T.I. has given Japan distinct advantages in setting up business in other territories. This has enabled the Japanese to find unerringly the weak spots in European markets whether in automobiles, television sets or ball bearings and then to exploit these swiftly and effectively. Similarly in South East Asia Japan has been able to give valuable advice on the inherent dangers of the damage to the economy and agriculture in this part of the world from the misuse of financial aid from the West. Many nations of the Third World in their hurry to industrialise without taking stock of the risks of overdoing this have lost arable land to a disastrous extent. A large number of aid projects have ended in disaster, especially in Africa. In Malaysia something like forty per cent of fish have vanished as a result of lead, mercury and cadmium poisoning of the rivers. The Japanese are not only well aware of these problems among their neighbours, but have stressed the vital importance of monitoring the environmental hazards of all new industrial developments in such countries as Malaysia and Indonesia. The Japanese were among the first to realise that the United Nations F.A.O. scheme to banish the tsetse fly from tropical Africa was potentially disastrous. For in trying to wipe out the tsetse fly by spraying, research has shown that fish and animals have been wiped out, too.

In 1981 it was reported that Japanese companies had invested £844 millions in Britain and that 200 of these companies with subsidiaries or offices in Britain were involved in some 600 projects. For the Japanese, Britain was the easy way into the European Community market; for the British, Japanese technology is enabling them to compete more effectively with some of their rivals. Thus Nippon Steel was asked to help in halting the decline of the British steel industry. But what is even more fascinating is the detailed ground work and research into labour relations and worker-customs which the Japanese undertake before operating overseas with foreign labour. Here again the Japanese study not only local trade union practices, management policies and use of plant, but the world of the worker himself—his role in the factory, his home, his secret desires and what gives him most satisfaction.

Some of the results of this diligent intelligence-gathering before setting up factories in Britain have been monitored by the London School of Economics' International Centre for Economics and Related Disciplines (I.C.E.R.D.). Overall, of 166 firms analysed (with a total 5,173 employees) Japanese workers made up 26.9 per cent of all staff and British 71.3 per cent, with just under 2 per cent drawn from other nationalities.[2]

The I.C.E.R.D. team found that over half the Japanese firms operating in Britain (80 per cent in the case of banks and 75 per cent of manufacturers) had pension schemes; 81 per cent provided sick pay; one in four subsidises lunches; 12 per cent (and 40 per cent of banks) offer mortgages; and 17 per cent (28 per cent for trading companies) provide travel season tickets. Another interesting point was that "a majority of firms (97 out of 166) reward key workers with trips to Japan, and not solely business trips".[3]

The N.S.K. (Nippon Seiko KK) ball-bearing factory set up in Durham has been highly successful. While Britain's largest ball-bearing factory of Ransome, Hoffman, Pollard, hit by the recession, closed its Annfield Plain plant in Durham, N.S.K. announced further expansion. With N.S.K. the firm's attitude to its workforce is that everyone from the plant director to the girl in reception and the shop-floor worker wear the same khaki uniform. There are no problems about job demarcation and everyone belongs to the same union, the A.U.E.W. Mr. George Arnold, divisional officer of the local branch of the A.U.E.W., stated that N.S.K. was "one of the companies around here with good industrial relations. They have been consistent employers with no redundancies."[4]

Another significant factor at N.S.K. has been that the man who makes the bearings follows the product through and tests the quality himself. "At the beginning and end of every shift workers meet to discuss any problems that might have arisen. There is a ten-minute overlap between shifts so that each worker has a chance to meet the one he is handing over to, or taking over from. Mr. David Smith, the production manager, says this minimises the risk of a man blaming his predecessor for anything that may subsequently go wrong, a familiar problem on many shop floors... the emphasis is on two-way communication rather than just downwards communication."[5]

One worker who was interviewed revealed that an example of the "family feeling" which the firm tried to engender was its custom of giving every worker a £2.50 gift voucher on his or her birthday. "Not a lot of money, perhaps, but it does show one is remembered," he added. But the "family feeling" goes much further than this: each month there are regular briefing sessions for all of the factory's three shifts. Not only are the workers fully briefed by their sectional leaders, but they are completely informed on the firm's trading results and any problems which may have developed.

All this and similar successes in establishing firms and offices in all parts of Britain have been achieved only after thorough research in preparing the ground. Labour relations problems which are endemic to Britain have been especially closely analysed. Indeed, intelligence on trade union affairs and the psychology of various work forces around the world has been given a high priority. In the case of the N.S.K. factory in Durham it has been so well evaluated that the firm now exports 85 per cent of the 1,600,000 ball bearings it produces each month.

It is interesting to note that the one quality in such foreign work forces for which Japanese managers look is "sociability". This they rate higher than almost any other qualification. But then this word in its Japanese context has a much deeper meaning than in English. It covers not merely affability and friendliness, but an ability to form consensual policies, to cooperate and inspire loyalty. In Japan many companies offer dormitory accommodation to their single male and female workers, as well as clinics, holiday facilities and even cheap land where employees can build their own homes. Not only is the Japanese executive usually seated in an open space, close to his colleagues so that there can be instant and frequent direct communication, but he considers it all part of his duty to drink with his staff occasionally, to attend and sometimes even to arrange their weddings as well as their funerals. The Japanese were at first horrified to note that in the class-structure system of many British firms there were as many as four different canteens for differing grades of worker. This they have remedied in their own factories in Britain wherever this has been feasible.

Not surprisingly the rest of the world has been gradually making up its mind to attempt to assess the secrets of Japanese productivity and sound labour relations. Belatedly, study missions have been making trips to Japan. The *Japan Economic Review* reported in 1981 that "Western study missions, since the start of this year, have been arriving in Tokyo almost every day ... The hottest focus of attention in almost all those Western approaches to Japan has been the problem of how the Japanese industrial enterprises have introduced their manpower-saving, advanced technological innovations and rationalisations and still successfully adjusted the resulting inevitable conflicts with the problem of maintaining their employment to minimise joblessness."[6]

So perhaps the Western World is beginning to say "Go east, young man" and reversing the century-old idea that all that was best lay in the west. Meanwhile it would seem that Japan retains a rather stronger belief in coming to terms with work forces in the West than many Western firms. Honda, for example, is planning to launch a new car factory in Ohio in 1982 despite the fact that it has had a few brushes with the United States Auto Workers union. The U.A.W., reports David Morris of the Anglo-Japanese Economic Institute, is aggrieved that Honda has not approved the wearing of U.A.W. caps by its non-U.A.W. workforce, this in itself a follow-up suggestion to its earlier call that Honda permit U.A.W. tee-shirts and badges for organised labour—rejected by the company lest the badges scratch or otherwise damage its products. Honda countered by saying that, in accordance with Japanese custom, all employees at the plant wore the company's own white uniform. But, in the traditional Japanese spirit of compromise, the company expressed the hope "that they would wear Honda caps, but did not prohibit U.A.W. caps."[7]

Nissan car company has not had a strike in Japan since 1953. This company even provides accommodation for workers as well as giving low interest loans to those who wish to buy their own homes. Some workers at Nissan may be seen wearing a variety of badges on their company caps. These may range from the shop steward's badge to various commendatory badges such as a specially struck medal for offering suggestions for improving production. A Japanese manager of a Tokyo firm operating in Britain, the U.S.A. and Brazil told me: "It is perfectly true that many of our policies towards our work forces are peculiarly Japanese. But we should be mad to think that we could thrust our ideas on every other nation and get away with it. We could not have achieved anything like the same business successes in Britain and the U.S.A., for instance, unless we had studied labour relations and workers' psychology beforehand. Industrial intelligence of this kind is probably worth as much as industrial espionage. Indeed, it is likely to produce the same results with less acrimony.

"We discovered early on that British management has seemed frightened of taking its workers into its confidence and positively afraid of asking shop floor workers to join in discussions for improving production. This is one thing we have tried cautiously to put right. We call it developing quality, making sure that if a worker has a nugget of gold tucked away in his mind, then we shall find it and reward him. This is easier for us because we make this participation by workers voluntary, but at the same time we try to train them in examining the problems of the shop floor. Perhaps it is not altogether understood as yet that if we succeed in Britain, you will be stronger not weaker. If Nippon Steel is able to give technical help to British Steel and Nissan creates more jobs in Britain, then so much the better for Britain.

"Our aim is strength through consensus, through regional agreements, joint productivity ventures with other nations. All this needs to be based on round-the-clock commercial intelligence from all over the world. It is much better doing business this way than in putting up quotas against one another. That plays into the hands of the Eastern Bloc. Of course, part of our industrial and commercial intelligence drive is to counter the blatant industrial espionage of that Bloc. We need a counter-commercial espionage programme as we have got to be more sophisticated to stop the Russians and the East Germans stealing our secrets. We have had to tighten our company security measures and in all this the aid we get from our government is all important. They have been able to warn us where the threat of commercial and industrial espionage is greatest. Up to two years ago the chief menace was East Germany which had its own scientific and technical espionage department. On this we were probably better informed than the West Germans until Werner Stiller, the East Berlin spy chief, defected to the West."

This was but one Japanese manager's view, but it is fairly typical. The drive for the kind of intelligence which will produce prosperity and stability will continue even at the expense of the defense budget. Certainly there is a general consensus that such intelligence is worth much more than, for example, possessing an independent nuclear deterrent, though without any doubt Japan could develop one speedily, if she wished. But Japan's special brand of intelligence causes her to look beyond the present East-West cold war and the stresses and strains this causes. She is concentrating on what to do when the current world situation changes radically. It is no exaggeration to say that the intelligence already acquired is largely responsible for so much of the almost futuristic planning now being undertaken—the development of robots in the factories, of pollution-control equipment, now rapidly becoming a big business in its own right, and the examination of activities which will need to be abandoned just as much as of new ones to be introduced.

Chapter Notes

CHAPTER 1
1 *The Talkative Muse*, Donald McCormick, Lincoln Williams, London, 1934. N.B.: this book was published under the author's real name and not his pen-name.
2 *A History of Japan*, Malcolm D. Kennedy.
3 *Saionji-Harada Memoirs*, Part xix, Tokyo, 1939.

CHAPTER 2
1 *A New Life of Toyotomi Hideyoshi*, Walter Dening.
2 *Ibid.*
3 Paper on *Hideyoshi & the Satsuma Clan*, vol viii, *Transactions of the Asiatic Society of Japan*.
4 Article by Dr. Sakatani Yoshihiro in *Nichi Nichi Shimbun*, 1901.
5 *A History of Japan During the Century of Early European Intercourse (1542–1651)*, James Murdoch.

CHAPTER 3
1 See preface to *Will Adams: the First Englishman in Japan*, William Dalton, A. W. Bennett, London, 1861.
2 *Memorials of the Empire of Japan in the 16th. & 17th. Centuries*, Thomas Rundle, the Hakluyt Society, London.
3 *Ibid.*
4 *Ibid.*
5 Cited by Kennedy in *A History of Japan*. Iyeyasu was not, of course, the Emperor, but he was frequently referred to as such by foreign visitors to Japan.
6 *Will Adams*, Dalton.
7 *The Soviet Union & Post-War Japan*, Swearingen.

CHAPTER 4

1 Part at least of this agent's message was actually shown to Sir Henry Brackenbury, Britain's first Director of Military Intelligence, for this is how it was revealed in a reference in the latter's own notes. Brackenbury commented: ". . . before passing on this information Imaru [sic] asked me for an explanation of what seemed to him to be incomprehensible incompetence." He did not say what explanation he gave.

2 *The Double Patriots*, G. R. Storry.

3 In some unpublished papers of Hiraya Amane there are painstaking sketches of all the various teacup, teapot and tray symbolic arrangements, as well as some in which bowls of food and rice are also employed. These appear to relate to the White Lotus Society and the Heaven & Earth Association. See also *Zhong-Guo Bi-mi She-hui Shi*, Amane.

4 *Secret Societies in China*, Jean Chesneaux.

5 For an authentic version of the *Genyosha* see *Genyosha sha-shi*, Tokyo, 1917. This book was an official history published by the society.

CHAPTER 5

1 *Krasny Arkhiv*, vol. ii.

2 *Twilight in the Forbidden City*, Sir R. Johnston.

3 Akashi's own work, *Rakka ryusui*, has been published in Japanese by the Gannando. One of the most illuminating and well-documented accounts of Akashi is contained in *Colonel Akashi and Japanese Contacts with Russian Revolutionaries in 1904–5*, by Michael Futrell in *St. Antony's Papers: No. 20 Far Eastern Affairs: No. 4*, edited by G. F. Hudson.

4 *Vinegar & Velvet*, Norman Thwaites.

5 See *Ace of Spies*, Robin Lockhart, and *A History of British Secret Service*, Richard Deacon.

6 Extract from a letter from Sidney Reilly to "E.C.F.", dated 3 December, 1902.

7 See *Tokyo Mail*, of 1896–7 for detailed reports of this strange trial of Mrs. Carew.

CHAPTER 6

1 *The Military Side of Japanese Life*, Kennedy.

2 *A Staff Officer's Scrap-Book*, General Sir Ian Hamilton.

3 *Ibid*.

4 *Ibid*.

5 Article entitled "Introduction to Thought Police" (*Shiso Keisatsu Tsuron*), Japan Police Society, 20 January, 1956.

6 See *Fran ofardstid och orologa ar*, 2 vols., Konni Zilliacus, Helsingfors, 1919–20.

7 *St Antony's Papers: No. 20 Far Eastern Affairs*: No. 4: See Futrell article.

8 Statement by Capt. Vincent cited by Hamilton in *A Staff Officer's Scrap-Book*.

9 See *Tokushu Joyaku*, a number of special treaties concerning East Asia, compiled by the To-A Dobun Association of Tokyo, 1904.

10 *Secret Servants*, Seth.

11 *The Times*, London, 25 October, 1904.

CHAPTER 7

1 *A Staff Officer's Scrap-Book*, Hamilton.

2 *Ibid*.

3 *Ibid*.

4 *Ibid*.

5 *The Genyosha*, an article by E. H. Norman, *Pacific Affairs*, vol. xvi, Sept. 1941.

6 Cited by Marius B. Jansen in *The Japanese & Sun Yat-sen*.

7 *Memoirs of a Soldier of Fortune*, Rafael de Nogales.

8 *Behind the Scenes of Espionage*, Winfried Ludecke, and *Memoirs of a Soldier of Fortune*, Nogales.

9 *A Staff Officer's Scrap-Book*, Hamilton.

10 Letter from Gen. Sir Ian Hamilton, 23 March, 1904.

11 Makiyo Ishimitsu compiled various notes on his adventures and career as an intelligence officer. These were subsequently edited by his son and published under his father's name as *Koya No Hana*, Tokyo, 1958.

CHAPTER 8

1 Cited by Capt. Francis Brinkley, R.A., former proprietor and editor of the *Japan Mail*.

2 *Broken Thread*, Maj.-Gen F. S. G. Piggott.

3 *Singapore: the Japanese Version*, Masanobu Tsuji, Constable, London, 1960.

4 *William C. Whitney: Modern Warwick*, Mark D. Hirsch. Also Benjamin F. Tracy Correspondence, Library of Congress, Box iii, File 12 M–1.

5 Letter from Charles H. Darling to Lt. H. Lloyd Chandler, U.S.N., 21 April, 1904, Naval Records Collection, National U.S. Archives, Confidential Letterbook No. 3.

6 *Genyosha sha-shi*.

7 *Homer Lea*, F. L. Chapin.

CHAPTER 9

1 *Twenty-Five Years*, Lord Grey of Fallodon, Hodder & Stoughton, London, 1929.

2 *Ibid*.

3 *Secret Intelligence in the Twentieth Century*, Constantine Fitzgibbon.

4 See *40 OB, or How the War Was Won*, Hugh Cleland Hoy.

5 Report from military attaché to British Ambassador, 12 April, 1919, Public Record Office, FO 371/3821.

6 This information obtained by the Japanese would appear to have been accurate according to Herbert O. Yardley: see *The American Black Chamber*.

7 *A History of Modern Espionage*, Allison Ind.

CHAPTER 10

1 The "firefly song" is a typical example of the many Japanese children's songs about insects and birds, many very similar to English nursery rhymes. The Japanese text of this song is: *Hotaru koi midzu nomasho: Achi no midzu wa nigai zo; Kochi no midzu amai zo; Amai ho e tonde koi!*

2 See *Toa senaku shishi kiden* (*Narratives & Biographies of East Asian Adventurers*), Yoshihisa Kuzuu, Tokyo, 1933–36. The author of this work became president of the Black Dragon Society in 1937 and he was also active in China-watching between 1911–16.

3 Cited by Kayano in his work *Chuka minkoku kakumei hikyu*, Tokyo, 1940.

4 Article by K. K. Kawakami entitled *"Sun Yat-sen's Greater Asian Doctrine"* in *Contemporary Japan*, Sept., 1935.

5 Attaché reports in the Naval Records Collection of the U.S. Navy show that in January, 1919, there were frequent reports on Japanese activities. The letter cited was to "Mr. Martin, State Department Operations," 7 Jan., 1919, File QQ, Box 482, Record Group 45, National Archives. It also referred to a Japanese demand for greater fishing rights off Siberia.

6 *The Protocols of the Elders of Zion* was first published in Russian by Sergye Nilus in 1902. It purported to tell of a Jewish conspiracy to take over the world. It was used both by the Czarist secret police and later by White Russian spokesmen as anti-Bolshevik and anti-semitic propaganda. It appeared in English under the title of *The Jewish Peril* in 1920, but has been subsequently denounced as a fake and forgery.

CHAPTER 11

1 Intelligence report from W. Somerset Maugham (Known as Agent S 6) from Petrograd to Sir William Wiseman, head of British Secret Service in U.S.A. in World War I, in private papers of Wiseman in the E. M. House Collection, Yale University Library, New Haven, Conn.

2 *Izvestia*, 23 November, 1918, reported that the revolution in Germany at the end of the war had put an end to a secret German-Japanese Treaty, the aim of which was "that a restoration [of the monarchy?] be carried out in Russia by the forces of Germany and Japan and a German-Russian-Japanese Alliance formed in which Russia should be subordinated to the other two partners in the Alliance".

3 Cited by James W. Morley in *The Japanese Thrust into Siberia*.

4 Japanese *Who Was Who*.

5 Wilton's widow sold this historic document at Sotheby's for £100 shortly after his death in 1925. It is now in the Houghton Library of Harvard University. See also *Nicholas A. Sokolov's Investigation of the Alleged Murder of the Russian Imperial Family*, John F. O'Connor, Robert Speller & Sons, New York, 1970.

6 Japanese *Who Was Who*.

7 Dispatch dated 11 July, 1918, included in Dmitri Abrikosov's Papers.

8 From photocopies of the "Chivers Papers". See also *The Rescue of the Romanovs*, Guy Richards.

9 *The Russian Revolution by a Witness*, Toshikazu Kaze, Shin Chosa, Tokyo, 1968.

10 See *File on the Tsar*, Anthony Summers and Tom Mangold, Gollancz, London, 1976.

CHAPTER 12

1 *Broken Thread*, Maj.-Gen. F. S. G. Piggott.

2 *With Japan's Leader*, Frederick Moore. Later Moore declared that the U.S.A. had made "a serious blunder in pressing Britain to break the Alliance . . . it weakened the influence of the Japanese naval men and gave the army men the dominant prestige."

3 *The Estrangement of Great Britain & Japan*, Kennedy.

4 *It Might Happen Again*, Admiral Lord Chatfield.

5 *The Second World War*, vol. i, Winston S. Churchill.

6 See *The American Black Chamber*, Yardley; *The Code-Breakers*, David Kahn; and *Secret Missions: the story of an Intelligence Officer*, Ellis M. Zacharias, Putnam, New York, 1946.

7 *Nichi Nichi*, Tokyo, 22 July, 1931.

8 *Ten Years in Japan*, Joseph Grew.

9 *Behind the Scenes of Espionage*, Winfried Ludecke.

10 U.S. Congress, Senate, *Unification of the War & Navy Departments & Post-War Organisation for National Security* (Eberstadt Report), 79th Congress, first session, 1945.

11 *The Military Side of Japanese Life*, Malcolm Kennedy.

CHAPTER 13

1 *The Menace of Japan*, Taid O'Conroy.

2 Cited by Professor W. G. Beasley in *The Modern History of Japan*.

3 See *Secret Societies in China*, Jean Chesneaux, and *Triad Societies in Hongkong*, W. P. Morgan, Hong Kong, 1960.

4 See *The Chinese Soviet Government's Appeal to the Association of Elder Brothers*, published in *Douzheng*, 12 July, 1936. This was the govern-

ment established in North China by the Chinese Communists after the
Long March.
5 Japanese *Who Was Who*.

CHAPTER 14

1 *Behind the Japanese Mask*, Sir Robert Craigie.
2 See *The Fugu Plan*, Marvin Tokayer & Mary Swartz. In 1934 the
   Japanese Foreign Minister, Arita, stated that Japan would not discrim-
   inate against the Jew. The settlement scheme was sponsored by Lew
   Zikman, a wealthy Manchurian Jew, with Japanese backing, and the
   talks involved Sir Victor Sassoon.
3 *Secret Agent of Japan*, Amleto Vespa.
4 Personal interview, 25 October, 1980.
5 *Secret Agent of Japan*, Vespa.
6 Reported in the *Literary Digest*, 28 October, 1933.
7 See *Twilight in the Forbidden City*, Sir Reginald Johnston, and *From
   Emperor to Citizen*, Pu Yi.
8 *Literary Digest*, 28 October, 1933. There is also confirmation of this
   in *The Double Patriots*, (Storry) in which the author states that Yoshiko
   Kawashima "was of help to the Kwantung Army when she escorted
   Pu Yi's wife from Tientsin."
9 *Literary Digest*, 28 October, 1933. This article also cites the London
   Sunday Express on the same theme.
10 *The Estrangement of Great Britain & Japan*, Kennedy.
11 *Broken Thread*, Piggott.
12 *Ibid*.
13 There is an account of Yoshiko's execution in *Underground Escape*,
   Masanobu Tsuji, Tokyo, 1952.

CHAPTER 15

1 *Inside Asia*, John Gunther.
2 *The Menace of Japan*, O'Conroy.
3 *Inside Asia*, Gunther.
4 *Behind the Japanese Mask*, Craigie.
5 *MacArthur's Japan*, Russell Brines.
6 *Thought Control in Pre-War Japan*, Richard R. Mitchell.
7 *The Amiable Prussian*, Charles Drage.
8 *Ibid*.
9 *Ibid*.
10 Article entitled *The Lost Colony*, by F. D. Morris in *Collier's Magazine*, 27 October, 1945.

CHAPTER 16

1 U.S. Congress, Senate, Eberstadt Report, 79th. Congress, 1st. session, 1945, on *The Unification of the War & Navy Departments and Post-War Organisation for National Security*.
2 *The Honourable Spy*, John L. Spival.
3 *Ibid*.
4 See *New York Times*, 14 Dec., 1938: 8, 11 and 21 March, 1939; 23 April, 1940.

CHAPTER 17

1 *Time Magazine*, 23 June, 1941.
2 Some writers, notably Ronald Seth, have stated that Rudolf Hess compiled an extensive dossier on Japanese Intelligence. However there are positively no documents referring to this in the Institut für Zeitgeschichte in Munich, nor do any of the many writers and researchers dealing with the life of Hess throw any light on this. It probably is that Hess claimed a certain responsibility for a report made for him on this subject by Albrecht Haushofer. The quotation referred to appears in papers which have simply been initialled "H". This almost certainly refers to Haushofer.
3 *Admiral of the Pacific: the Life of Yamamoto*, John Deane Potter.
4 See *Spy-Counter-Spy*, Dusko Popov, Weidenfeld & Nicolson, London, 1974, for confirmation of his extraordinary relationship with Hoover.
5 *A History of Modern Espionage*, Allison Ind.
6 Some documented accounts of Yoshikawa's coded messages are to be found in *The Code-Breakers*, Kahn.

CHAPTER 18

1 *Inside Asia*, John Gunther.
2 *The Second World War*, vol. ii, Churchill.
3 *Singapore: The Japanese Version*, Masanobu Tsuji.
4 *Ibid*.
5 *Two-Gun Cohen*, Charles Drage.
6 *Borrowed Place, Borrowed Time*, Richard Hughes.
7 Article entitled *Bubbles: Chinese woman a Japanese spy*, by Emily Hahn, *New Yorker*, 22 April, 1944.

CHAPTER 19

1 Letter to the author, 11 March, 1970.
2 See *Spy!*, by Richard Deacon, B.B.C. Publications, London, 1980, and *The Double-Cross System*, Sir John Masterman.
3 Extract from diaries of Dr. Goebbels, German Propaganda Minister, in the *Institut für Zeitgeschichte* in Munich.

4 This statement fully bears out Professor Richard Storry's contention that Saionji was never a member of Sorge's intelligence ring, as has sometimes been alleged, and indeed as this author originally suspected.

CHAPTER 20
1 *The Code-Breakers*, David Kahn.
2 Joseph C. Grew, U.S. Ambassador in Tokyo in 1941, noted in his diary of 1 August in that year that "Prince Konoye knows that I would like to talk with him oftener, just as the President does with Admiral Nomura, but it is the fear of leakages and publicity which has prevented such interviews; it was indicated that any reports which our Embassy might send to Washington would of course become known to the Japanese authorities": *Ten Years in Japan*, Joseph C. Grew.
3 *Newsweek*, 7 August, 1944.
4 *Ibid*.
5 *Time*, 13 April, 1942.
6 *Ibid*.
7 *Secret Sources*, Wythe Williams.
8 *Ibid*.
9 Interview with Farago, 30 October, 1971.

CHAPTER 21
1 *The End of the Imperial Japanese Navy*, Masanori Ito.
2 *Ibid*.
3 *A Secret War: Americans in China 1944–45*, Oliver J. Caldwell.
4 *Ibid*.
5 *Time*, 20 November, 1944.
6 *Time*, 15 January, 1945.

CHAPTER 22
1 *The Amiable Prussian*, Charles Drage.
2 Article entitled "Putting Teeth into the Law" by Kazuo Kuroda in the *Japan Times*, 4 December, 1965.
3 Article entitled "Japan is a Target for Espionage" by Tazuo Furuya, in *Keizai Orai*, March, 1969.
4 *The Espionage Establishment*, David Wise and Thomas B. Ross.
5 Verbatim minutes of the Allied Council for Japan, 12 June, 1946.
6 *Japan Weekly Times*, 8 February, 1975.
7 *Japan Weekly Times*, 28 October, 1976.

CHAPTER 23
1 See *Newsweek* for months of Sept–Oct, 1976 and *MiG Pilot: the Final Escape of Lieut Belenko*, John Barron, McGraw-Hill, 1980.

2 *Guardian*, 12 February, 1977.

3 "Chinese Spy Ring Broken", *Daily Telegraph*, 6 August, 1978.

4 *Herald-Tribune*, 2 November, 1979.

5 Statement made in an interview with Clare Hollingworth, *Daily Telegraph* Defence Correspondent in Tokyo, 1980.

CHAPTER 24

1 *Japan's Revenge*, Hakan Hedberg.

2 *Japan Today*, William H. Forbis.

3 *Japan's Revenge*, Hedberg.

4 *Time*, 14 December, 1962.

5 *Fortune*, 27 February, 1978: article entitled "The Japanese Spies in Silicon Valley", by Gene Bylinsky.

6 *Japan Today*, Forbis.

7 *New York Times*, 12 March, 1972, article by C. L. Sulzberger.

CHAPTER 25

1 *Japan Weekly Times*, 26 January, 1980.

2 *Anglo Japanese Economic Institute Review*, No. 72.

3 *Ibid*.

4 Article by Robin Gedye entitled "One union and uniforms for all spells expansion", *Daily Telegraph*, 11 February, 1981.

5 *Ibid*.

6 *Japan Economic Review*, 15 March, 1981.

7 *Anglo Japanese Economic Institute Review*, No. 72: article by David Morris entitled "See How They're Run".

Bibliography

ABRIKOSOV, Dmitri: *Revelations of a Russian Diplomat*, University of Washington Press, 1964.

AMANE, Hirayama: *Zhong-Guo Bi-mi She-hui Shi*, translated from Japanese into Chinese, Shanghai, 1912.

ASAKAWA, Dr. K.: *The Russo-Japanese Conflict: Its Causes & Issues*, Houghton Mifflin, New York, 1904.

AXELBANK, Albert: *Black Star Over Japan*, Hill & Wang, New York, 1972.

BEASLEY, Professor W. G.: *The Modern History of Japan*, Praeger, New York, 1972.

BRINES, Russell: *MacArthur's Japan*, J. B. Lippincott, New York, 1948.

BRYANT, William E.: *Japanese Private Economic Diplomacy: An Analysis Of Business-Government Linkages*, Praeger, New York, 1975.

CALDWELL, Oliver J.: *A Secret War: Americans in China 1944–45*, Southern Illinois University Press, 1972.

CHATFIELD, Admiral Lord: *It Might Happen Again*, Heinemann, London, 1947.

CHESNEAUX, Jean: *Secret Societies of China*, Heinemann Educational Books, London, 1971.

CHURCHILL, Winston S.: *The Second World War*, The Educational Book Company, London, 1951.

CRAIGIE, Sir Robert: *Behind the Japanese Mask*, Hutchinson, London, 1946.

DALTON, William: *Will Adams: the First Englishman in Japan*, London, 1861.

DEACON, Richard: *A History of Chinese Secret Service*, Federick Muller, London, 1974.

DEACON, Richard: *A History of Russian Secret Service*, Frederick Muller, London, 1971.

DEACON, Richard: *A History of British Secret Service*, Frederick Muller, London, 1969.

DE GRAMONT, Sanche: *The Secret War: The Story of International Espionage*, London, 1962.

DENING, Walter: *A New Life of Toyotomi Hideyoshi*, the Kyobun-Kwan, Tokyo. 1904.

DE NOGALES, General Rafael: *Memoirs of a Soldier of Fortune*, Wright & Brown, London, 1931.

DORE, Professor Ronald P.: *Aspects of Social Change in Modern Japan*, edited by, Princeton University Press, 1967.

DRAGE, Charles: *Two-Gun Cohen*, Jonathan Cape, London, 1954.

DRAGE, Charles: *The Amiable Prussian*, Anthony Blond, London, 1958.

DULLES, Allen: *The Craft of Intelligence*, Weidenfeld & Nicolson, London, 1963.

DUPUY, I. N., *Asian & Axis Resistance Movements*, F. Watts, Illustrated History of World War II, 1970.

DUUS, Masayo: *Tokyo Rose Orphan of the Pacific*, Kodansha International, Tokyo, 1979.

FAIRBANK, G. K., REISCHAUER, E. D. and CRAIG, A. M.: *East Asia: The Modern Transformation*, George Allen & Unwin, London, 1965.

FITZGIBBON, Constantine: *Secret Intelligence in the Twentieth Century*, Hart-Davis McGibbon, London, 1976.

FORBIS, William H.: *Japan Today; People, Places, Power*, Harper & Row, New York, 1975.

GILCHRIST, Sir A.: *Bangkok Top Secret: Being the experiences of a British Officer in the Siam Country Section of Force 136*, Hutchinson, London, 1970.

GREEN, J. R.: *The First Sixty Years of the Office of Naval Intelligence*, American University, Washington, D.C., 1963. Master's Thesis.

GREW, Joseph: *Ten Years in Japan*, Hammond, Hammond, New York, 1946.

GUNTHER, John: *Inside Asia*, Hamish Hamilton, London, 1939.

HAMILTON, Lieut.-General Sir Ian: *A Staff Officer's Scrap-book during the Russo-Japanese War*, vols. I and II, Edward Arnold, London, 1907.

HAMILTON, Peter: *Espionage & Subversion in an Industrial Society*, Peter A: Heims, Leatherhead, 1979.

HASWELL, Jock: *Spies & Spymasters*, Thames & Hudson, London, 1977.

HEDBERG, Hakan: *Japan's Revenge*, Pitman Publishing, London, 1972.

HUDSON, G. F.: *St. Antony's Papers: No. 20, Far Eastern Affairs*, Oxford University Press, 1967.

IND, Allison: *A History of Modern Espionage*, Hodder & Stoughton, London, 1965.

IND, Allison: *Spy Ring Pacific*, Weidenfeld & Nicolson, London, 1959.

IRVING, David: *Breach of Security*, William Kimber, London, 1968.

ITO, Masanori: *The End of the Imperial Japanese Navy*, Weidenfeld & Nicolson, London, 1962.

JANSEN, Marius B.: *The Japanese & Sun Yat-sen*, Stanford University Press, California, 1954.

JOHNSTON, Sir Reginald: *Twilight in the Forbidden City*, Gollancz, London, 1939.

KAHN, David: *The Code-Breakers*, Weidenfeld & Nicolson, London, 1968.

KENNEDY, Malcolm D.: *The Military Side of Japanese Life*, Constable, London, 1924.

KENNEDY, Malcolm D.: *A History of Japan*, Weidenfeld & Nicolson, London, 1963.

KENNEDY, Malcolm D.: *The Estrangement of Great Britain & Japan 1917–25*, Manchester University Press, 1969.

LAWSON, D.: *The Secret World War II*, F. Watts, 1978.

LUDECKE, Winfried: *Behind the Scenes of Espionage*, Mellifont Press, London, 1949.

MASTERMAN, Sir John: *The Double-Cross System in the War of 1939–45*, Yale University Press, 1972.

MENDELSSOHN, Peter de: *Japan's Political Warfare*, Arno Press, New York, 1972.

MITCHELL, Richard H.: *Thought Control in Prewar Japan*, Cornell University Press, 1976.

MOORE, Frederick: *With Japan's Leaders*, Chapman & Hall, 1943.

MORLEY, James William: *The Japanese Thrust into Siberia 1918*, Columbia University Press, New York, 1957.

MORRIS, Dr. I. I.: *Nationalism & the Right Wing in Japan: A Study of Post-War Trends*, Oxford University Press, London, 1960.

O'CONROY, Professor Taid: *The Menace of Japan*, Hurst & Blackett, London, 1933.

PALMER, Frederick: *With Kuroki in Manchuria*, Methuen, London, 1904.

PIGGOTT, Maj-Gen. F. S. G.: *Broken Thread*, Gale & Polden, Aldershot, 1950.

POOLEY, A. M.: *The Secret Memoirs of Count Hayashi*, Eveleigh Nash, London, 1915 .

POTTER, John Deane: *Admiral of the Pacific: the Life of Yamamoto*, Heinemann, London, 1965.

PRATT, Fletcher: *Secret & Urgent: the Story of Codes & Ciphers*, Robert Hale, 1939.

RICHARDS, Guy: *The Rescue of the Romanovs*, Devin-Adair, Old Greenwich, Connecticut, 1975.

ROWAN, Richard Wilmer and DEINDORFER, Robert G.: *Secret Service: Thirty-three Centuries of Espionage*, Hawthorn Books, New York, 1967.

SETH, Ronald: *Secret Servants*, Gollancz, London, 1957.

SPIVAL, John L.: *The Honourable Spy*, Modern Age Books, New York, 1939.

STORRY, G. R.: *The Double Patriots*, Chatto & Windus, London, 1957.

STORRY, G. R.: *The Case of Richard Sorge*, Chatto & Windus, London, 1966.

SUMMERS, Anthony and MANGOLD, Tom: *The File on the Tsar*, Gollancz, London, 1976.

SWEARINGEN, Rodger: *The Soviet Union & Postwar Japan*, Hoover Institution Press, Stanford University, 1978.

TOKAYER, Marvin and SWARTZ, Mary: *The Fugu Plan*, Paddington Press, London and New York, 1979.

TSUJI, Masanobu: *Singapore: the Japanese Version*, Constable, London, 1960.

VESPA, Amleto: *Secret Agent of Japan*, Left Book Club, Gollancz, London, 1938.

WHITE, John Albert: *The Diplomacy of the Russo-Japanese War*, Princeton University, 1964.

WILLIAMS, Wythe: *Secret Sources*, Ziff-Davis, New York, 1943.

WILLOUGHBY, Maj-Gen. Charles A.: *Shanghai Conspiracy*, E. P. Dutton, New York, 1952.

WISE, David and ROSS, Thomas B.: *The Espionage Establishment*, Random House, 1967.

WOHLSTETTER, Roberta: *Pearl Harbour: A Warning Decision*, Stanford University, California, 1962.

YARDLEY, Herbert O.: *The American Black Chamber*, Bobbs Merrill, Indianapolis, 1931.

Also consulted:

Japanese Ministry of Foreign Affairs: 1868–1945.
   Documents relating to investigations of intelligence offices in various foreign countries (*Shogaikoku ni okeru joho kankei kancho chosa ikken*), Library of Congress, Washington D.C. Check List S 1.3.1.0–2.

Archives of the School of African and Oriental Studies, London University.

Japanese *Who Was Who*; the Public Records Office, London: *Time* Magazine; *The Times*, London; *New York Times*; *Popular Science*; *Living Age*, *Literary Digest*, *New Yorker*, *Reader's Digest*, *Pacific Affairs*; *Newsweek*; *Saturday Evening Post*; *Nation*; *Business Week*.

Archives of the International Institute for Strategic Studies.

Index

MEN AT WAR!

Gritty, gutsy, fascinating, real, here are stories of World War II and Vietnam— -and the men who fought in them.

THE NEW YORK TIMES BESTSELLER
PULITZER-PRIZE WINNING AUTHOR OF
<u>ADOLF HITLER</u> AND <u>THE RISING SUN</u>

JOHN TOLAND

INFAMY

PEARL HARBOR
AND ITS
AFTERMATH

A Selection of The Literary Guild and
The Military Book Club with 16 pages of photos

0-425-07664-4 · $4.50   Price may be slightly higher in Canada.